THE ENGLISH LANGUA

THE
ENGLISH LANGUAGE
PAPER

A Handbook for Candidates

★

Denys Thompson

1958

CHATTO & WINDUS

LONDON

PUBLISHED BY

Chatto & Windus Ltd
42 William IV Street
LONDON WC2

★

Clarke, Irwin & Co Ltd
TORONTO

First Published 1956
Reprinted 1957
Revised 1958

CONTENTS

Papers Actually Set (*continued*)

ACKNOWLEDGMENTS

FOR permission to quote copyright passages the author wishes to thank the following authors, or their representatives, and publishers: Andrew Buchanan and Phœnix House (*Going to the Cinema*); Arthur Bryant, A. D. Peters and Collins, Sons & Co. (*English Saga*); Apsley Cherry-Garrard (*The Worst Journey in the World*); E. M. Forster and Sidgwick & Jackson (*Collected Short Stories*); Sir John Hunt, Hodder & Stoughton, the Joint Himalayan Committee of the Royal Geographical Society and the Alpine Club (*The Ascent of Everest*); Dr. David Lack (*The Life of the Robin*); Col. J. H. Williams and Rupert Hart-Davis (*Elephant Bill*); Her Majesty's Stationery Office (*Report of the Royal Commission on the Press*); The Cambridge University Press (George Sturt's *The Wheelwright's Shop*); Siegfried Sassoon and Faber and Faber (*Memoirs of an Infantry Officer*); the Editor of *The Observer*; Clough Williams-Ellis and Geoffrey Bles (*England and the Octopus*); Col. F. Spencer Chapman and Chatto and Windus (*Living Dangerously*); and Martin Lindsay and Cassell & Co. (*Sledge*).

The author also wishes to thank the following examining bodies for supplying copies of examination papers and for permission to reproduce the whole or part of papers set in English Language in the General Certificate of Education: The Associated Examining Board, The University of Bristol, the University of Cambridge Local Examinations Syndicate (for the first half of English Language, Paper II, July 1953, and the second half of English Language, Paper II, December 1952), the University of Durham, the University of London, the Northern Universities Joint Matriculation Board, Oxford Local Examinations, the Scottish Universities Entrance Board, the Welsh Joint Education Committee, and the Educational Supply Association, who publish the Welsh papers in their series, *Past Examination Papers*.

TO THE TEACHER

THIS book provides a complete revision course for the English Language Paper. It is based on experience in teaching for three of the examinations and on the detailed study of papers set by all the examining bodies. The candidate who works through the book should have a good prospect of success.

The passages for précis and comprehension are longer than those found in examination papers, and are sufficiently substantial and interesting to stand on their own. The purpose of including longer passages is to avoid the scrappy effect of studying nothing but very short extracts of examination length, and to encourage the reading of the books from which they are taken. It is hoped that some of the reading recommendations will be followed up; they should make the work more interesting and increase the candidate's chance of passing. The well-read candidate rarely fails.

Chapter 1

TO THE CANDIDATE

WHY THE LANGUAGE PAPER IS SET

THE aim of this book is to make sure that you pass the English Language Paper.

This paper is a more recent one than most of the others that are set in the General Certificate of Education. It was started because examiners found that candidates did not know their own language well enough to answer clearly the questions set in History, Geography, the Sciences and so on. There was an English Literature Paper, but it was not compulsory, and many candidates must have thought that because there was no English Language test they need not bother about English. The subject was neglected, and other work suffered as a result.

The Language Paper was therefore brought in to make sure that all candidates reached a reasonable standard in the writing and understanding of English. To take it was compulsory; and to pass it was essential, for a candidate who failed in this paper could not be awarded a certificate however well he or she had done in other subjects. Nowadays no subject is compulsory, but nearly all candidates take English Language and Mathematics (or a Science), because passes in these subjects are required by the bodies which control entry into the professions, the Universities, the Services and other occupations. For example, many such bodies set their own examinations, but they will now accept passes in the G.C.E. instead. So that a boy or girl who has done reasonably well in the G.C.E. has in his certificate the key to a wide range of callings. When the various professional and technical organisations set their own entry tests, a fifth form at school might contain a dozen or more candidates for a dozen entry examinations, as well as a number of boys or girls who had not made up their minds about a career. The common factors among all these requirements are English Language and Mathematics; whatever your career, passes in them are likely to be required before you can enter it. In short, the English Language Paper is almost compulsory again.

THE USE OF ENGLISH

That is one motive for passing it. There is another reason why everyone who speaks English ought to be able to pass the paper, whether his or her career requires it or not. English is a key subject. You cannot enter or do well in any career you are likely to take up without a good knowledge of your language, from the moment you write your letter of application to the day when you fill in your claim for a pension. First, you will need to make yourself clearly understood by other people, both in your work and outside it. Only in the humblest occupations is it possible to get on without the ability to express oneself. And of course the more responsible the post you hold, the more you need to be a clear "transmitter".

The second reason is another aspect of the first. All of us need to understand fully what other people mean in their speech and writing. For example, consider the difference in meaning between "Made in England" and "British Made". There is no doubt about the former; but the latter may mean "Put together in N. Ireland with parts imported from U.S.A.", or "Made in Holland by British workmen" or "Made in Italy by a firm run on British capital". And when we read that a certain product "contains glycerine" or is "made with olive oil", we have to think what important information we are not being given.

So far we have considered "bread and butter" arguments for understanding what other people write and say, and for being able to make oneself fully understood by others. Civilisation is complicated; to run smoothly it needs exact measurement and precise two-way communication.

APART FROM EXAMS

A good standard of reading and writing will get you through the paper we are discussing. But there is more to it than just passing examinations. We learn arithmetic in order to give and receive the right change, to keep our own money affairs in order, to decide what is the best investment for our savings. Passing an arithmetic paper is only a stage in becoming a person who can stand firmly on his or her own feet. So with English. Men are higher than animals in that they can think more, see more and feel more; in addition they have the power to record their thoughts and sights and feelings in words. These records— in the form of history, fiction, poetry, science, biography and so on—are of value to anyone who can read properly. The less effective human beings are at communicating, the nearer they are to animals.

One result of this ability to make records is that a large number of books and periodicals are being produced. Perhaps not many of them are worth preserving, but there is enough good reading matter in any civilised language to keep a man or woman busy for a long time. None of us wants to limit his activity to reading, but without reading matter we should most of us find life rather tedious. A book or magazine meant to last only a month or two does not require very much effort to produce or to read. But any pursuit worth taking up requires some trouble, and this applies to reading. Writings of permanent value demand more from their reader than the mere effort to turn pages over; practice is needed for getting the most out of reading. What is meant to last only for a single day—e.g. a newspaper—can be read very easily. It has to be, for its readers often consume it in a bus, standing up in a train and in odd moments. On the other hand, a real book requires the reader to sit down for some time, to concentrate on the matter in hand, to be deaf to the radio and blind to T.V. This ability to read steadily is likely to be found in anyone who passes the Language Paper.

HOW TO PASS IT

There is one answer in the sentence just above. A practised reader is unlikely to have any trouble with the Language Paper. And that is the best way: to be so good at your own language that you can take an English examination in your stride. There are thousands every year who do pass it with no special preparation, though most of us cannot do it so easily. Anyone, however, can enormously improve his or her prospects of success by steady and sensible reading. For this reason one feature of this handbook is a section of samples from books worth reading; the idea is that you should get hold of some of the books yourselves. There is, in fact, enough practice material in these pages to help anyone to pass in the Language Paper without further reading, provided that he learns from the correction of his mistakes; the book can be used as an intensive short course. But the more interesting course and possibly the safer from the examination point of view is to use it in the way designed: to do the reading as well as the drill.

In reading a good book, you are likely to make progress in several directions. You are improving your skill at comprehension work. You are stocking your mind with material which will help you to write an interesting essay, for reading supplies you with information and accounts of experiences which are unlikely to come your way. You are improving your own writing; you will acquire a larger vocabulary, and be able to express yourself with fluency and variety. You come to see things from a fresh angle; Andrew Buchanan's *Going to the Cinema*, for example, enables its readers to look at films in a new light and with fuller understanding. This good reading makes life more interesting to the reader and makes the reader himself, or herself, more interesting to other people. Reading produces thoughtful and clear-sighted individuals.

To sum up: the book tries to equip you for success in the Language Paper. This can be achieved by using these pages as a drill that will enable you to go through the motions of passing the examination. But you will get more out of the work and improve your chances if you read a number of the books that are recommended.

Chapter 2

OF WHAT THE PAPER CONSISTS

THE Language Paper is designed to test your ability to understand a passage of English, and your capacity to write sense and make yourself understood.

If you wish you can now turn up Chapter 17. Here are given ten papers set by the ten examining bodies; you can pick out the one that belongs to the particular examination you are working for. Note that there is no guarantee that exactly the same type of paper will be set every year; in fact, some examinations show changes from year to year. It may well be that the paper you eventually take will be quite different from the example of "your" examination given in Chapter 17. But however different the paper of one year may appear from that of another, the ability that the examiners are trying to test remains the same. Thus practice on any previous papers will be of value. Similarly, the working out of answers to a paper set by examining body X is good practice for taking the paper set by examining body Y; both examiners in English are out to find the answer to the same question: whether the candidate can use and understand the English language. Therefore try all or several of the papers given in Chapter 17; do not limit yourself to the paper set in your particular examination. If you do restrict yourself, you will be too specialised, and not flexible enough to cope with the questions that you meet on the day.

About two-thirds of any English Language Paper is on much the same lines as two-thirds of any other. In each English Language test the essay is compulsory, and probably accounts for about one-third of the total marks. Some examinations set you a separate essay, allowing for it an hour, an hour and a quarter or an hour and a half. Others set a long paper of two and a half hours, including the essay, on which you are expected to spend about an hour.

The other compulsory one-third that is common to all Language Papers is accounted for by the précis. It usually consists of a passage 350 to 500 words long, and you are asked to reduce it to a third of its length. Sometimes you are given a maximum number of words that must not be exceeded.

The remaining third is taken up by tests of Comprehension, Vocabulary, Grammar, Expression and Miscellaneous Items. Of these the Comprehension test is the most important; in over half of the examinations it is compulsory. Sometimes the questions are set on the précis passage; in other cases a separate piece of prose is provided. Knowledge of Vocabulary is tested in a number of ways. You may be asked to fill in the blanks in a short passage with words from a given list; to replace a compound verb like "send across" by a single verb such as "transmit"; to give dictionary definitions; or to supply synonyms. In several examinations such a question is compulsory.

Grammar appears in most papers and is compulsory in one or two. It almost always consists of some form of clause analysis. The tests of Expression are rarely compulsory. The commonest question is the punctuation of a given passage; others require you to rewrite simple sentences in the form of a complete sentence, or to rewrite ungrammatical or badly expressed sentences.

The Miscellaneous Items include comprehension tests on a piece of poetry, the explanation of proverbs and figures of speech, and further questions on the précis passage.

THE PLAN OF THIS BOOK

In short, you are likely to have in your Language Paper: I. An Essay; II. A Précis; III. A Comprehension test; and

IV. Further Questions, allowing you a choice, in Grammar, Vocabulary and Expression. In preparation for these the next three chapters deal respectively with essay, précis and the remaining items.

Then come eleven chapters, all on the same plan. They are arranged on the lines of a Language Paper, and with the ten papers actually set in a recent year they provide a full year's practice for the examination. However, there are two differences from actual examination papers.

(1) Rather more questions of the miscellaneous type are offered than are found in the papers set. The aim is to provide a selection of all types of question normally set; thus, if you gather that your examination never sets clause analysis, you can leave out the grammar question every time. In this way, from each of the chapters, slightly longer than the paper you will eventually take, can be formed a test paper that closely resembles your own particular type.

(2) Instead of fairly short passages of about 350–500 words, much longer passages are provided, for several reasons. First, preparation for an examination can become very tedious, if it consists only of studying a large number of short passages, which do not mean very much by themselves. Secondly, the extracts act as samples of books worth your reading. Moreover, they supply you with material for essays.

Chapter 17 contains papers set by the ten examining bodies in a recent year.

Appendix A is a list of commonly mis-spelt words; Appendix B contains pairs of words to be distinguished; Appendix C consists of examples of the principal Figures of Speech; Appendix D contains further passages for précis-writing, intended for candidates taking examinations (such as that of the Oxford and Cambridge Joint Board) which include harder and longer extracts.

Last of all come the Final Hints. It may be worth reading them twice; in fact, the first time might well be now. I emphasise this, because more than once I have spent half a period or so before the examination in giving such hints, only to find, when collecting the papers for posting to the marker, that some candidates had neglected all the advice given a day or two before.

Chapter 3

THE ESSAY

TIME AND LENGTH

In the hour that you have for this question you are expected to write about two or three pages; some examiners suggest a length, others leave it to you. If a length is mentioned, keep to the amount stated or a little over. If no length is given, work to a maximum of about three pages of examination paper; in an ordinary exercise-book this will work out at more than three.

Length matters. If you write too much, you are only taking time away from the rest of the paper, and you will not earn any more marks for the extra writing. But if you write too little, you are bound to be penalised. However good your material and however clear and logical its arrangement, a hurried marker, correcting scripts with one eye on the clock, is very likely to be quite automatic in marking down, as "thin" or "inadequate", an essay below the standard length.

The two factors, time and length, make it necessary for you to be able to produce a composition of the right length in the time allowed. Practice will help considerably in this. You must get used to writing at the required length, just as a hurdler or long jumper must take a certain number of strides of the right length in order to take off in the right place. The three-page length—or a little more, because you can always cut down—must become habitual.

It is advisable, too, to go further and become accustomed to writing about the same number of paragraphs. In the case of a three-page composition, you will need to have an opening paragraph and a conclusion of about half a page each. The remaining two pages can be divided up into about three or four or five paragraphs. Avoid a string of short paragraphs; they give an impression of short-windedness and scrappiness. It is probably best to keep in mind a structure of five or six paragraphs all told, and to form the habit of writing essays in these proportions. (If all your preparation is done in the commonly used 8-in. by 6½-in. exercise-book, a length of four pages should be aimed at.)

CHOOSING A SUBJECT

In recent years the tendency has been to include "easier" subjects. Subjects, that is, within the range of experience and interests of most candidates. You have every chance of finding, among the five to ten topics offered, one that suits you reasonably well. Below are a large number of those actually set; they have been sorted out into four main types, thus:

Subjects requiring some specialised knowledge

The features that you would like to see in a newly planned town

Mining to-day

The contribution of music and song to the life of your country

The importance of the scientist

The improvements that could be made in the transport system of your country

The achievements of a great man or woman whom you admire

The importance and interest of recent discoveries and inventions

Famous scientists and their work in promoting health and comfort

The achievements, and the future, of aviation

A country inn in the old days

The Olympic Games

Subjects within the experience of most candidates

The Youth Association to which you belong

Your favourite living author

A criticism of a film or play or broadcast you have recently seen or heard

How the Coronation was celebrated in your district

How to organise a school debating society

A novel which has given you a vivid impression of a period or way of life other than your own

Describe the most exciting match you have ever played or seen

A day when everything went wrong

The last day of a holiday

A visit to the theatre

Topics on which you are expected to have views

The career you hope to follow, and your reasons for choosing it

The kind of entertainment which gives you most pleasure

Compulsory military service

The advantages and disadvantages of doing paid work during term time and in the holidays

To which part of the world, and why, would you wish to emigrate?

Journalism as a career

Your views on the keeping of pets

The holiday you hope to have some day

In what ways would you like to develop the activities of your school's societies?

General (imaginative, descriptive, reflective)

The sky in winter

Birthdays

"Nothing venture, nothing win"

Travelling companions

Bridges
Safety First; Live Dangerously. Which do you prefer?
Waste
An imaginary meeting with a tramp or an old fisherman
New ideas
Queer people
Visitors
Good manners
Colour
Christmas-cards
The scene in a city or market-town, 12 noon to 2 p.m.
Tell a story about . . .

Of course this classification can only be rough and ready; some readers might sort them out quite differently. But you can see that among them are a large number of subjects on which you should be able to have something to say. As for the way they may be combined in an examination, here is an example of an essay paper from one of the 1953 examinations:

Write a composition (which may be in the form of an essay, a straightforward account, a speech or a letter) on one only of the following subjects:

(a) The way in which your town or village celebrated the Coronation
(b) Bridges
(c) The Olympic Games
(d) How to organise a school debating society
(e) The repair of war damage

This is not a particularly easy set, but even so you should find one topic to suit you. (It looks better for boys than it does for girls.) It is worth noting, too, that the examiners, as well as setting a good range of subjects, make the choice even wider by suggesting that there are several ways of treating the subject open to you. Later, more will be said about the choice of subject.

ARRANGEMENT

One of the examining bodies tells its candidates that marks will be given specially for style, subject-matter and arrangement. Others do not give instructions, but in either case you can be certain that one of the points that all examiners look for is arrangement. In spite of the fact that a good deal of time is given to practising the arrangement of essays, many candidates are weak at it. For this reason we are again going over ground which you may have covered in the last year or two.

If you practise the planning of the skeleton essays we suggest in these pages, you may possibly find, when it comes to the examination, that you have an essay, with some material already arranged, almost at your finger-tips. It is more likely that the subject on which you eventually write will not be exactly the same as one you have done in preparing for the examination, but a variation or close relative.

Obviously you need something to arrange before you can start sorting things out. If you have chosen a narrative or descriptive approach, then of course the arrangement decides itself and the material is ready in your mind. But in most cases it is best to keep to the good old method of free association; it can put flesh upon the driest and most unpromising skeleton of a subject. Jot down the first thing that comes into your head in connection with the chosen subject, and let it lead quickly on to dozens of others. Never mind how trivial or even silly they appear; get them all down, anything and everything. You will probably make use of everything you've noted down, when it comes to writing the essay. If you have the material cut and dried already, so much the better. Then you need only write down about half a dozen main points.

Next comes the sorting out of your notes, and if you cannot think of a scheme of your own there are two ways of drawing one up. First, some subjects in the way they are set suggest a structure for your essay. For example, with such a topic as "The features to be desired in a newly planned town" you have to think of three or four important features, put the most important first, let the others lead on from it (e.g. site, separation of business and residential quarters, street planning), and supply a conclusion. Much the same applies to "The improvements that could be made in the transport system of your country" and "The achievements, and the future, of aviation".

Secondly, there are a number of stock arrangements which may come in handy. The most obvious of these is the pros and cons scheme; this might apply to such a topic as "Compulsory military service", and to many others. Another plan is to sort your material under the three heads, "Past, Present, and Future". Look back to the list of essays and see if there is any subject that calls for this approach. Then there are such ways of handling matter as comparing the ideal with the actual, the historical treatment, the contrast between English and foreign and the classification into types. If at any time during the year you are stuck for a scheme of arrangement, look up these pages again, and see if one of the suggested plans will help you. There is no need to feel that in using a stock method of arrangement you are failing to be original. It does not matter very much what a peg is like, so long as it holds up what is hung on it. The examiner will not worry if your arrangement is a commonplace one, provided that your views and information and experiences are of some interest.

Next we shall collect and sort out material for the subject, "Are the chances of adventure growing greater or less in the world to-day?" Here is the list of notes just as they came into the writer's head:

      1. writers
      2. speech day speeches
         elderly always telling the young that they're
         not adventurous enough.
         Why do they?

A   3. types of adventure, detectives
Bi   4. discovery, America
         Northwest Passage
Bi   5. driving to Pole
Bi   6. climbing Everest
      7. lost in cave
Bi   8. shipwreck
      9. forced landing
    10, 11. fire, burglary
A   12. real adventure
A   13. fictitious adventure
    14. why do some people seek adventure?
Bi 15. exploring Central Africa
         S. America
    16. accidental adventure
    17. intentional adventure
Cii 18. social security against
Ci 19. population increase, fewer open spaces
    20. passports
D   21. discovery penicillin
D   22. inter-planetary flight
A   23. adventure on films, T.V.
    24. what is an adventure?—
         a chance happening of interest and excite-
         ment
    25. must there be danger?
Bi 26. Stefansson avoids adventure
    27. "The Worst Journey in the World"
    28. adventure in war
D   29. Outward Bound Schools
A   30. manufactured by Press

After looking twice through the material above, I thought it might—most of it—go under four headings, thus:

A. Popularity of adventure stories, both real and fictitious

This rather suggests that there is less chance of real adventure.

B. i. **Compare adventures in the past:**

ii. On consideration, they were not sought intentionally.

Purpose: Discovery. Explore unknown.

C. i. World smaller now, therefore less chance of adventure.

ii. Social security.

D. Conclusion

May be room for new types of adventure, scientist.

But for the few. For the masses, not much adventure likely, unless they go and look for it.

Of course the material could yield other schemes of management, but I have given the one which occurred to me as I did the example. Once the outline is set down, the material can be set in its right place within it. I find that the best way to do this is to put the letters of my main headings against my list of items, until there are few or none left without a letter. In this case I have put the letters of the scheme against most of my items, but not all. Look back to the list to see if you agree with the sorting-out, and decide if the non-lettered items can be found a place within the scheme. If you do not like the scheme or the distribution of material, try something better on your own.

While the ideas about arrangement are fresh in your mind, try this example, orally or in writing: (1) Read through the items below, suggested by the subject "Smoke", and draft a scheme for an essay, with four, five or six main headings. (2) Then distribute as much of the material as you can under the headings, using merely the numbers.

Smoke

1. Cigarettes go up in . . .
2. Tax on tobacco, big
3. Bad for sight, taste, sense of smell
4. Perhaps bad for lungs
5. "Smog" certainly bad for lungs, causes deaths
6. What smog is
7. See any town at about 5–6 p.m. in late autumn
8. Factory smoke
9. Could be consumed—ships had to in wartime to conceal themselves from submarines
10. Ordinary fires cause about two-thirds of the smoke trouble
11. Cost of painting stations
12. 240 tons of soot fall on every square mile of London each year
13. Useful substances in coal lost as smoke
14. Smokeless fuel, from which creosote, etc., is removed
15. Central London in winter gets only half the sunlight that reaches Kew Gardens
16. Sheffield, Manchester
17. Acid of soot kills grass, bites into glass
18. London spends £1 per head of its population every year on coping with soot
19. Iron bridges constantly need painting
20. Makes clothes dirty
21. Siting of factories
22. Example of St. Louis, in U.S.A.
23. Fifteen years ago one of the world's smokiest cities now smokeless
24. By use of smokeless fuel and smoke-consuming equipment, diesel engines
25. Better health, cleaner buildings, fresh air
26. Soap bill

27. Traffic paralysed; accidents
28. Soot damages stone, paint and brickwork
29. Smoke-screens
30. Smoke signals

PARAGRAPHING

A good scheme makes sure that you write one essay on one subject, not bits of several essays stuck haphazardly together. It gives unity to your composition. Unity is necessary, not only to the general idea, but also within the components of the essay, i.e. the paragraphs. You will almost certainly in the past have done a good deal of work on paragraphing, and we need not spend very long on it here. A composition of any length is normally divided into paragraphs, for the convenience of both the writer and the reader, and especially the reader. Any piece of writing is more easily absorbed if it is consumed by mouthfuls, in between which the reader can pause. Thus you will find that a popular paper, like *Picture Post*, tends to be written in short paragraphs, very easy to take in. A serious novel, a work of history or science, will be composed of much longer paragraphs. But the two types, the long and the short, have one thing in common: each is a unit, and deals with only one aspect of the matter in hand.

Each paragraph then has a unity of its own, which is made clear by the theme or topic sentence that announces the subject of the paragraph and sums it up. Thus every sentence of the paragraph must have some bearing on the theme sentence. To remind you, here is a paragraph from Martin Lindsay's *Sledge*, the account of a three-man trip across the Greenland Ice-cap:

The technique of sledging is probably more intricate than that of any other form of travel. Our equipment was of a highly specialised order and everything from the tent to the snow-glasses was the result of years of experience and hours of careful thought and trial. The efficiency of every item was of supreme importance, since the punishment for the breakdown of any article might have been death by cold or hunger. The penalty of error in sledging has only one parallel elsewhere, and that is in war. So every detail had to be scrupulously examined before we set out, and every eventuality guarded against. Nothing was too trivial for the gravest consideration, for all the little things count. Misfitting dog-harnesses or damp matches might have made just the difference between success and disaster. Under these conditions there was no room for anything but neatness, neatness of thought and neatness of execution. Sledging calls for certain qualities that do not necessarily show to great advantage in ordinary life, and tidiness and forethought are just as important as cheerfulness in the face of adversity. Fortunately all three of us were fairly tidy people, for an untidy man would have been not only a nuisance but a disaster.

Obviously the subject of the paragraph is stated in the first sentence—"The technique of sledging . . . is intricate . . ."—and a glance will show that everything which follows links up with it. In fact, a diagram might be made of the paragraph, just like that of a complete essay or chapter, on these lines:

Technique of sledging very intricate
  Equipment highly specialised
    Every item must be efficient, or death may result.
    Careful planning and neatness
  Men, too, need to be neat and careful

There is, of course, no need—nor is there time—to draw up a plan for each paragraph. Your scheme, if worked out thoroughly, will give you a subject for each paragraph; if you can, start off each one with a sentence containing an idea from your plan, and the rest should follow naturally. Précis and essay work help each other here; if you develop the habit of writing paragraphs with a unity of their own you will be better able to see the bones of the paragraphs in précis passages.

If practice in the writing of paragraphs is needed, one or two of the following exercises should be done:

1. Rearrange the material below in the form of a paragraph. You can rewrite, join or shorten the sentences, and add anything needed to make the paragraph clear.

   (a) Second great advantage is that copies can be made and sent all over the world.
   (b) If a film is taken of the operation, every stage is recorded in actual moving pictures.
   (c) Specialists are employing films more and more in their research, and in recording it.
   (d) The third advantage is that only a few students can see all of an actual demonstration, whereas a film enables hundreds of people to see everything perfectly.
   (e) Specialist medicine and surgery are examples of this.
   (f) But the actual operation is over and cannot be repeated.
   (g) Imagine that an important operation has been performed, and that afterwards the surgeon wishes to lecture upon it to his students.
   (h) That recording of every stage in pictures that can be shown again and again is the first great advantage.
   (i) He will have to rely on his power of speech to describe it to the students, with the aid perhaps of some photographs or charts.

   (Based on p. 89 of Andrew Buchanan's
   Going to the Cinema)

2. Write a paragraph of eight or more lines of writing to develop one of these theme sentences:

(a) Dogs and cats have very different ways of showing their intelligence.

(b) Swimming is one of the best forms of exercise.

(c) Thus the General Certificate sometimes affects the whole career of the girl or boy who takes it. (This theme sentence will come at the end of the paragraph.)

(d) It is not always the collection with the biggest and brightest stamps that has the most interest.

(e) T.V. is still one of the most argued-over pastimes.

BEGINNING AND ENDING

Beginning

Any writer or speaker who wants a hearing will be careful to start in a way that will help to engage the attention of his audience; and schoolmasters have been known to start a period with something in the way of a joke, especially if a difficult language or maths. problem was to follow. If you glance at a newspaper or note the next wireless talk you hear, you will probably find that the writer or speaker is careful how he starts. With a book it does not matter so much; a good book can survive a poor start. But a talk or newspaper article intended for immediate consumption must catch the hearer's or reader's attention.

Much the same applies to essay writing in examinations. A good impression at the beginning counts for something, and a bad impression likewise—there is not much time or space, as there is with a book, to retrieve a poor start.

One method is to visualise; to see at a glance what the mind's eye will suggest. When I applied this method to the subject we looked at earlier in this chapter ("Are the chances of adventure growing greater or less in the world to-day?"), I pictured Stefansson the explorer carefully avoiding adventures (which are a sign of bad planning), and next a railway bookstall displaying piles of adventure stories. Either or both might help with the opening; I will try both:

The explorer Stefansson disapproved of adventures; he said that no one who planned an expedition properly would have much use for adventures. But to judge by the measure of thrillers that can be seen on any book-stall, and by the posters shown outside cinemas, many people do not agree with him. Adventure stories of all kinds are very popular, true as well as made up, for there is nothing the newspapers like so much as an up-to-the-minute account of some real adventure. Perhaps this demand for excitement in films and print is caused by the lack of opportunity for actual adventures.

You may, of course, find it easy to introduce the subject of your essay. But if not you might consider other possible ways of opening. You could start with an anecdote—a very brief one—or by quoting a proverb and going on to show how the truth of it was proved for you. . . . You could explain the scheme and scope of your essay. The latter approach is very much in place when you have to handle a subject about which volumes might be written. The subject "Bridges", for instance, is a large one and an essay-writer will have to restrict himself; he could for example deal with Old Bridges, the History of Bridges, Some Famous Bridges, Bridges in History, or The Science of Bridge-building. Whatever approach is used, the essay on Bridges could start with a short paragraph stating that of the many aspects of the subject, the writer has chosen (say) The History of Bridges, because . . .

Ending

The ending of an essay gives the last impression that the reader will take away with him. As a reader of essays I have found that, so long as the scheme is adequate, a good start and conclusion make all the difference when it comes to awarding the marks. A few feeble sentences at the end can spoil the effect of an otherwise good essay, and the essay which just stops dead is equally unsatisfactory to the reader. Such poor endings are very common.

To make sure of an effective ending, you can make use of the suggestions made for starting an essay, though with a different purpose, according to the type of subject you are writing on. If it is a descriptive piece of writing, end with a paragraph that gives the general impression of the scene or events you have presented. If your aim is to put across a particular case (as in the type of essay "What changes would you like to see made in . . ."), you could end with a telling piece of evidence, or a specially convincing reason. Again, with this subject you could finish by saying something on the lines of:

> All these changes would make Bridgetown a better place to live in. It would be cleaner, more conveniently planned and a good deal healthier. In fact it would be a place to be proud of, not a place to be sorry for.

Other possibilities are: balancing the pros and cons—in an essay in which you are discussing advantages and disadvantages; suggesting the outlook for the future, or comparing with the past; summarising, in different words, what you have said in the body of the essay. Here is a specimen conclusion to the subject for which an outline was suggested on p. 25, on the chances of adventure in the world to-day:

> So with the opening up of the world and the establishment of social security schemes, there seems less chance of adventure. There will almost certainly be opportunities for the scientist, and the men who apply the discoveries of science to everyday life—rocket-flight is an obvious example. But these are for the few. For the masses of ordinary people there is not much possibility

of adventure in everyday life, which is so much securer and better-policed than it used to be. Adventures will have to be looked for; they will not come by chance.

CONNECTION

It is no use having a good arrangement unless the reader, and rather a hasty reader at that, can see it quite clearly. So you must let your scheme appear, and the way to do this is to use connecting links, pointers, summing-up phrases and similar devices. We shall look briefly at half a dozen groups of these. Something of the sort placed at the beginning of a paragraph, probably as part of your theme sentence, can often sum up what has just been said, look forward to what is coming, and help the reader to keep your scheme in mind. There are many others besides those words and phrases listed below.

For example, if two paragraphs set out *cause* and *effect*, one of the following devices might open the second:

> Thus
> Therefore
> The result was . . .
> Because of this . . .
> This being so . . .
> For these reasons

The last of these could sum up more than one paragraph.

Again, if you are *listing a number of points*, you can hold them together and show that they are all parts of a whole by links such as:

Another advantage . . . (feature, problem, etc., etc.)
Examples of this habit . . .
Other illustrations can be found in . . .
But the most interesting animal of all . . .

You will notice that all of these phrases both connect up with what has gone before and look ahead to what is coming.

A *sequence of events* can be connected and made clearer by words and phrases like these:

> Next morning . . . (day, etc.)
> After some time . . .
> The next step . . .
> Once this problem had been overcome . . .
> Now that the preparations were complete . . .
> Once the . . . was over, we could think about . . .
> Eventually

When there is some contrast between the contents of two paragraphs, there are many ways of coupling them:

> On the one hand . . . on the other . . .
> However, nevertheless
> But there is another side to the picture . . .
> A different type of penguin . . .
> In spite of all these setbacks . . .
> But that afternoon turned out . . .
> We have dealt with the A's: now we must consider the B's.

Next, some examples of phrases that sum up items and introduce a fresh step:

> Under these circumstances . . .
> In view of what had happened . . .
> All these events led us to . . .
> Encouraged by these successes, they . . .

And lastly some phrases and clauses for use in narrative:

> At this height . . .
> Once we had reached . . .
> At (name of place previously mentioned)
> The journey accomplished, we . . .

TYPES OF ESSAY AND HOW TO APPROACH THEM

When you face your list of subjects in the examination, it is worth spending a minute or two on choosing what is, for you, the right subject. There have been cases of candidates who have picked a subject hastily, started work on it, and then changed their mind because the subject has not been at all manageable. This is disastrous. Time is very short, and you can save time and choose your subject much more readily if you have some idea beforehand of the range of topics likely to be offered in your particular examination. You should then be able to decide your subject quickly and confidently.

Some subjects lend themselves to good arrangement and suggest the material that could be used. Others appear easy, but require a good deal of thought and care when it comes to writing on them. A glance at an actual list of subjects will suggest what to bear in mind when choosing your subject, and some possible approaches to different types. Here are the subjects offered recently in the Scottish Leaving Certificate Examination; the time allowed was one hour, and 35 per cent of the total English marks went to the essay. The instructions are printed as well:

Write legibly and neatly, and leave a space of about half an inch between the lines.

Marks will be deducted for bad spelling and bad punctuation, and for writing that is difficult to read.

The title must be copied out accurately, as printed in the paper.

Write a composition of *about three pages in length* on any *one* of the following subjects:

(*a*) The causes and prevention of road accidents.
(*b*) "If I were a millionaire . . ."; "If I were a Member of Parliament . . ."; "If I were a cinema pro-

prietor ..."; "If I were school captain ..." Imagine yourself in *one* of these positions, and tell some of the things you would like to do.

(c) Write a letter to a friend whom, owing to illness or absence from home, you have not seen for a long time, proposing an expedition or outing such as you know will appeal to you both.

(d) A description of *one* of the following: A factory; an art gallery; a large store; a dog show; the wonders of the seashore; a summer afternoon in a garden.

(e) "One man's meat is another man's poison." Discuss and illustrate this proverb with reference to any *one* of the following: spending a holiday; the reading of books; listening to music; furnishing a house.

Clearly (a) is the subject which provides its own arrangement; a six-paragraph essay is an obvious and symmetrical possibility, on these lines:

I. *Introduction*
   The seriousness of the problem

II. *Causes*
   1. Failings in roads and vehicles
   2. Failings in people

III. *Prevention*
   1. Better roads; remedying congestion
   2. Better attitude and more care in drivers and road users

IV. *Conclusion*
   Again stress seriousness of problem, suggest which are the remedies to be started now, and which later. Advise the individual what he can do.

Though the arrangement here is ready to hand, the material may not be, and you need an interest in and some knowledge of the problem before you can attempt it. Both "causes" and "prevention" may be pitfalls. It is no good inventing causes which the examiner or anyone else knows to be quite unreal; nor is it any use proposing fantastic and impracticable remedies. Both information and good sense are needed here.

(b) is one of the subjects that are most attractive at first glance, for all of us enjoy day-dreams in which we occupy an important position or wield great power. Again, information and good sense are required. According to which of these you chose, you will have to know some of the disadvantages and restrictions that may trouble a millionaire, and to have some serious idea of what money alone can achieve; to have some knowledge of an M.P.'s duties and position and influence; or to be knowledgeable about cinema audiences and the supply of films. With the last of the possibilities, you should have the necessary knowledge, since the examiner will be specially on the look-out for practical and sensible proposals. For an opening to this subject you could briefly say what your first thoughts suggest, and then go on with "But on thinking it over, the things I should really like to do are . . ." For a conclusion you could sum up the general purpose of your plans and the enjoyment you expect to get from realising them.

In (c) the examiners would expect you first to use the right method of setting out a letter, and the right mode of address to a friend, and then to plan something of interest. As the letter form of composition is frequently set, remember the main points:

1. *Address* about one-third of the page from the right, no inverted commas for name of house, name of town quite clear. Put date below, because it is a good habit to get into.

2. *Beginning and Ending*

(i) Business letters, or letters to complete strangers: Dear Sir, or, Dear Madam . . . Yours faithfully,

(ii) Letters to people you know fairly well, such as members of school staff, clergymen, friends of your father or mother, person in charge of a tour abroad: Dear Mr, or Mrs, or Miss . . . Yours sincerely,

(iii) Letters to friends and relatives: Dear Aunt Mary, My dear Bill, and so on . . . Yours ever,

Avoid facetiousness in beginning or ending; what seems funny when you first think of it can look very dead after twelve hours in the post.

3. *General:* suit the style and matter to the occasion and the person addressed. In business letters be quite clear and to the point; avoid business English and pomposity. In type (ii) above you can be more colloquial; still more so in type (iii). In all of them see that your signature is clear and level.

(*d*) offers a good opportunity to nearly every candidate, if he or she takes care. The temptation here is to dash into describing one of the scenes or experiences suggested, without selecting the right material and without shaping it in any way. The subjects do not suggest the way they should be treated, so the form of the essay demands special attention. Again, all are subjects on which a very lengthy composition, perhaps even a book, could be written. The right choice will have to be made from the material to hand, and you will specially need to remember this if you pick on a subject you are enthusiastic about. For example, if you know much about a particular breed of dog, it will be useless to make the Dog Show an opportunity merely of airing your knowledge and enthusiasm. Instead you need to make your essay interesting to the general reader. Again, you may visit a factory where something of absorbing interest to you—cars or silk stockings—is made, but it will be a mistake to spread yourself on the technical side of the process, when what is wanted is a description that will hold the attention of a reader to whom a car is a piece of ironmongery on its way to the scrap heap and silk stockings a lot of money for a very little material.

It is then essential to have an angle of approach when dealing with one of these rather general subjects on which much could be said. With the "factory" subject, for example, a satisfactory composition might consist of an introductory paragraph mentioning the factory visited, what it makes and how you came to go over it, followed by an account of the process whereby the raw material became the finished product. This might be enough. But it would be more interesting if you were to comment, either in your conclusion, or as you go along, on any special impressions—the cleanliness, noise, speed of the place, the complexity and ingenuity of the machinery, the safety precautions and the welfare of the workers. If it were a big factory, you could show how mass-production involves splitting up the making of a car or sewing-machine, or whatever it is, into thousands of small operations. Instead of one man making one complete machine, thousands of men—and women—make thousands of little pieces; they may hardly know what they are making or why. Some essay-writers may wish to go further and use their visit to answer the question "Is mass-production killing craftsmanship?"

(e) requires not only some knowledge and experience (and in three of the subjects rather specialist knowledge) but also imagination, because you are required to discuss two different sets of preferences. "Spending a holiday" might be discussed without any specialised knowledge, but the others it will probably be best to leave alone unless you are well informed about one of them.

Chapter 4

THE PRÉCIS

PASSAGES for summarising are normally set in the Language Paper. This suggests that précis-writing is generally thought (i) to be good for candidates, and (ii) to equip them with skill which will be useful to them.

Probably in the past you will have done a good deal of work in summarising, perhaps without realising why the exercises were set. We shall therefore briefly consider why the various examining bodies are unanimous about the value of précis-writing.

The first reason is that it is a good exercise for the mind and makes it more capable of following an argument or a narrative. A précis is never as good as the original, unless there is something wrong with the latter. Why then should one make a good piece of writing worse? The answer is that the act of making a précis ensures that the reader has really grasped what the writer has to say. It is one of the best methods of getting to understand an author's meaning. It is, incidentally, an exercise which ought to bring satisfaction to the précis-writer; there is a feeling of "something accomplished, something done" in producing a convincing summary, in which every word fits into place and helps to bring out the point of the original. It is rather like completing a successful piece of cooking or carpentry from material provided; in this it is different from essay-writing, in which you have to provide your own material.

The first reason for précis-writing, then, is that it increases a reader's power of understanding; he has not only to come to grips with a passage, but also to prove to others that he has grasped it. The second reason is that the art of summarising is needed in many careers. A lawyer has to read through and condense long accounts of legal actions; an historian has to read through the full accounts of parliamentary debates that are found in *Hansard* and perhaps boil down hours of discussion to a brief paragraph; a journalist has to produce a simplified version of a technical account of a scientific discovery; and a firm specialising, say, in radar equipment will need to make and keep précis of articles in the various scientific journals that have some bearing on its products. Many more examples could be instanced; and other professions, even if they do not involve the making of summaries, require the skill in taking and making notes that comes from practice in précis.

When we consider the various purposes in life that involve summarising, it is clear that they will result in summaries of different types. The historian reading *Hansard* may reduce pages of wordy argument to a hundredth of the original length; the politician, running through an opponent's speech, will pick on certain themes and neglect others; a film company in search of a story may see only half a page of plot in a 500-page novel; while a particularly difficult piece of scientific or mathematical reasoning may be quite impossible to shorten at all. The nature of a summary will vary according to the purpose it is intended for, and according to the point of view of the person at work on it. There is really no such thing as an ideal summary; a speech made at a prize-giving, for instance, will be dealt with in very different ways by the reporter for a local newspaper, the reporter of a "national" newspaper (if the speaker is important enough), the writer of the account for the school magazine, and the fourteen-year-old girl or boy, whose parents ask her or him what the speaker said.

We have discussed the reasons for précis-writing, because some candidates regard it as a pointless drill. It is not; it has a useful purpose, and like the exercise of any skill it can be enjoyable.

PRÉCIS IN EXAMINATIONS

In real life summaries vary greatly: but the requirements of examinations vary only a little. A glance at some papers shows that in one certificate examination a passage of 353 words is set, and has to be brought down to not more than 125 words; in another, 500 words have to be reduced to not more than 170. You can find out the requirements of your own examination; it is fairly certain that you will have a passage of somewhere between 250 and 600 words to be brought down to about one-third the length of the original. But there is nothing sacred about this 3:1 ratio; and if after leaving school you have summaries to make, fix the length by the needs of the job in hand.

Usually the instructions run something like this:

Read the following passage carefully, and then write a summary of the whole in not more than 150 words, taking care to give a continuous connection of ideas, and using your own words as far as possible. State the number of words you have used, but note that failure to keep *within the limits of* 150 *words* will be penalised.

One or two examinations employ a slightly different formula. They may, for instance, provide an extract from an article on football pools, and ask the candidate to summarise the writer's views for or against pools, or his views on their consequences. Here you will have to be particularly careful to give what is asked for, and nothing else; you may have to concentrate on a special section of the passage, or to pick out certain ideas.

In any case, whether the passage you are set is long or short, the examiners wish to see the line of thought made clear; the sequence of ideas must be shown by the way in which your own sentences are connected. (We shall deal later with ways and means of achieving this.) It is no use just picking out the important sentences and setting them down without links; a version on these lines shows that the candidate has not really grappled with and understood the passage. It is to make sure that candidates understand the writing before them that the instructions commonly advise the candidate to use her or his own words. Anyone who has marked a number of précis will tell you that nothing gives away a candidate's failure to understand a passage so much as a number of sentences or groups of words taken over from the original extract. They stick out like uncooked lumps of oatmeal in porridge.

METHOD

If you have studied the method thoroughly and know the "drill" off by heart, you can leave out the suggestions made here and go straight on to practise some examples. But however familiar it may be, the method is being set out again here because it is important, and because some readers may have forgotten how to approach a précis, or have had little practice in the work.

First read the passage quickly. Then give it one or more slower readings, and when you are getting hold of it, underline the important points and connecting links. Look over these marked points, find the backbone of the extract, and see how everything fits on to it. Then write your précis so far as possible without referring to the original. The memory is a very good sieve of what is important, and the less you look at the original the more completely you will be able to recast it in your own words. Then read through what you have written to make sure (i) that it is clear and connected, (ii) that nothing important is left out, and (iii) that it is not too long.

The habit of reading, and of understanding what you

read, is a great help in précis-writing: but practice is essential until you are proficient. Practice will get you into the habit of keeping the rules that follow. Include only what is important; if, for instance, the extract quotes another writer, you will probably be right in leaving out the quotation and the name of the author. Again, if evidence from a work of reference is given in some such form as:

Whitaker's Almanack for the years 1950, 1952, 1953, 1954, 1956 and 1957 gives sets of figures which show that . . .

or

The *Nautical Almanack* in its recent editions supports the local belief that rough weather is to be expected in this area at about the end of September

you can omit the source of the facts and reduce the mention of material from reference books to something like:

Recent evidence shows that . . .
Rough weather occurs here at the end of September.

Use as few words as possible, without sacrificing the sense. A sentence such as:

In actual fact, the trees we had been tending with so much care produced a far better yield of fruit than at one time we had expected.

will come down to:

With careful cultivation the trees yielded surprisingly well.

If you save words without loss of meaning you will have room to add the connecting links which help to make the thread quite clear.

Direct speech, in the form of dialogue or quotation, must be turned into indirect speech or summarised. For example:

At the end of his talk the careers adviser answered a number of questions, such as "How can I train for physiotherapy?" "Where can I obtain information about forestry?" "At what age does one get into scientific instrument making?"

will have to appear in some such form as this:

In answer to questions he told them where information about various careers could be obtained.

Do not include anything you do not understand, and remember not to take over unaltered sentences from the original.

EXAMPLES

We shall now work through two examples, one a fairly long extract, and the other of the shorter kind in which you are asked to summarise only a part of the material provided.

Give a clear, connected summary of the passage below, which contains 615 words. Your version must not contain more than 200 words.

I

The country houses were the headquarters of what was still the chief industry of England—agriculture. From their estate offices a great national interest was directed. During the past eighty years its productivity had been immeasurably increased. New and revolutionary methods of farming and stockbreeding had been introduced and nearly seven million acres of waste land had been reclaimed by enclosure. A German traveller in the eighteen-twenties was amazed on each successive

10 visit to England to see vast tracts of formerly unculti-
    vated land transformed into fine corn-bearing fields.
    It was during these years that Tennyson's northern
    farmer was engaged on his long and manly task of
    stubbing "Thurnaby waste". It was all part of a
15 tremendous national achievement. Though the popula-
    tion had doubled itself since 1760 and England had
    ceased to be a corn-exporting country, more than
    three-quarters of its total wheat and nearly all its barley
    consumption were being met by the home producer.

2

20 By their agricultural activity and inventiveness the
    English had not only given an example to the world but
    saved themselves. The new methods of breeding stock,
    the increase of grazing, the use of fodder crops on lands
    formerly left fallow, fencing, building and draining,
25 contributed as much to the defeat of a militant and
    revolutionary France as the broadsides of Trafalgar
    and the stubborn squares of Waterloo. Without them
    the rising populations of the new manufacturing towns
    could never have been fed nor the power of Napoleon
30 humbled. The accumulated experience of all this
    mighty effort had now been elevated into a science: the
    annual gatherings at Holkham to toast the great Coke
    of Norfolk who had turned thousands of acres of rabbit
    warren into a smiling countryside, the ceaseless output
35 of books on improved methods of farming and the
    foundation of the Royal Agricultural Society in 1838
    were among its many symptoms.

3

    One best saw the industry in its corporate capacity on
    market day in any country town—the old market hall,
40 the country women's stalls and baskets spread about the
    roadway, the gentry and tenant farmers in their John
    Bull tophats, loose open frock-coats, vast collars, white
    waistcoats and breeches and heavy top-boots. One saw
    it, too, in the great fairs that sprang up annually

45 throughout the countryside, where a whole neighbourhood of peasant and farmer folk would assemble to buy,
gossip and junket, and when those who wished to be
hired for service for the coming year proudly carried
the symbols of their trade—the carter his whip, the
50 milkmaid her pail and the cook her ladle. The lads or
lassies hired received a shilling as testimony of accept-
ance and stuck a ribbon in cap or hair in honour of the
bargain. "I took the shilling, put a bit of ribbon in mi'
hat to show as I were hired like 'tuthers," said an old
55 farm labourer recalling the days of his strength and
pride, "and went and spent the rest of the day at the
pleasure fee-ar." And as night fell and the drums and
bugles outside the painted, lit booths sounded over
lonely down and far watching valley, the rustic fun
60 waxed fast and furious. A national industry was relaxing.

4

If the apex of the agricultural community and of its
ordered industry and culture was the country house, its
basis was the cottage. It was here that those who reaped
65 and sowed were born and bred. Their homely virtues
were as vital to their country's splendid achievements
as the genius and assurance of the hereditary aristocrats
who led them. On the field of Waterloo the great Duke
gave his calm orders, and with equal calm and fortitude
70 the rustics who manned the battered squares obeyed.

ARTHUR BRYANT, *English Saga*

At first reading, these probably stick in the mind:

    Paras. 1 and 2: Agriculture, Progress of
    Paras. 3 and 4: Examples

On a second reading, more ideas will be retained:

    Para. 1: Country houses, centres of agriculture
        Agriculture much improved,
          new methods, enclosures,
          examples,
          results

Para. 2 : New farming saved England in war,
provided for bigger population

Para. 3 : On market day could be seen all the
people engaged in agriculture
At fairs too, for fun and hiring

Para. 4 : Humble people in cottages the foundation of this achievement

The next step is to underline the important words, such as:

Para. 1 : Country houses, headquarters
Agriculture
productivity ... increased
new methods of farming
land reclaimed,
transformed
population doubled
more than three-quarters of . . .
wheat
[*Mental note:* the German traveller and
the northern farmer are examples and
can be severely cut down]

Para. 2 : Agricultural activity and inventiveness
English saved themselves
new methods defeat France
rising populations ... fed
agriculture a science
[*Mental note:* Coke, books on farming,
and Royal Agric. Soc. are evidence, and
can be cut down]

Para. 3 : Industry in corporate capacity
market day
Great fairs, too ... to buy, gossip ...
to be hired
National industry relaxing
[*Mental note:* Meaning of "corporate
capacity?" How express it in own
words? Much of this para. consists of
picturesque examples]

Para. 4: Basis was the cottage
             vital to country's achievement

> [*Mental note:* rest of paragraph is example]

At this stage we go back and consider the underlinings and doubtful points. For example, should "country houses" be mentioned at the beginning? Most of paragraph 1 deals with agriculture; therefore the country houses should not be mentioned. But on second thoughts they must be brought in, because the cottage and its inhabitants which complete the agricultural scheme are mentioned in the last paragraph. Again, what is the meaning of "corporate life" (para. 3)? How far shall particular illustrations or examples be reduced, if they are included at all?

Next follows my first version, which is on the long side. But I have left it unshortened, and suggested possible cuts in the comments at the side.

1. Agriculture, centring round the country houses, had become very much more productive in the last eighty years. For this, new methods of farming and stockbreeding and the recovery of waste land were responsible; nearly seven million acres more were brought into cultivation, to the amazement of visitors from abroad. As a result of this achievement, England produced most of her wheat and barley at home, though

"Country houses" comes first in the opening sentence of para. 1; why has the order been changed?

"For this" both sums up what has gone before and connects.
"and stockbreeding" can be omitted; it is a part of farming.

"millions of acres" would be shorter.

"to the amazement . . . abroad" may have to be cut. Or "visitors from abroad" could be reduced to "foreigners". "As a result" is needed as a connecting link.
"Of this achievement" may have to go out. "most of her wheat and barley at home" could be cut to "her own corn".

the population had doubled since 1760.

"Despite a doubled population" would save three words.

2. By all this energy and ingenuity England had saved herself, in addition to setting an example to the world. The new methods of stockbreeding and cultivation were just as important as the army and navy in the defeat of France, and they enabled the increasing population of the new towns to be fed. In fact, agriculture had become a science; this could be seen in the respect paid to Coke for his recovery of waste land, in the many books on farming, and in the founding of the Royal Agricultural Society.

"Thus" could replace "By all . . . ingenuity" and it would still sum up and connect.

"In addition . . . the world" might go out.

The word "For" could be inserted before "The new methods" to introduce and link up the explanation that follows.

"of stockbreeding and cultivation" could either go entirely or be replaced by "farming".

"the army and navy" could be replaced by "the forces".

"they fed" could replace "they enabled . . . to be fed".

"In short" (a summing-up phrase) might be better than "In fact".

The examples given here could be reduced thus: "as is shown by such evidence as the founding of the Royal Agricultural Society ".

3. The individuals who made up this industry could be seen together on any market day, when farmers assembled and the country folk sold their produce. They could be seen too at the annual fairs, where people met for trade and enjoyment, and labourers came to hire their services. These fairs were the main entertainment of farming people.

Once again "this" connects.
"together" brings in the idea of "corporate".
Much of this paragraph consists of illustrations, which are omitted.

To save words, the last sentence ("These fairs . . .") might be omitted. It gives the general idea of the last third of the paragraph.

4. The farm labourer was the foundation of this prosperity, as the aristocracy was the peak; and the victory at Waterloo showed that his strength was as important as the talent of his leaders.

"cottage" has been omitted, on the ground that it is the people who live in it that matter most.

"prosperity" is intended to sum up "the agricultural community . . . its ordered industry and culture".

This final paragraph is rather short to stand by itself, and were it not that the subject matter changes it could be joined on to the previous paragraph.

Some examining bodies combine précis and comprehension questions on one passage; in such cases the candidate is asked to summarise only a part of the extract given, on these lines:

Summarise in not more than seventy of your own words the author's views on the value of adventure to-day.

I believe that by recognising the sense of adventure that lives in every one of us, and by providing opportunities for people to experience the fullness of life, and the inner satisfaction that comes from facing and over-
5   coming danger, one will be doing something to prevent the frustration which helps to create war, and possibly to provide an alternative to that sense of heightened living which some people seem only able to achieve through war. And it is possible, even in the space of a
10   few weeks, to create conditions which give people companionship, the delight in exercising a craft, the background of natural beauty and the spice of adventure and danger.
These conditions can be provided at sea and among
15   mountains and to a certain extent on a horse, in a canoe, or a glider, and, yes, on a coal-face too. A man masters himself by mastering hazards from which there is no escape. And as long as he is reasonably fit and has learnt the necessary technique—whether it is map-
20   reading, sailing, or climbing—he will come to no harm. This is as attainable for the townsman as for anyone else—nearly all Wingate's men came from towns, most

of them from Liverpool—and it is most needed by those
whose lives are spent in dull indoor jobs—nor is it
25   necessary to go to the ends of the earth in search of
adventure.

If you get a group of boys together—and probably girls
too, though this is beyond my experience—even if they
come grossly unfit from a desk or a factory, within a
30   month they can sail a boat and find their way over
thirty or forty miles of mountainous country with no
strain at all; and if the weather is bad and it is a little
difficult to navigate with map and compass, they get a
tremendous sense of achievement and self-confidence
35   which, I believe, stays with them for the rest of their
lives. They know the difference between doing a thing
themselves and just watching other people doing it.
They have learnt in fact how to enjoy life.

F. SPENCER CHAPMAN, *Living Dangerously*

We need not apply to this passage the lengthy procedure that we used above. A glance at the extract shows
that most of what Col. Spencer Chapman has to say about
the value of adventure to-day comes in his first paragraph.
But not all; a hasty worker could easily miss the two
sentences in the second paragraph that bear on the topic,
even if he did notice that the second half of the last
paragraph is relevant. So if there is anything fresh on the
subject in paragraphs two and three it must be worked in.
This is my effort:

Everyone can gain happiness
and satisfaction from giving
rein to his sense of adventure
—this is especially good for
people with dull jobs. To face
risks produces self-discipline
and a lasting feeling of
achievement and self-confidence. By overcoming danger

"happiness" = *"to experience the fullness of life"*.

"dull jobs": this seems an importan
point, from para. 2.
"self-discipline" = *"A man masters
himself..."*
"lasting" = *"stays with them ... lives"*

people learn how to enjoy life, and will not suffer the frustration which breeds war. Adventure to-day can provide the excitement which some people find only in war.

"excitement" = *"that sense of heightened living"*.

CONNECTION

You may be able to pick out the right ideas and express them in your own words, but still your version may not be readable and convincing because of the lack of connection. Without connecting links a précis will read disjointedly; the relation of the sentences to each other will not be clear; the version will not hold together. You will find useful such methods of connection as:

> These proposals . . . (or aims, or actions, or events. Words like these also sum up what has gone before)
> To achieve this . . .
> After this . . .
> The result of . . . was
> The next step . . .
> Eventually . . .
> In the end . . .
> Therefore . . .
> In fact . . . } { (contrasting with something only
> Actually . . . } {   planned or proposed)
> However . . . (connecting by contrast)
> Moreover . . .
> In addition . . .
> Another reason . . .
> But nowadays . . . (connecting by contrast with the past)

Below is a version worked by a candidate who has managed his connections well; nearly every sentence grows naturally out of what has gone before.

Erosion of the vital top-soil is a very great problem confronting the men of many nations; it was brought on by the carelessness and negligence of earlier generations. Their greed caused them to overcrop their lands, resulting in the gradual destruction of vast areas, which became deserts through the continual exposure to wind, rain and frost. Once this erosion starts it is very difficult and costly to stop.

It is foolish to think that now there is nothing to fear because we have more advanced implements and methods, for to-day there are millions in the East eking out a miserable existence with very little food. To feed all of them adequately it will be necessary to utilise all the land possible and to tend it carefully for many years to return it to its former condition. More grass and trees must be planted to hold the soil together and preserve the moisture; humus must be introduced by keeping stock; and where violent storms prevail, terraces and dams must be built. These aims can best be achieved by many small self-sufficient farms, and by making erosion a common foe, against which all men can unite.

"great" is a vague word; problems are "serious", "difficult", "urgent", etc.

"Their" connects.

"this erosion" connects and sums up.

"now" connects by contrast with the past.

"all of them" connects.

"More grass . . .": there is no word to connect here. There is no need, for the sentence clearly develops the idea of the previous sentence.

"These aims" connects and sums up.

In short, the first essential in précis-writing is to understand the passage set; the next is to have a sufficient vocabulary to recast it in your own words.

ORAL PRACTICE

The examples below can be used for written work, but they are intended mainly for oral "limbering-up". In other parts of this book there are numerous passages for précis, and if time is short now some of the questions set below can later be used on these longer passages.

1. (a) Summarise in five words:

It is a matter of general agreement that in cases where two or more courses of action are possible, it is desirable to select the alternative involving the greater degree of honesty. Such a policy, it has been found, is preferable on practical grounds, and for reasons of expediency, as well as in theory.

(b) Summarise in six words:

When matters relating to the repair of woven fabric garments are under discussion, it has been observed that a single stitch, applied to the appropriate part of the item of clothing concerned in time, will normally avoid the necessity of an additional nine or more further stitches at a later date, if the repair in question is further deferred.

2. (a) Give a title to the passage that follows.
   (b) Give one title to the first pair of paragraphs, and one to the second pair.
   (c) Give a title to each of the four paragraphs.

Grave warnings of a future world famine have come from Lord Boyd Orr and other authorities, and some American writers are given to very gloomy prophecies. On the face of it these warnings seem justified: the world's population is rising by 20,000,000 a year

(54,000 a day), and estimates of the earth's total area suitable for tillage—even if the continuing ravages of soil erosion can be checked—are not very reassuring.

But there is talk also in America of other possibilities of food almost unlimited from the sea and quite unlimited from the air. Science, it is hoped will come to the rescue; new methods will supersede the cultivation of the soil. How far is this prospect to be taken seriously, and how should we regard it?

One of the new methods, hydroponics, or culture without soil, is already in use. It began in the laboratory a long time ago, when plants were grown in nutrient solutions in order to study their use of mineral salts. In the 1930s the method was taken up commercially; greenhouse crops were grown in tanks; and during the war the idea was applied to vegetable culture in arid places (notably Ascension Island) where troops had to live.

Whether this food is in every way as healthy as naturally grown food is perhaps an open question, hard to test and not yet fully tested. But in any event it seems unlikely that hydroponics will be used for the production of basic foods on a large scale; too much costly equipment, covering large areas and needing skilled attention, would be required. Probably the future of hydroponics lies in the cultivation of vegetables and specialised foods, chiefly where they could not otherwise be grown.

CHARLES DAVY, part of article "Science and World Famine", *The Observer*, 19th June 1949.

3. *Either* summarise the following extract from *Hansard* in forty words, *or* summarise it in not more than fifty words of which none, except "Indian" and "government", is more than two syllables in length.

It has long been the policy of successive British Governments to work towards the realization of self-government in India. In pursuance of this policy an increasing measure of responsibility has been devolved on Indians and to-day the civil administration and the Indian Armed Forces rely to a very large extent on Indian civilians and officers. In the constitutional field the Acts of 1919 and 1935 passed by the British Parliament each represented a substantial transfer of political power. In 1940 the Coalition Government recognized the principle that Indians should themselves frame a new constitution for a fully autonomous India, and in the offer of 1942 they invited them to set up a Constituent Assembly for this purpose as soon as the war was over.

His Majesty's Government believe this to have been right and in accordance with sound democratic principles. Since they came into office, they have done their utmost to carry it forward to its fulfilment. The declaration of the Prime Minister of 15th March last, which met with general approval in Parliament and the country, made it clear that it was for the Indian people themselves to choose their future status and constitution and that in the opinion of His Majesty's Government the time had come for responsibility for the Government of India to pass into Indian hands. . . .

c. r. attlee (Prime Minister), House of Commons, 20th February 1947.

4. Write out the words and phrases that you would mark at the underlining stage in making a summary of the following:

1. Let us consider for a moment how such industrial towns and villages as Oldham and its neighbours and satellites grew up.

All through the eighteenth century cotton-weaving had gone on in the valleys of these Lancashire moors. When cotton-spinning machinery was invented there were streams ready to turn it. Markets were discovered, and the demand for labour was sharp. It was as a rule no part of the system for the mill-owners themselves to provide housing for their operatives, or if they did they provided it, as it were, in their private capacity and as a side-line which they hoped to make profitable. Under the current system they were perfectly entitled to build as bad a house and charge as high a rent for it as they could get away with. If they did provide honest houses, it was as a work of supererogation, and they were under no obligation to do so; for in theory, at any rate, the operative was entirely free not to live in their houses if he thought them too bad.

2. Countless houses of mean streets on the grid plan were incontinently run up, no notice being taken of the contour of the ground or of existing trees or other amenities, each estate being developed quite independently of the other, usually without any drainage. The extent, by the way, to which our industrial towns are innocent of adequate drainage would be a surprise to those who have not personal knowledge of them.

When the speculator decided to run up his house, he was usually able to buy his land quite cheaply, and his grid plan was often arranged fairly amply; so that each house had a longish strip of garden at the back of it— all the gardens forming a kind of square. But in days when there were no trams and no bicycles, the demand to be near the works was very great, and our speculator quickly found that all his houses were occupied, and that more were demanded.

3. The value of land had meantime gone up in the neighbourhood, and he saw that if he wanted to buy more of the land, whose value the growth of the town had appreciated, he must pay a very heavy price for it. He therefore cast his eye back on the plot that he already had, and found that either by building back to back with the original houses or by planning a little inner street down the middle of what used to be the gardens, he could do what was held to be his whole duty in life—that is, to double his income.

CLOUGH WILLIAMS-ELLIS, *England and the Octopus*

5. Summarise each of the following very briefly; the first, for example, should be reduced to six words:

(a) The Colonial Office, the Foreign Office, The Dominions Office, The Ministry of Health, The Home Office and the Board of Admiralty are all situated in or near Whitehall.

(b) *The Fish Trades Gazette*, *The Fruitgrower*, *The Furniture Record*, *The Hairdressers Weekly*, *The Pianomaker* and *The Toy Trader* are not regularly found on the average bookstall.

(c) The Institute of Chartered Accountants, the Institute of Chemical Engineers, the Institute of Electrical Engineers, the Institute of Municipal Treasurers and Accountants and the Royal College of Physicians set their own entrance examinations.

(d) A good General Certificate of Education is needed for pharmacy, librarianship, mechanical engineering, radiography and meteorology.

(e) But for teaching in grammar and similar schools, the administrative grades of the Civil Service, university lecturing, the priesthood and scientific research a degree is essential.

(f) In the storm her smokestack was blown out of the true, a life-boat was stove in, two hatches were flooded, and a good deal of glass and light woodwork was smashed.

6. What can be sent in the form of small packets and samples? Are there any restrictions as to contents? For safety reasons, certain types of item have been prohibited, e.g. things which may soil or damage correspondence or be dangerous to post office employees on account of their nature or packing, such as drugs, explosive and inflammable matter and—what would not have occurred to one at first—live animals, with the exception of bees, leeches, silkworms, and parasites or enemies of insect pests when exchanged between officially recognised institutions for campaigns against insects; the parcels containing them must of course be carefully packed, and their contents clearly indicated on the wrapping.

Oral Questions:

May explosives be sent by post? Give reason.
May silkworms go by post?
May parasites of insects go by post? Give reason.
Summarise the paragraph in one sentence suitable for display as a notice in a post-office.

7. Formerly each country had its own postal service, which it administered as it thought fit. To enable a letter to be conveyed from one country to another, a treaty was needed to regulate the postal relations between the two countries concerned; thus a separate agreement had to be made with each country with which correspondence was exchanged. The sender's country levied a fee on letters for carriage by its own postal service from the place of dispatch to the frontier; and a further charge was made by each country through which the letter passed, and by the country of destination. This meant that every time a letter was sent, a complicated sum had to be worked out to find the total postage payable by correspondents. The cost differed according to the route by which a letter was sent; and weight rates varied from country to country. All these complications seriously slowed up exchanges of correspondence, and prevented their proper expansion. This state of affairs had to be remedied and some agreement had to be reached internationally, in order to unify and simplify the postal services.

Oral Question:

The paragraph above might be précised on these lines; fill in the blanks to complete the sense:
When each country . . . foreign correspondence was costly because . . ., complicated, because . . ., and slow, because . . . This state of affairs was remedied by . . . (two words only).

Chapter 5

OTHER ELEMENTS

AFTER the Essay and Précis, your Language Paper is likely to be made up of some of these: Comprehension test, Vocabulary work, Grammar, Punctuation, and—to a less degree—explanation of proverbs and figurative expressions, and correction of sentences. With Essay and Précis, the theory is important; you need to know something about aim and method before your practice will be of any use. But with most of the remaining elements in the Language Paper, practice is everything, except in the grammar questions. Of course you can get used to the types of question you are likely to meet, but in the main these miscellaneous questions test, not the teaching a candidate has had, but the candidate, herself or himself. They are very much a practical examination, like the practical part of woodwork or cooking. Theory helps little; you need practice to attain the necessary degree of skill, and then probably most of you need do no more. As with riding a bicycle—once learned, it is never forgotten —so with the Language Paper. It is your skill in understanding and handling words that is being examined, not the amount of information you have taken in. And, once again, this skill is acquired by practice, practice mainly in reading.

This chapter touches on all the types of question you are likely to meet; but you will certainly not have to attempt all the types discussed here. Therefore you must find out, from the syllabus, and from back papers, which parts of this chapter are the most important ones for you. The items in the chapter are arranged roughly in their order of frequency in examination papers.

COMPREHENSION TESTS

These are compulsory in all examinations but one. Sometimes a separate prose passage is provided, sometimes the questions are set on the extract used for the précis question. The remarks above about the unimportance of the theoretical side particularly apply to work in comprehension. There is no advice to give, other than that which applies to all examinations: study the question set; keep your head; answer the question set. A little practice is what is required. Most likely you will have had far too much comprehension work; because it is set in the certificate, it tends to be part of the English syllabus for years before the examination. This is unfortunate, because one of the aims of studying English is to read good books, and whole books. The continual examination of snippets of prose is a tedious business, and—more than that—a waste of time. For there is no evidence that a pupil who has done five years of comprehension questions is any better at answering them than one who has done only five weeks. The reading of real books with reasonably close attention is as good a preparation as any for comprehension work, as well as for many of the other questions commonly set in the Language Paper.

For those who need some immediate practice, a few examples are provided below.

A

An interesting question concerns the origin and significance of the plumage variations. . . . Why, for instance, should the robins of Tunis and of England be similar in plumage, while those in the large area between are
5 different? Can the environment in which robins live be similar in England and Tunis but different in between? Or has the resemblance in plumage some quite different explanation? It seems too close an agreement to be due to accident. Why, again, should the robins of the

10 western Canary Islands look extremely similar to those
of Sweden 2,000 miles away, but extremely different
from those of the central Canary Islands only 20 miles
away? Could it be that the distinctive Tenerife robin
superbus is an earlier race which, like the human
15 Guanches of the same islands, has been largely ex-
terminated by later evolved types from the mainland?
These and many other problems await solution. The
robins' skins lie in museum drawers, but the answer to
these problems must be sought in the field.

DAVID LACK, *The Life of the Robin*

1. The word "origin" (l. 1) could be explained by replacing it with a direct question "How did the plumage start to vary?" Similarly replace "significance"
(l. 1) with a direct question.
2. What possible explanation is suggested for the likeness in plumage of robins in England and Tunis?
3. Do the robins of France resemble the robins of Tunis
in their plumage?
4. Does the "distinctive Tenerife robin" live in the
western or the central Canary Islands?
5. What may be the explanation for the difference
between the robins of the central and western
Canary Islands?
6. Complete this re-writing of the last sentence of the
paragraph: "The answer to these problems cannot
be found by research in museums, but by . . ."

B

He rose from supper a giant refreshed; and, changing
his seat to one nearer the fire, began to examine the
other guests with an eye to the delights of oratory.
There were near a dozen present, all men, and (as
5 Joseph exulted to perceive) all working-men. Often
already had he seen cause to bless that appetite for dis-
connected fact and rotatory argument which is so
marked a character of the mechanic. But even an

audience of working-men has to be courted, and there
10 was no man more deeply versed in the necessary arts
than Joseph Finsbury. He placed his glasses on his nose,
drew from his pocket a bundle of papers, and spread
them before him on a table. He crumpled them, he
smoothed them out; now he skimmed them over,
15 apparently well pleased with their contents; now, with
tapping pencil and contracted brows, he seemed
maturely to consider some particular statement. A
stealthy glance about the room assured him of the
success of his manoeuvres; all eyes were turned on the
20 performer, mouths were open, pipes hung suspended;
the birds were charmed. At the same moment the
entrance of Mr. Watts afforded him an opportunity.

R. L. STEVENSON and LLOYD OSBOURNE: *The Wrong Box*

1. Explain in your own words:

    (*a*) with an eye to the delights of oratory (l. 3).
    (*b*) assured him of the success of his manoeuvres
    (l. 18).

2. Why did Joseph "exult" to see his hearers were
working-men?

3. What is the meaning in their contexts of "courted"
(l. 9), "deeply versed" (l. 10), "exulted" (l. 5)?

4. What was the aim of the "manoeuvres" (l. 19)?

5. Mention the evidence for the statement that the
"birds were charmed" (l. 21).

6. The word "mechanic" has changed its meaning since
1889, but you can tell its meaning in the passage
because it is interchangeable with another word.
What is the other word?

7. Write one sentence describing the characteristic of
Joseph mentioned in this extract.

C

Going to the movies is to-day as ingrained a habit as
smoking cigarettes or drinking alcohol, and it serves

very much the same purpose: while seeming to stimulate it dulls the nerves. Grandiose narcotic! As we turn
5   the corner into the high street there it rises in fantastic
splendour, Odeon or Palladium, bigger, newer, more
expensive than the buildings round. It spreads a carpet
of light over the pavement, and inside the carpets are
thicker than elsewhere. Great staircases or corridors
10   with gilded mirrors and artificial flowers suck in the
payer of 2s. 4d. A musical-comedy footman passes us
on to the musical-comedy chorus who light us to our
seats. We are wrapped round with warmth, twilight,
ease. Relax, says the twilight, let go. In moments when
15   the screen is empty an organ rises out of the depths to
hum and whinny chromatic tunes. The lights change
from green to magenta. It might be a parody of a church
service, like those innocuous cabaret turns labelled
"Enfer" for the benefit of pre-war tourists to Mont-
20   martre. All this—and the people guided in and out, the
interlocked couples—we have learnt to take for granted:
the wrapper on the packet, the label on the bottle.
Whatever the picture we are about to see it will have
been voted in advance the greatest, the most astound-
25   ing, most vibrant, most human drama ever filmed.

Made for Millions, "The Film", by G. W. STONIER

1. What features of the cinema "dull the nerves"
   (l. 4)?

2. What evidence is given for the statement that films
   pretend to stimulate?

3. What do you consider to be the meaning of narcotic
   (l. 4) in this context?

4. What is there about the commissionaire and usher-
   ettes that leads the writer to describe them as
   "musical-comedy"?

5. "The wrapper on the packet, the label on the bottle"
   (l. 22). What is the wrapper and what is in the
   packet?

6. Who will have done the "voting in advance" (l. 24), and how?
7. Have you yourself noticed anything of the kind described in the last sentence of the paragraph?

GRAMMAR

The grammar questions set in the Language Paper are rarely compulsory. They are of two kinds: (a) Analysis, sometimes with parsing, and (b) correction of sentences containing grammatical errors.

In analysis questions you may be given a complete sentence and asked to "Analyse it into clauses, stating the kind and function of each". Remember that there are three kinds of clause: (1) Noun clauses, (2) Adjectival clauses and (3) Adverbial clauses.

(1) For example, in the sentences:

I can't understand your *game*
I can't understand *what you're playing at*

the italicised words are the objects; and in the second sentence a clause is acting as a noun. Such noun clauses may also be the subjects of sentences; they can do all the work done by a noun.

(2) In these examples:

The *most popular* books to-day are works of travel.
The books *that are read most to-day* are works of travel.

the words in italics describe "books", the second example containing of course an adjectival clause. "That", and the other relative pronouns "who", "which", "what" together with the relative adverbs "where", "whence", "whither" introduce (i.e. begin) adjectival clauses. Remember, in doing analysis, that the relative pronoun is often omitted in English, e.g.

The town I live in isn't very old.
Where's the book you got out for me?
The man I saw yesterday didn't return.

(3) Of adverbial clauses there are eight main kinds, always introduced by a subordinating conjunction—a conjunction, that is, which makes the clause that follows an appendage to the main sentence. Here are examples, with alternative labels, of the kind used in Latin grammar, in brackets:

TIME (temporal): *after, before, when, until, as, since,* etc.
You must decide *before the baker comes.*

PLACE (local): *where, whither,* etc.
Leave the injured man *where he is.*

PURPOSE (final): *that, in order that, so that* (. . . may, . . . might)
They took a taxi *that no time might be lost.*

RESULT (consecutive): *so . . . that, so that, with the result that*
He has heard that tune so often *that he never wants to hear it again.*

CAUSAL: *because, since, as*
She's buying matches *because her lighter is broken.*

CONCESSIVE, i.e. clauses in which some allowance is made: *although*
Though he had no oxygen, he climbed fast.

COMPARATIVE: *as, than*
At your age I couldn't swim *as you do.*

(*N.B.*—The verb is often omitted, and must be understood, in comparative clauses:

You have more stamps *than I* (*have*).)

CONDITIONAL: *if, unless, so long as*
Don't cross the moor *if the red flag is flying.*

When you are given a complex sentence for analysis, bracket off the clauses and decide which is the main clause. Then give a label (one of those above) to each subordinate clause and say what its work in the sentence is. For example:

> *Analyse the following sentence into clauses; state the kind, and give the exact grammatical function of each:*
>
> When they had reached the summit, Hillary took photographs with his camera, which he had kept in his clothing so that it shouldn't freeze up.

The brackets will be placed thus:

    i. (When they had reached the summit)
   ii. (Hillary took photographs with his camera)
  iii. (which he had kept in his clothing)
  iv. (so that it shouldn't freeze up)

The main clause can usually be picked out because it is the only one that will stand by itself and make sense—in this case clause (ii). Clause (i) is an adverbial clause of time modifying *took* in (ii). Clause (iii) is an adjectival clause qualifying *camera* in (ii). Clause (iv) is an adverbial clause of purpose modifying *had kept* in clause (iii). Note that:

> an adjectival clause *qualifies* the word it goes with,
> an adverbial clause *modifies* the word it goes with.

For practice turn back to Question 4, on page 57, and in section 1 find an adverbial clause of time, and two adverbial clauses of condition; in section 2 find an adjectival clause and a noun clause; in section 3 find a noun clause and an adjectival clause.

One or two examinations still offer parsing questions. To parse a word is to give an exact grammatical description of a word and its function in the sentence of which it is a part. In parsing, the first requirement is to say what part of speech is the word in question, and then to proceed thus:

Nouns
State the case and the number; and give the reason for the case. The gender may also be given.

Pronouns
State kind of pronoun, person, case, number; and give the reason for case. With relative pronouns state the antecedent.

Adjectives
State kind of adjective (qualitative, numeral, etc.); degree (positive, comparative, superlative); what it qualifies.

Verbs
State transitive or intransitive; person, number, tense, mood, voice; subject.

Adverbs
State kind of adverb (simple, interrogative or conjunctive) and what it modifies.

Prepositions
State what word it governs.

Conjunctions
State kind of conjunction (co-ordinate or subordinate) and what words or clauses it connects.

For example:

Parse the words in the sentence "I know the reason for his departure".

I:	personal pronoun, first person, nominative singular, subject of "know".
know:	transitive verb, first person, singular, present indicative active; subject is "I".
the:	definite article, qualifying "reason".
reason:	noun, accusative singular; object of "know".
for:	preposition, governing "departure".
his:	possessive adjective, qualifying "departure".
departure:	noun, accusative singular, governed by preposition "for".

As well as clause-analysis, a large number of miscellaneous grammar questions are set; sometimes sentences including one or more mistakes are provided for correction. A reading of a number of examination papers shows that questions involving mistakes in number, case, and tense occur frequently, as well as many questions on usage and idiom. Some characteristic sentences-for-correction now follow, with the correction and explanation in brackets.

Number

Neither John nor Mary want to play.
(*wants*, because the two subjects are considered separately.)

Everyone must realise that what is best for themselves may not suit others.
(*himself*, because it refers back to the singular "everyone".)

The result of long training and hard practice by the Oxford team were many victories.
(*was*, because the subject "result" is singular.)

Roberts, with his friends Willoughby and Smith, were first on the scene.
(*was*, because there is only one subject.)

Anyone can dine at the Ritz provided that they have the money.
(*he has*, because "anyone" is singular.)

We must expect these kind of sheep in southern markets.
(*this* kind, because "kind" is singular. This mistake, found in many good writers from Shakespeare onwards, occurs because the writer is thinking ahead to the plural word.)

Albert Schweitzer is one of those rare figures who puts service to humanity first.
(*put*, because the antecedent of "who" is the plural "figures".)

Case

You play tennis better than him.
> (*he*, because the verb "plays" is understood; or *he does*, where "does" equals "plays".)

He is one of those whom I think will succeed this year.
> (*who*; nominative needed for subject of verb "will succeed".)

After a month in the sun he looks like you and I.
> (*me*, because "like" here acts as a preposition and governs the accusative case.)

There's no difference in appearance between you and I.
> (*me*, because it is governed by the proposition "between".)

I think it was him who won the Amateur Championship in 1953.
> (*he*, not *him*. *He* completes the idea of the verb "was"; it is the nominative complement, not the object of a verb.)

Tense

I should have preferred to have gone by myself.
> (*to go*; the second perfect tense is superfluous—a common error.)

It is expected that play would continue till 6.40.
> (*will continue*; wrong sequence of tenses.)

I shall have much pleasure in accepting the invitation.
> (*I have*; the pleasure in the acceptance is now.)

Idiom

First aid for animals is not particularly different than first aid for human beings.
> (*different from* is correct.)

I prefer ginger ice, if I can get it, than chocolate.
> (*to chocolate*.)

Nylon is superior, for some purposes, than cotton.
> (*superior to* is correct; "than" follows a comparative adjective, e.g. "better", but "superior" is positive.)

The doctor was disgusted at the quack remedies offered to sufferers with rheumatism.
> (*disgusted with, sufferers from*.)

Finally there is a large chamber of horrors from which howlers are brought out to test a candidate's knowledge of English usage. Commonest perhaps is the floating participle:

Opening the cupboard door, the skeleton fell out on us.
(*When we opened the cupboard door* . . .
As the sentence stands, it means that the skeleton opened the door.)

Frequent in poorly spoken English are various forms of tautology (saying the same thing twice) and superfluity. For examples:

Both gazed at each other.
(*They gazed* . . . "each other" implies that two people are concerned and makes "both" superfluous.)

He drives equally as well as his father.
(*equally* is superfluous.)

The only alternative . . .
(*only* is superfluous, because "alternative" means one of two choices.)

Those interested may care to look up pp. 327 and 328 of Eric Partridge's *Usage and Abusage*, where there is a fine display of tautologies, from which I take a few examples:

> co-operate together
> final completion
> new innovation
> original source
> repay back

Every year examiners, in their reports, complain about the bad English of certificate candidates, and I had intended to print a museum collection of all these errors, so that they might always be shunned. But it would take up too much space, so I will group together a few "howlers" which have appeared, and then deal with a final half-dozen or so types of error. The howlers are:

I can't hardly . . .
The snow lays on the ground . . .
He don't . . .
She learned her pupils . . .
The bell has rang . . .
Literally glued to their chairs with fright . . .

An error which examiners used to be fond of setting is the misuse of "due to". "Due" is an adjective, and is correctly used in:

The collapse of the bridge was due to flooding.

where "due" is an adjective qualifying "collapse". But it is wrong to say:

Due to flooding, the bridge collapsed.

The adjective "due" has nothing to go with, and we must use instead a word that has become a preposition, "Owing to . . ." Actually "due to" is so commonly used, that it is likely to be considered good English fairly soon.

The misuse of "like" is another popular mistake. You must not say:

Put your money in the bank like I do.

because "like" is an adjective and cannot (at present) be used as a conjunction. Two sentences are being connected, and the conjunction "as" is needed.

Now consider this sentence:

He didn't like me fiddling with the radiator.

What "he" disliked was the "fiddling", but grammatically it means that "he" disliked "me", which may not be true. Since it is the fiddling that is disliked, the sentence must be corrected to:

He didn't like my fiddling with the radiator.

In the correct version "fiddling" is a verbal noun, object

of "didn't like"; in the wrong one "fiddling" is a participle agreeing with "me".

Another mistake about which examiners complain is the transposition of qualifying phrases, and with it I shall include the misplaced "only". Taking "only" first, consider the different meanings obtained by placing "only" in various places in the sentence, "A man could do that". The rule is that "only" must go next the word it modifies. As for qualifying phrases, this example (which Mr. E. H. Blakeney records) shows what can happen when they are wrongly placed:

> Erected to the memory of . . .,
> accidentally shot, as a mark of
> affection by his brother.

Some of the errors above are due to a speaker's or writer's forgetfulness. A sentence is started in one way and concluded in another. This may account for floating participles, and even for the omission of the subject. Forgetfulness or carelessness accounts for the misuse of "and" before "which". Thus

> Bannister covered a mile in four minutes at Oxford in May 1954—a splendid achievement under not very favourable conditions, and which gave a great impetus to other attempts to get within four minutes.

The word "and" here is meant to connect "a splendid achievement" with the clause beginning "which . . ." But no connection is needed; the relative pronoun is itself a means of connection with its antecedent. "And" must be used to connect two likes, e.g. two nouns, two adverbs, two main sentences, etc. The only case where "and which" is permissible is when two relative clauses are being connected:

> The rhinoceros, which Dürer drew and which was unlike any real animal, was for many years copied by artists.

REWRITING

Your examination may offer passages for rewriting, in one of three ways. First, a short paragraph without any stops may be provided for rewriting with punctuation. Second, a number of short sentences may be set out, and the candidate asked to combine them into a single complex sentence. Third, a passage of direct speech may be set for turning into indirect speech. All three are good exercises, quite apart from the use that examiners make of them.

Punctuation exercises are usually well carried out by candidates; there is not much to go wrong. Three mistakes are sometimes made. First, a single comma is inserted between subject and verb:

The breakdown gang and the police, eventually got the lorry on to the road again.

There should be no comma, for there is no need. A pair of commas between subject and verb is needed, for example, when a phrase in apposition or an adjectival phrase or clause occurs, thus:

Gerbault, unlike many other famous voyagers, spent a year sailing alone in the Mediterranean.

The commas here do the work of brackets. Next, candidates forget that a question mark counts as a full stop and must be followed by a capital letter; and thirdly they tend to omit the commas required when direct speech is quoted, as in this example:

"Please give me six coppers," she replied, "I want to telephone."

Here is a short passage if practice is wanted at once; punctuation and capital letters are to be inserted:

theres a kettle of hot water charity said i thought perhaps youd like to wash before supper and then i can wash afterwards as emma said nothing she added i think we *ought* to wash tonight we didnt yesterday and not much the day before

EMMA SMITH, Maidens' Trip

A second type of rewriting, sometimes set, is on these lines:

Combine the following sentences into a single complex sentence:

We lay on our bunks. We tried to cheer each other with happy reminiscences. Every now and then we came back to our present position. We tried to find out if there was anything more we could do. Suddenly into the cabin fluttered two bedraggled little swallows.

You are expected to restore the piece of writing to the state it was in before being mangled for examination purposes, thus:

We lay on our bunks, trying to cheer each other with happy reminiscences, every now and then coming back to our present position and trying to find out if there was anything more we could do, when suddenly into the cabin fluttered two bedraggled little swallows.

HUMPHREY BARTON, Atlantic Adventures

For immediate practice, if required, there follow further examples. Each group of sentences is to be turned into a complex sentence, by the addition of conjunctions and by other small changes:

The Mounted Police were always in and out. They left cheerful chaos alone. They quickly interfered. The aim was to prevent serious disorder. They sensed real commotion at once.

A. GRAHAM, The Golden Grindstone

There was a bad harvest. An unusually wild winter followed. Such storms had not been known for thirty years. They swept over the country. They brought a hard frost and biting wind. The wind pierced to the very marrow of your bones.

K. FITZGERALD, They Lived in County Down

They sailed round the coast. Pocahontas's excitement grew. She was eager to be quit of the ship. She was eager to plunge into the heart of England. She was not disappointed. Rolfe said they would go to Heacham at once.

D. GARNETT, Pocahontas

The third type of rewriting that may come your way is introduced by a question on the lines of:

> *Turn the following passage into Reported Speech, beginning with the words "He said that":*

The rules for turning Direct into Reported Speech after a verb in the past tense are:

1. Tenses of verbs must be changed—Present into Past (Perfect); Perfect into Pluperfect; Future into Conditional.
2. First and second person Pronouns are changed into the Third Person.
3. Adverbs and Demonstrative Adjectives will need altering to fit the change of tenses (e.g. "now" becomes "then", "this" becomes "that", and so on).

The working of rule 2 may cause confusion, thus:

Direct: I will not endure your interference or his rudeness.

Indirect: He said that he would not endure his interference or his rudeness.

The reported version uses the same word *his* to refer to two people, presenting the reader with an ambiguity. This can be avoided by adding a proper name, thus:

He said he would not endure his opponent's interference or Mr. Smith's rudeness.

You may be given a piece of dialogue, and in this case you will have to add such expressions as "X replied", "Y went on", "Z retorted".

The passage that follows is for turning into Reported Speech:

I am very ready to make a statement on this subject, but the situation in Geneva is now so uncertain that I think it would be better to wait till Monday. I will then give the fullest answers which are possible.

This will become:

He said that he was very ready to make a statement on that subject, but the situation at Geneva was then so uncertain that he thought it would be better to wait till Monday. He would then give the fullest answers which were possible.

The next example for rewriting is a piece of dialogue:

Captain Edwards now looked sane enough: so Abraham ventured to ask him:
"Why won't you allow my men on board?"
Edwards turned red as a colonel.
"I allow no man on board without my permission."
"Why?" said Abraham bluntly. "Have you got an infectious disease on board?"
"If I refuse permission, no man on earth has a right to ask my reason!" cried Edwards, thumping the table.

When turned the dialogue appears in this form:

He stated that Captain Edwards at the time had looked sane enough, so Abraham had ventured to ask why he would not allow his (Abraham's) men on board. Edwards had turned red as a colonel and emphasised that he would allow no man on board without his permission. Abraham had again asked the reason, bluntly enquiring whether they had an infectious disease on board. At this Edwards had thumped the table and cried out that if he refused permission no man on earth had a right to ask his reason.

Some further examples are printed, for immediate practice:

Turn the following passage into Direct Speech:

The Rev. John Gedge, Rector of Mundesley, today expressed his conviction that unless a solid sea wall was built, the parish church, the hall and other buildings would in time disappear over the cliff or become so near it as to be too dangerous for use. He claimed that the existing revetment at the west end would not halt erosion because the method did not give the requisite degree of stability to the base of the cliff. Only a solid sea wall, he said, would do that.

Turn the following adapted quotation from "The Times" into Reported Speech, beginning "Mr. Shinwell asked the . . ."

Mr. Shinwell: Is the Prime Minister aware that the Belgian Government is proposing to reduce the period of conscription to 18 months, and that the United States Government is considering a reduction to six months; and, as both these Governments are associated with N.A.T.O., will he consider an early reduction in the length of national service?

Sir Winston Churchill: I am aware of the proposals of the Belgian Government. The Right Hon. gentleman is mistaken in suggesting that the United States Government is considering a reduction to six months' whole-time service. Our own period of national service must be determined by our own requirements. But, as was said in this year's Statement on Defence, the Government are keeping the question under review.

Turn the following passage into Reported Speech, beginning with "Racksole then wished Jules good-day . . ."

'Good-day, then. You have my good wishes and my admiration, so long as you keep out of my hotel.'

Racksole got up.

'Good-day, sir. And thank you.'

'By the way, Jules, it will be useless for you to apply to any other first-rate European hotel for a post, because I shall take measures which will ensure the rejection of any such application.'

'Without discussing the question whether or not there aren't at least half a dozen hotels in London alone that would jump for joy at the chance of getting me,' answered Jules, 'I may tell you, sir, that I shall retire from my profession.'

'Really! You will turn your brains to a different channel?'

'No, sir. I shall take rooms in Jermyn Street, and just be content to be a man-about-town. I have saved some twenty thousand pounds.'

ARNOLD BENNETT, *The Grand Babylon Hotel*

VOCABULARY

The ability to communicate precisely is what distinguishes man from other animals. The latter can show their feelings but not much more. For man, words are the tools of communication, and the more complicated and subtle his needs, the greater the number of words needed, and the greater degree of precision required. A good vocabulary and the ability to use it are the signs of a civilised human being, and for this reason tests of vocabulary and idiom are provided in many language papers. A good vocabulary is acquired by practice in the use of words for reading and writing. There are no rules to be laid down, but an analysis of the questions set shows that three types recur: (i) Formation of words from other parts of speech; (ii) Questions on meaning (this is by far the largest class); and (iii) Questions on idiomatic use of words.

(i) Questions requiring word-formation:

Give the abstract nouns connected with the following words:

acquiesce, oblivious, indifferent, irate, slow, probable, tranquil, grow, strange, rapid.

Form verbs from the following nouns:

inscription, danger, peril, black, glory, antagonist, facility, trench, guile, application.

Add the suffix -able, or -ible, to each of the following words, making any necessary changes in spelling:

present, divide, pay, reverse, notice, eat, manage, sink, avert, bear.

(ii) Questions are also asked on these lines:

Find a single word to express the idea of each of the following:

that which cannot be divided
without having made a will
to make amends to a person for damage done
a written authorisation to make an arrest
one who pretends to foretell the future by the stars
one who runs away from the reach of the law
occurring at the same time
the hour for extinguishing fires and lights in the evening
supply which exceeds the demand of the market
the curved track of a heavenly body

Give the opposites, by adding or removing a prefix, of:

similar, connected, consistent, acceptable, animate, qualification, eligible, literate, movable, illegible

Give a brief definition of:

museum, television, detergent, monopoly, taxation, bacteriology, encyclopedia, epic (noun), opera, pleat (noun)

State the difference between the words in each of the following pairs, adding a sentence or example to illustrate your definition:

eminent, imminent
notable, noticeable
famous, infamous
disinterested, uninterested
wisdom, knowledge
disgusting, distasteful
access, excess
differ, defer
insensitive, insensible
secret, secrete

Under the heading of "meaning" come the non-comparable or non-qualifiable adjectives. Questions requiring a knowledge of these are often set in the form of errors for correction. A sentence such as the following may be set for rewriting or comment:

Bannister's achievement is absolutely unique, but in the number of records broken Wooderson is more supreme.

Here "unique" and "supreme" are wrongly used. "Unique" means "unequalled, without any of the same kind". A thing is either unique (one of its kind) or it is not; there is no half-way house. So it cannot be compared; you cannot say "A is more unique than B" if there is only one of "A". If there is more than one "A", "A" cannot be unique. Similarly, there is no point in adding "absolutely" to "unique". Again, a person or thing is either "supreme" or not; there is only one apex to a pyramid.

Other such adjectives are: complete, empty, fatal, full, indispensable, inferior, perfect, priceless, simultaneous, superior and unanimous.

(iii) Lastly under the heading "Vocabulary" we find questions on the correct usage of certain words, as in this example:

What prepositions normally follow the words listed below?
Write a short sentence to illustrate the correct use of each word:

aim	liable
acquiesce	replete
averse	suspicious
derived	tolerant
opposed	void

One caution is needed to those who have to answer vocabulary questions: make quite sure that you answer the question. This sounds obvious enough advice, but it is a fact that many candidates, who have the right answer somewhere in their heads, fail to convince the examiner. If, for example, you are asked to give dictionary definitions of words, then you must give a noun phrase to define a noun, an adjective phrase to define an adjective, and so on. If the word you are asked to define comes from a given passage, then it should be possible to remove the word and replace it by your definition, so that the passage still makes sense. For example, you might be asked to explain the words italicised in:

In this unsatisfactory manner the *penultimate* message of Cavor dies out. One seems to see him away there in the blue *obscurity* amidst his apparatus *intently* signalling us to the last.

H. G. WELLS, *The First Men in the Moon*

The equivalents should be on these lines:

penultimate: last but one
obscurity: indistinctness, or state of dimness
intently: with a look of concentration, or, in an earnest manner.

But what candidates often do is to offer an adjective or adjective phrase where a noun or noun phrase is required, defining, for instance, "obscurity" as "very indistinct".

The same rule applies to the giving of synonyms or

opposites; a similar part of speech must be chosen. For example, a synonym for "dignity" is "stateliness", not "stately", and the opposite of "spacious" is "cramped", not "narrowness". It is important to answer such questions in the right way, and a few examples are therefore given below, for practice in providing equivalents. Remember that if you are asked to provide a one-word synonym for a given word, you must give a similar part of speech; if you are required to give a dictionary definition, you may give a synonym, if you can think of one, followed by a phrase, thus:

> blindness: sightlessness, condition of being blind.

Remember too that if you are defining a verb, your equivalent should be in the infinitive, i.e. your answer must start "To . . ."

The following examples are for practice in producing the equivalent phrase or part of speech.

> *Give a definition, in a single phrase, of each of:*
> highway, grip (verb), torrential, quietly, brush (noun and verb), comfortably, ready, peel (verb), book.

> *Think of one-word synonyms for:*
> permanent, agitate, ponderously, somnolent, normally, fissure, endeavour, rescued, demonstrate, courteously.

PROVERBS AND FIGURES OF SPEECH

What has been said above about producing, as near as can be, the exact equivalent applies also to the explanation of proverbs and figures of speech. The following is a characteristic question.

> *Explain the meaning of the following proverbs:*
> (*a*) A stitch in time saves nine.
> (*b*) The more haste, the less speed.

(c) Good wine needs no bush.

(d) You can take a horse to the water, but you can't make him drink.

(e) Penny wise, pound foolish.

(f) It's an ill wind that blows nobody good.

Below are three attempts to explain (a); which of them is the best?

(i) A remedy applied as soon as it is needed will save trouble later.

(ii) A garment which needs mending should be mended quickly, or it will need more mending afterwards.

(iii) If you see your mudguard loose it will be best to tighten it up quickly or it may come off and get into the spokes.

All of these attempts show that the writers have some idea of the meaning of the proverb, but only one is really good. A proverb usually applies to events or circumstances that may come about at different times, in different places, and to different people. The explanation of a proverb must therefore be in general terms so that it can be widely applied. Only explanation (i) passes this test; it fits any situation where immediate action will save trouble later on; (ii) merely puts the proverb in other words without explaining its general meaning; it refers only to "garments", and, unlike (i), it could not be used by a man noticing that a tile on his roof was loose and that it ought to be secured before the wind loosened others; (iii) also applies only to a particular instance; it gives an example of a special situation to which the proverb could be applied, but it does not explain the proverb in terms that could be used of any situation where a speedy repair is required.

The following are offered as explanations of the remaining proverbs:

(b) An action taken in a hurry is likely to mean delay in the long run, because lack of thought and care will make a fresh start necessary.

(c) A sound and reliable product does not require any advertising. (A bunch of ivy used to be hung outside a house where wine was for sale.)

(d) You can offer a person advantages and opportunities, but you cannot compel him to make use of them.

(e) It is unwise to be stingy over spending small sums, if the saving only means that much greater amounts will have to be spent later.

(f) However unwelcome an unfortunate turn of events may be to most people, it may still do good to someone.

When dealing with figurative expressions it is necessary to decide whether the phrase amounts to a noun, an adjective or a verb, and to give the right equivalent. Consider this typical question:

Explain the meaning of each of the following figurative expressions:

(a) a wolf in sheep's clothing
(b) to shut the stable door after the horse has got out
(c) as pleased as a dog with two tails
(d) to make a mountain out of a mole-hill
(e) nipped in the bud
(f) a bull in a china shop

The questions include the equivalents of two nouns, two adjectives and two verbs. Note in the answers suggested below that the form of the answer must be varied to suit the question: sometimes all that is needed is to provide an alternative expression; at others, as in (c), (e) and (f), a word or two of explanation is needed. When in doubt use the full form of explanation given in these answers.

(a) a person who conceals evil intentions under a mild and innocent exterior
(b) to apply a remedy too late to be of any use
(c) highly delighted; a dog shows pleasure by wagging

its tail, so that an animal with two could show double pleasure

(d) to exaggerate the difficulty caused by a very small obstacle

(e) checked at the very beginning; this applies to plans which are soon frustrated, just as the bud of a plant is stopped growing by the nip of a frost

(f) an awkward and clumsy person in a situation where he is likely to do a great deal of damage, just like a bull which has found its way into a china shop

Here are some examples for immediate practice:

Explain in your own words the meaning of the following proverbs:

(a) Don't count your chickens.
(b) You've made your bed and you must lie on it.
(c) Pride goes before a fall.
(d) Once bitten, twice shy.
(e) A fool and his money are soon parted.
(f) Keep your breath to cool your porridge.

Briefly define the meaning of the following phrases:

(a) to sit on the fence
(b) to show the white feather
(c) to sail under false colours
(d) to worship the golden calf
(e) a rough diamond
(f) to stick to one's last

Chapter 6

THE PROBLEM OF EVEREST

[JUST before the Coronation of Queen Elizabeth II in 1953 Hillary and Tenzing reached the summit of Everest. Their achievement was the apex of a pyramid of thorough and careful planning. The problem, the plan, and the achievement are all set forth in Sir John Hunt's *The Ascent of Everest*, from which the extract below is taken.]

1. What is the problem of Everest? What were the weapons with which the mountain had so long succeeded in holding at bay so many resolute men? By last autumn, when we were preparing to tackle it, the nature of the undertaking had already been largely exposed; indeed, in a sense it was almost solved, with only the last 1,000 feet unclimbed. It was romantic to suppose that some spell had been cast over the final keep, that a barrier had been reached at about 28,000 feet beyond which even such stout spirits as Norton, Smythe, Wyn Harris and Wager, Lambert and Tenzing could not pass. It might appear that the problem was confined to the breaking of this spell, the forcing of this invisible obstacle, a point in space comparable with the barrier of sound. Although perhaps true in a physiological sense, to follow this line of thought would be to give a totally false impression, just as it would be untrue to say that, with the climbing of the mountain this year, there is no further problem for future aspirants to reach the top. Others had gone before us to approximately the same height on opposite sides of the final peak, but they had not been turned back by any physical obstacle beyond their technical skill to surmount. The terrain was passable; in descriptive mountaineering jargon,

"it would go". Some among this select band maintain that they could have gone farther but for lack of time. I will return to this point later; it is enough to say for the moment that they had been defeated by the cumulative effects of altitude, effects which had been telling both on them and on their supporting comrades from a much earlier stage.

2. There are three factors of awe-inspiring magnitude facing those who seek adventure among the high peaks. They are this matter of vertical scale, the climatic conditions and the climbing difficulties. Let us look at altitude first.

3. The rarefied air surrounding the upper part of Everest, or any other of the big peaks, obviously makes movement, even over easy ground, much more difficult. Lack of oxygen also slows down and blurs the mental processes. Beyond a certain point life itself is no longer possible. On the other hand, it is now sufficiently proved that the ill-effects of altitude on the climber may at least be retarded by a careful regimen of what we call acclimatization, a gradual getting used to increased height over a certain period of time. Individual performances on a mountain naturally vary, but it may be said that those among us who are best adapted to climb high mountains, provided they follow this policy of gradualness, can reach an altitude of at least 21,000 feet and remain there without serious detriment—at any rate long enough to make a supreme final effort to reach a higher point, provided it is not too far above.

4. Trouble begins above that height, which is one main reason why the really high peaks—those of 26,000 feet and over—are in a different category of difficulty from any lesser ones. The policy of gradualness breaks down, for the muscle tissues begin to deteriorate fairly rapidly and the climber's resistance to cold, his fortitude in the face of wind and weather, are weakened. He tends to

lose the promptings of appetite and thirst and he is denied the relaxation of normal sleep. In fact, from about 21,000 feet onwards, he really needs greatly to speed up the rate of his progress and employ "rush" tactics. But this he cannot do. On the contrary, he is increasingly handicapped by the height as he climbs and his progress becomes painfully slow; the mental effort, like the physical, is infinitely greater. If this is true of easy ground, it is the more so when difficulties arise, even minor ones which would not deter a moderate performer at a lower height. A slight change of gradient may be a straw which will break the camel's back. Considering that Everest is over 29,000 feet and that some 8,000 feet have to be climbed above this established level of successful acclimatization, one aspect of our problem, which also played an important part in defeating former expeditions, becomes clear. It would be very desirable, in order to minimize the factor of physical deterioration, to climb those 8,000 feet in a day, or at most two; but this is clearly quite out of the question. For so slowly does the climber move by his own unaided efforts, that four or five days would be required to get up, quite apart from the subsequent descent, and by about the fourth day at the latest, he would already be so weakened, mentally as well as physically, that he would be unlikely to have the strength or the determination for the last lap—just when he needs it most. This is what had happened before at about the 28,000-foot level.

5. But the problem is much more complex than this. These days above 21,000 feet involve the establishment of a number of high camps, and these in turn represent tents, sleeping-bags, mattresses, food, cooking equipment and fuel, as well as climbing gear. All this must be carried up, and because of the need to provide even a modicum of comfort and—more important—protec-

tion against the cold, some of this baggage is inevitably fairly heavy. The loads would be far beyond the capacity of those destined to climb to the top, who should be spared as much as possible for their mission; they must be carried up by others in a supporting rôle. Moreover, in order to keep the size and stocks of these high camps to a minimum, the baggage parties must be staggered in time; the loads must be shifted upwards over a period of days. This period in turn is likely to be protracted because the amount any man can carry at high altitude is so small. So climbing Everest takes a long time, not only because of the need to acclimatize slowly up to a certain point, but also because of the slowing down of the final effort by lack of oxygen.

6. And in the final stages particularly, the saving of time is vital, not only because of physical deterioration but also because of another factor, the most important of all —weather.

7. On all but the smallest mountains, or those on which no serious difficulties are met, the weather obviously plays a big part in mountaineering plans. It imposes a serious handicap on the climber's ability to negotiate difficult ground; it slows his progress and exposes him to cold and wind. He may lose his way and stray on to even more difficult territory, and he may become benighted. The dangers of bad weather on a mountain need no further emphasis, and I mention them only to introduce their more deadly effect on the biggest mountains of all. The periods when weather conditions may be fair enough to permit a serious attempt on the summit of Everest are not only brief and few in any one year; they appear to be rare as assessed over a number of years. Throughout the winter, from November to March, a fierce gale blows constantly from the northwest. It is strong—wind speeds of at least seventy to eighty knots are probable—and it is desperately cold. It

scours the northern flanks of the range and deposits snow on the southern faces; and snow thus overlaid on the existing layer is usually unstable and dangerous, for it is apt to peel off in avalanches. During the winter this great westerly wind rules supreme in these high and lonely places. It is scarcely possible to climb a major Himalayan peak at this season, unless it be by some quite exceptionally protected and straightforward route.

8. In the early summer—it may be late May or the beginning of June, depending on the position of the mountain along the range—a countering element comes up from the south-east in the form of the monsoon. This warm, damp wind from the Bay of Bengal deposits heavy snow on the higher flanks of the mountain barrier; it is particularly intense in the south-east part of the Himalaya, on which it unleashes its force soon after reaching the head of the Bay, and it is in this area that Everest is situated. Monsoon conditions normally continue to prevail in this region until towards the end of September. Some climbing may be done during this period, but the difficulty of climbing all high peaks, particularly in the south-east Himalaya, is greatly increased by the handicaps and dangers of the deep new snow. The chance to get up Everest is probably limited to the gap, or lull, between the departure of the one Fury and the onset of the other; these lulls may occur in May and early October, that is, just before the monsoon sets in, and when it dies away. Nearly all attempts to climb Everest have been made in the pre-monsoon period, although the Swiss last year went back to the mountain in the autumn. While there is no conclusive evidence against it, this second period would seem to offer very small chance of success, for the heavy snow must first be swept off the mountain by the westerly wind, and this wind, when it reaches its full force, is beyond human endurance. Whichever the

period, it is short. Indeed, there is no assurance of any
lull occurring at all between winter conditions and the
oncome of the monsoon. This situation was encountered
by each of the Everest expeditions in 1936 and 1938.

. . . .

9. These two factors, the altitude and the weather, tend
separately and together to defeat the climber. The
height weakens, slows him down; it forces him to spend
days and nights in the course of his assault on the summit; the weather, besides adding to the demands on his
energy and moral fortitude, conspires to deny him the
time he needs to complete his mission. Whereas in
lower mountains and on easy ground the weather may
be no more than a handicap, in the high Himalaya it
is decisive, regardless of terrain.

10. The deduction to be drawn from these two factors was
clear enough. We must either so fortify ourselves that
we could continue, without detriment, to live and have
our being above the limit of natural acclimatization, or,
better still, we must solve the problem of speed. It was
desirable, in fact, that we should meet both these
requirements and thus give to those chosen to attempt
the summit and to their supporters some measure of
insurance against the vagaries of the weather, for safety
in mountain climbing is as much a matter of swiftness
as of sureness of foot. Either or both could be achieved
only by the administration of oxygen in sufficient
quantities to make up for the deficiency in the air, and
for the duration of the upward journey above the limit
of successful acclimatization. In other words, oxygen
may be looked on as a height-reducer, producing conditions comparable with climbing on more familiar
mountains.

11. This need of oxygen on Everest was no new problem;
it had been well known for many years past, although

all climbers had not admitted it was essential; some even considered it undesirable on ethical grounds. It had been used on the first expedition ever to make a serious attempt on the summit, by Finch and Bruce in 1922. But the equipment used hitherto had not brought climbers within range of the summit in much better shape than others who had been climbing without it, owing to the small amount of oxygen provided for a given weight. This question of weight at great heights, unless more than compensated by the oxygen supply, is of capital importance. It would seem that all earlier equipment did comparatively little to reduce the effects of strain, fatigue and deterioration. Our problem was to produce apparatus markedly better in performance than this. The lighter the apparatus, provided always that it would enable the climber to continue for reasonably long periods without replenishing his oxygen supply, the faster we would be able to climb.

SIR JOHN HUNT, *The Ascent of Everest*

Précis and Comprehension

1 Write a clear and connected summary of paragraphs 3 ("The rarefied air . . ."), 4, and 5 (to ". . . lack of oxygen") inclusive.

The remaining five questions are on paragraph 1.

2 What reasons for the failure of previous expeditions are mentioned by the author, but not accepted by him as the real reason? Answer as briefly as possible.

3 What, in the author's view, really prevented previous expeditions from reaching the summit?

4 Write down words that might replace, in their context, each of the following:

resolute, exposed, confined, approximately, select.

5 Write a short explanation of the meaning of each of the words that follow; your answer may take the form of a

dictionary definition, a phrase to replace the given word, or a comment of your own.

romantic, aspirants, terrain, jargon, cumulative.

6 (a) What was "true in a physiological sense"? (l. 15).
 (b) Give the meaning, in your own words, of "not beyond their technical skill to surmount". (l. 23).

Vocabulary, Punctuation, Grammar

1 Seven of the following phrases can be replaced by single words from paragraph 5 of the extract from *The Ascent of Everest*. Find the words and list them, with the number of the equivalent phrase against each:

(i) to become used to the physical conditions of a new environment
(ii) the largest possible amount
(iii) consisting of a number of parts
(iv) a small quantity
(v) in a way that is sure to happen
(vi) appointed work
(vii) to need more and more food and air
(viii) prolonged
(ix) placed at intervals

2 Rearrange the following passage in dialogue form, adding the necessary punctuation, inverted commas and capital letters—"aunt" should be given a capital throughout:

aunt charlotte pounced on the gooseberries fly had in the lap of her pinafore what are you going to do with these ripen them said patsy you cannot ripen green gooseberries said aunt charlotte indeed you can said fly you squeeze them till they are soft and then you suck them till they are sweet i am sure your nurse cannot allow you to do anything so disgusting said aunt charlotte

K. FITZPATRICK, *They Lived in County Down*

3 (i) List all the finite verbs in the following passage; you will then have as many clauses as you have finite verbs.

(ii) Against each verb state the kind of clause in which it occurs, and in the case of subordinate clauses say what the clause modifies or qualifies.

> The first thing I saw when I got back to the ship was Ransome on the quarter-deck sitting quietly on his neatly lashed sea-chest. I beckoned him into the saloon, where I sat down to write a letter of recommendation to a man I knew on shore. When I had finished I pushed it across the table. "It may be of some good to you when you leave the hospital."
>
> JOSEPH CONRAD, *The Shadow-Line*

4 Combine the following simple sentences into not more than three complex sentences, making any alterations you find necessary:

> Stores were landed at the base station. Atkinson was the senior member of those left behind. He took over the dogs. This was according to Scott's directions. He went to Hut Point on 13th February. He was kept in camp by bad weather till the 19th. On this day Crean reached the hut. He brought the news of my breakdown at Corner Camp. A blizzard precluded a start for the purpose of relieving me. This expedition was undertaken as soon as the weather abated.
>
> Based on *South With Scott*

5 Turn the passage below into Reported Speech, after an expression such as "He told his hearers . . ." You may have to add a similar expression later on.

> It is my sincere hope that all road users, whether pedestrians, drivers or riders, will study the Code and respect its provisions. To do so is, in fact, a moral duty. If observance of the provisions of the Code, and the spirit of tolerance and consideration underlying them, became a habit, road accidents would rapidly decrease. They are a social evil which can only be overcome by the co-operation of everyone.
> Please do not glance at the Code and decide that it

does not apply to you: it applies to everyone, and I ask you to study it and act upon it and encourage others to do so.

From the Foreword to *The Highway Code*

6 Explain the meaning of five of the following sayings:

(a) There's many a slip 'twixt the cup and the lip.
(b) It's no use crying over spilt milk.
(c) One swallow doesn't make a summer.
(d) Out of the frying-pan into the fire.
(e) It's a long lane that has no turning.
(f) Manners makyth man.

Subjects for Essay or Discussion

1 Are attempts to break speed records on land, on water, and in the air justified?

2 Is the interest in records in games and athletics a good thing for sport or not? Put your view in the form of a letter to a newspaper.

3 Give an account of any book you have read, or film you have seen, that deals with a feat of exploration or record-breaking, and say why it appeals to you.

4 Use all or some of the following points in an essay on the suggestion that "The spirit of adventure is dead".

Crime is the only opening for adventure now.
Most people have always preferred a comfortable life.
There are still opportunities but people don't take them.
Life is a routine matter with no scope.
Anyone can seek adventure if he or she really wants.
Sailing, climbing are within the reach of many.
The world's surface is well mapped.
Wars provide ample opportunity.
It's a good thing if the spirit of adventure is dead, because it produced pirates and wars.
Outward Bound schools for mountaineering and sailing.

5 Time spent on games and athletics in girls' schools is completely wasted.

6 What could be done, without great expenditure, to make the town or village you live in a pleasanter and safer place?

Books Recommended

GERTRUDE BELL, *Letters* (Penguin selection).
See pp. 94–105 for an account of how Gertrude Bell led to safety, after fifty-three hours on the rope, a climbing party which had been caught in a blizzard.

SPENCER CHAPMAN, *Living Dangerously.*

M. HERZOG, *Annapurna.*

SIR JOHN HUNT, *The Ascent of Everest.*

H. W. MURRAY, *The Story of Everest.*

F. S. SMYTHE, *Kanchenjunga Adventure.*

E. WHYMPER, *Scrambles Among the Alps.*

SIR FRANCIS YOUNGHUSBAND, *The Epic of Mount Everest.*

Chapter 7

GOING TO THE CINEMA

[THE passage below comes from a book planned and written specially for readers of about sixteen.]

1. Do you ever read what the film critics say about a film before you go to see it? It is very interesting to find out whether your opinion agrees with theirs. Re-read their criticisms on your return from the cinema, to refresh your memory on certain points. It is not often a film critic is really wrong in his or her judgment, but you should bear in mind that a critic may be applying standards which are not your own.

2. Some critics do not analyse films so much as estimate their entertainment value and popular appeal. Others judge by very high standards indeed. Each newspaper appeals to a certain type of reader. Some are for those who are not very selective, or who are not interested in the development of film as an independent art; others are for the more serious-minded. You will find it helpful, to begin with at any rate, to study as many different critics as you can. Not only should you compare what a critic says with your own private opinion of a film but you should also compare the critics with each other.

3. The film industry has its own professional papers and magazines which are published both daily and weekly, and they contain criticisms of all films shown to those in the film trade. These criticisms are read by the renters and exhibitors, and greatly influence the bookings of the films. Consequently, the trade paper critics have a most responsible task, and they carry it out with

great ability and impartiality, based on long experience.

4. Do not, of course, confuse a review written by a film critic with a write-up about a film. Write-ups are published in local and provincial papers, and tell you what forthcoming films are about, and who the stars are. Write-ups usually make the films sound inviting, because they are a form of publicity, and back up advertisements of local cinemas in the papers. They are written up from material provided by the renters of the films. You will realise, therefore, what a wealth of difference there is between a brief article which is really advertising this week's or next week's programme, and a careful analytical criticism of films by impartial critics.

5. We began by discussing why we go to the cinema, and decided that most of us go to be entertained, to be taken out of ourselves, and that in time it may become a habit to go without bothering very much about what we are going to see. I then tried to show you how, nice as it is to be entertained, it is nicer still to be entertained in a really worthwhile way.

6. But whether the films we see are important or unimportant, they all influence our outward and visible life. Americanisms have crept into our speech because we have been listening to so many American characters on the screen. Americanisms, or slang, are very expressive and terse, even though they do not claim to be either beautiful or musical. They combine slovenly forms of expression with a brisk way of speaking.

7. Similarly, films influence our manners, and our fashions. It would be difficult to find anyone to-day beyond the influence of the cinema. Feminine hair styles, make-up, and manicure all over the world have followed the fashions set by the stars. In remote country places one sees styles which, before the coming of the cinema, the country people would never have heard of. Not all such influences are undesirable. Whilst any thinking

person realises that to introduce American slang into one's conversation is nothing to be proud about, on the other hand the attention paid to personal appearance and the general smartening up which has occurred during recent years, despite shortages of so many things, are largely the result of the influence of the film. Although a great many feminine fashion whims result in an artificial appearance, and conceal the real person, attention to such details in moderation is better than a complete disregard for one's appearance.

Can we see Real Life on the Screen?

8. Do films truly interpret the age we live in? Documentary films, yes; news reels, to a small degree; fictional feature films, no, or perhaps it would be more correct to say that most feature films give a false picture by exaggerating dramatic and comedy situations, and setting characters in backgrounds which are not always true to life.

9. It is the documentary or factual film that shows us the world in which we live, and here the film comes into its own, for its backgrounds are the real world, and the players ordinary people. As I have said before, it is most unfortunate that documentary films can't be seen in the majority of our cinemas, but it is to be hoped that there will be a place for them in the programmes of the future.

10. Meanwhile, as the documentary film of real life is obviously the true film, and does not show artificial or exaggerated situations, it stands to reason that a blending of the methods used to produce the documentary film with those used in feature production would result in the ideal type of film. Already, as we have seen, there are a few examples of great fictional feature films which are, to some extent, documentary also, because their stories are set against natural backgrounds. This is a

far more life-like kind of film than most of the ordinary 'features', and the more of such films we have the better. The only way for us to get them is to go to see any that come our way, thus showing that they are the sort of film we want.

11. You will find that the average feature film often ignores most of the major problems of life and, instead, encourages us to forget them. Such films are called escapist. They are popular because they enable millions of people to forget the difficulties of everyday life and to relax. To enable them to do this it is obvious that the screen stories must not be too closely related to life. This escapism seems justifiable when you first think of it, but it does not help in the long run because one cannot escape from life. The most intelligent directors and script writers see that there is often drama, heroism, suspense and humour in the lives of ordinary people, and they show this in their films. They give us stories in which we can recognise the sort of people we know, or have met or have heard about—people in which we can *believe*. *Millions Like Us* was that sort of film. The truly great film is the kind that will help us to escape from escapism and meet truth face to face, and help us to understand life better. If we spend all our spare time escaping we may be quite sure that the situations from which we try to escape will surround us on our return.

12. That is why the documentary film is doing such an excellent job. And it is telling us not only about what is going on in our country, but also about other countries. If we can only see sufficient documentary films, and read what we can about the subjects they deal with, our general knowledge will open a whole new world to us.

13. We want entertainment, of course, and the screen can give us that. But it can give us so much more. It can tell us things and show us places which we should most

likely know nothing about otherwise. It can make these things most interesting and exciting. There never was such a chance, before films came, of seeing for ourselves what is going on in the rest of the world. Not to make the most of this chance is throwing away one of the greatest advantages of living in a modern world. Fifty years ago or more the chance wouldn't have been there. If the public shows that it appreciates these films and wants more of them, it will get more of them.

Why are Poor Films made?

14. Perhaps you have sometimes asked yourself, after seeing a particularly feeble film, how it ever came to be made. To be fair, it is not very often we do see films that are poor in every way. A film is not necessarily feeble or bad just because it does not happen to appeal to us, for it may appeal to many other people. But sometimes a film appeals to no one. It may be badly acted, and have totally unconvincing situations. Well, you can be sure it was not produced by any of the great film companies either here or in America, for they make certain that their productions reach the highest possible standards of entertainment. Absolute rubbish is usually made by small producers who are concerned with footage and not with quality. By footage, I mean they regard film in terms of length only, like selling so many yards of cloth and, knowing there is a shortage of films the world over and that most films of feature length (and anything over 3,500 feet counts as a feature film) are fairly sure of a market, they make their poor films as quickly and as cheaply as they can. There are bound to be such films, but one need not bother about them, nor use them as an excuse for criticising the cinema as a whole. The majority of films to-day are excellent in every way, except that the stories they are based upon are not always worthy of all the time and money spent

to produce them. You notice how we always come back to the *story*—the subject-matter—the foundations.

15. If the average screen story had reached the same high standard as technical ability, the film of to-day would be infinitely greater, more worthy of our respect, and nearer to being an independent art form. Instead, stories are borrowed from all other possible sources because of their successes *as* stories or plays, and nothing hinders films from developing on the lines most suited to them so much as this does.

When the Star is too Dazzling

16. But whether features have good, weak, or unsuitable stories, their producers put the necessary ingredients into them to make them box office successes, and the first of those ingredients is, of course, the star. As I have said, one need not entirely condemn the star system, nor the habit so many of us have developed of selecting films *because of the stars in them*, even though we are sometimes missing the best films by merely following the stars. But it is true that, while the cinema-goer's *first* thought in choosing a film is ' Who's the star?', the film itself will not improve.

17. The Soviet film-makers go to the other extreme; they make the story the feature, and the players more or less anonymous. Even when a Soviet film features an actor who plays in, say, a screen biography, such as that of Lenin, so much care is taken over casting, make-up, direction, and acting, that the actor entirely sinks his personality into the character he is playing, instead of being encouraged to remain the star he is, and indulging in all his famous mannerisms. This impersonal type of production is far more true to life and, of course, far less artificial than the story which features a world-famous star. Then we are conscious all the time that the

part is not being played by the actual character the star is representing, but that the character is being used as a vehicle to enable the star to shine with his or her accustomed personal brilliance.

18. But the box office demands stars, spectacle, thrills, and musical numbers and so, by hook or by crook, feature films are written so as to contain them.

19. It would be foolish for those producing costly films to ignore the fact that they must bring in money, but it is even more foolish to sacrifice all imagination, good taste, and intelligence for box office receipts because, in the long run, the purely commercial entertainment film will cease to satisfy an increasingly critical public. As people realise more and more clearly what the film can do they will grow impatient when it does not do it.

20. If, both in the immediate future and in the years to come, you develop and apply your critical faculties, you will be surprised how, in time, whilst enjoying a film as a whole, you will also be separating and analysing the story, the direction, the camerawork, the lighting, the recording, the editing, the art direction, and the acting.

21. You cannot achieve that critical standard all at once, of course, but you can begin immediately, and you will find it very helpful to keep a book containing your observations on the films you see, noting whether they appealed to you or not, and why. It will provide an invaluable record for the future, not only enabling you to check the progress made by, say, a particular Director, but also by showing whether the films that appealed to you become classics. I think you will find, over and over again, that the weakness of a production is in the story, that it is unconvincing or not suitable for the screen.

22. If, in your Club, or in the special kind of non-theatrical film shows which you attend, you become more familiar with documentary films, you will be seeing *two* kinds

of productions simultaneously—two kinds which run *parallel*, the theatrical and the non-theatrical.

23. The rising generation of film-goers—that is, *you*—will decide the sort of film we shall have in the future. So far, in films, as in everyday life, material progress has out-distanced our spiritual progress; film has advanced technically to a much greater degree than it has artistically, imaginatively, and internationally.

24. We can be sure that films will go on improving technically. There will be more and better colour photography, greater depth and solidity of people and objects—or stereoscopic values as this is called—and other effects. What we shall have to watch is that the subjects of the films and their treatment reach the same high standard. We want more films in which the stories are set against real backgrounds, where fact and fiction are blended, but where it is quite clear which is fact and which is fiction. We want films in which what we see is always more important than what we hear, and dialogue has a secondary place. The stage is the place for dialogue to be given first importance. Films are too important in their own right to copy the theatre, or to borrow material from the pages of novels. The cinema, too, can present all nations to all other nations, and really show us how the other half of the world lives.

How can we get more of the best kind of film? First of all by knowing what is the best, and then by choosing to see it whenever we get the chance.

I hope that, after reading this book, you will get even more pleasure and excitement out of going to the cinema than you did before.

ANDREW BUCHANAN, *Going to the Cinema*

Précis and Comprehension

1. Write a précis of not more than 120 words of paragraphs 16–19 inclusive.

2. *Either* say why the writer considers it desirable that there should be more films with "documentary" interest, *or* say what in his view goes to make a good film.

In each case set out the points in numbered tabular form.

3. Briefly explain in your own words the meaning of five of the following in their contexts above:

applying standards (para. 1)
entertainment value (para. 2)
popular appeal (para. 2)
professional papers (para. 3)
the difference between a write-up and a review (para. 4)
escapism (para. 11)
independent (para. 15)

4. Write not more than ten lines on one of:
   (*a*) Does your observation of why people go to the cinema agree with the author's?
   (*b*) Give examples from your own observation of the influence of films on fashion, speech, behaviour and so on.
   (*c*) Describe any film you have seen that was either completely or partly documentary.
   (*d*) How do films need to be improved, apart from technical developments such as colour and stereoscopic effects?

Vocabulary, Punctuation, Grammar

1. Give a word opposite in meaning to twelve of:

critical   imaginative
responsible   normal
taking sides (cf. para. 4)   encourage
desirable   enable
excess (cf. para. 7)   sufficient
worth nothing at all (cf. para. 21)   regard
satisfy   personal

2. Rewrite, adding any necessary punctuation, capitals and inverted commas:

the first lord wavell told us that among his favourites were mr sponges sporting tour the best of surtees hunting novels samuel butlers fantasy erewhon hermann melvilles extraordinary story of whale hunting moby dick and almost anything of kiplings especially puck of pooks hill and the jungle books

3. Analyse paragraph 20 of the extract from *Going to the Cinema* into clauses, writing out each clause in full. Give the grammatical description of each clause and state its function in the sentence.

4. The following passages consist of short sentences that would better be combined into one. Rewrite each so as to form one readable sentence, avoiding the use of such conjunctions as "and" so far as possible. You may alter the wording but not the sense.

   (a) I clung to the machine. It swayed and vibrated. I did not heed how I went. I brought myself to look at the dials. I was amazed to find where I was.

   (b) It was a very hot morning. I think it was the fourth. I sought shelter from the heat in a colossal ruin. It was near the house. I slept and fed in this house. A strange thing happened.

   Based on H. G. WELLS, *The Time Machine*

5. Correct any mistakes you find in the following sentences; you need not write them out in full unless your answer requires it. Do not change the constructions more than you can help.

   (a) A meeting of the villagers, held in the hall, were very unanimous that a new bus shelter was the best of the two proposals.

   (b) The engine began to intermittently cough and practically started, but due to water in the petrol it failed entirely.

   (c) Glaring at each other, both boxers could not hardly wait to chose his corner.

   (d) He should have preferred to have gone with Mary or I, but actually Jane suited him equally as well.

6. Rewrite the italicised phrases so as to bring out their meaning:

(a) *At a conservative estimate* there were 100 present.
(b) Most of them were *blackcoated workers*.
(c) The speaker *gave them the rough edge of his tongue*.
(d) But they *did not turn a hair*.
(e) For he was *in the autumn of his years*.
(f) And they did not grudge him *his place in the sun*.
(g) They knew *his bark was worse than his bite*.
(h) And that very soon he would be *a back number*.

Subjects for Essay or Discussion

1. Describe any memorable film you have seen, and say why you liked or disliked it.

2. What subject or story would you like to see made into a film? Suggest how it should be treated.

3. If you have seen a good play performed, say what advantages the theatre has over the cinema, and then what advantages the cinema has compared with the theatre. Given the opportunity would you prefer to go regularly to a theatre or a cinema?

4. What are Saturday morning film clubs, and what do you think of them?

5. From your knowledge of history, show how the entertainment industry has developed in England. Is there now too much entertainment?

6. Use the following points, or replies to them, in an essay on The Average Film:

"My objections to the Hollywood film are:
That its values are sordid and its morals squalid.
That its stories are silly, its romance tinsel, and its humour infantile.
That it has debased the English language and corrupted the speech of our own youth.
That it unscrupulously revises the facts of history in favour of America.

That it has lowered the prestige of the white man throughout the world."

Quoted from *The Observer*

7. Place the following occupations in the order of their usefulness to mankind:

confectioner   nurse
journalist   professional games player
film-star   doctor
brewer   postman

Give some reasons; then consider whether the order of their popularity is the same as the order of their usefulness.

Books Recommended

ADRIAN BELL, *Corduroy*.

ANDREW BUCHANAN, *Going to the Cinema*.

JAN and CORA GORDON, *Stardust in Hollywood*.

JOHN MADDISON and PHYLLIS LADYMAN, *Living Pictures* (Penguin).

R. MANVELL, *The Cinema* (Penguin).

F. NAUMBERG, *We Make the Movies*.

E. RICE, *Voyage to Purilia* (Penguin).

Chapter 8

THE SPIRIT OF THE JUNGLE

[IN *Living Dangerously* F. Spencer Chapman recounts some of his adventures—driving reindeer in Lapland, kayaking off Greenland, climbing in the Himalaya, living in Lhasa, parachuting, fighting the Japanese, being captured and escaping from them into the jungle.]

1. One of these days, I dare say, somebody will succeed in getting to the moon, and if he manages to get back again, what difficulty he will have in trying to describe the lunar landscape! I experienced the same difficulty in trying to conjure up, for those who have never been there, a picture of the Malayan jungle—indeed more than a picture, for it is not only the visible monotony of greens and browns, but the jungle noises, the jungle smells, and above all the uncanny feel of the jungle that makes it almost impossible to describe it. I have called my book about these years *The Jungle is Neutral* because I think the essential neutrality of the jungle is its most characteristic quality. Allowing for a certain amount of luck, it is your mental attitude to the jungle that decides whether you go under or not. But it took me almost a year to discover this neutrality of the jungle. In the early days I felt it was hostile, actively hostile, and at times altogether terrifying.

2. Imagine me one evening, a few months after the fall of Singapore, walking along a hard-beaten, muddy track, so narrow that the leaves brushed my bare legs. I wore only a pair of ragged khaki shorts and a shirt, and carried an ancient 12-bore hammer gun. I had been out after monkeys, because we were existing at that time on rice,

diluted with tapioca, and various kinds of leaves fried up with coconut-oil and salt. So a dish of stewed monkey was always a valuable addition to our diet. I was tired, depressed, and what was more—I was scared stiff. In the first place, I was not sure if I was on the right track. Surely I had passed that detour caused by a fallen tree several times already? The sun was setting, though I could not even see the sky, much less the sun. After the short tropical twilight it would be dark, and I was terrified of spending the night alone in the jungle. At eye-level I could not see more than twenty or thirty yards in any direction, and higher up I could see only the great tall tree-trunks rising up all round me, shutting out the fresh air and the light. Far up above me they met in an almost impenetrable ceiling of leaves. Many of these tree-trunks rose straight and symmetrical, like the pillars of a cathedral; others were festooned with creepers, some with stems a foot thick and fleshy leaves. And there were hanging gardens up there, where huge-leaved ferns, orchids and other parasitic growths flourished in a world of their own. I had to watch the track carefully in case I put my foot on a snake, or on a scorpion—I had seen them as big as tea plates, obscene creatures with shining black claws and poisonous sting waving in the air; a loathsome red centipede, six inches long and as thick as my finger with venomous fangs like two black thorns. And leeches too: as I brushed past the leaves they attached themselves to my bare legs, and fed between my toes, so that I left a trail of blood as I walked. Others, I was sure, had crawled up beneath my clothes and were even now sucking my blood, but the sight of bloated leeches stuck to my body filled with me such revulsion that I preferred not to look, knowing that when they were replete they would drop off and the wound bleed less than if I pulled them off so that their mouths remained, to fester later.

3. At twilight there is an uncanny hush in the jungle, just before the evening chorus of crickets, cicadas and other insects starts up. It was deadly still, when suddenly a tall palm in front started swinging madly backwards and forwards for no apparent reason. For some time I had had the uneasy feeling that I was being followed. I heard a stealthy sound behind me, but when I stopped to listen the rustling stopped too. I was sure it was a tiger. I could feel the hair standing up on the back of my neck, and my nerves pricked and tingled all over. Suddenly a stick snapped. I wanted to run, but after all I had a gun. True, I had only four home-made cartridges and they were so old and damp that misfires were frequent, but it gave me confidence and I made myself walk. Anyway, it was no good running. I might bump into a Jap patrol or a party of aborigines with their blow-pipes and poisoned darts. I heard an elephant trumpeting ahead of me, a noise which seemed to fill the jungle, starting off in a shrill neigh then coming right down the scale to a deep, deep note, which seemed to set the very air vibrating. I remembered having heard that if once an elephant decides to pursue you, nothing can save you unless you can get up a tree. I shivered, and wished I were back in camp. But I got back all right, just as night fell.

4. A year or two later, how different the jungle seemed! But the change was in me, not in the jungle. By this time I knew the aborigines, I knew that the last thing they would want to do was to shoot a poisoned dart at me or at anybody else. They are the most gentle and friendly people. And I was not afraid of running into a Jap patrol, because experience had taught me that they travelled so noisily, and that their reactions were so slow, that I was always able to see them first, and to step off the path and hide till they passed. Snakes, centipedes and scorpions I was no longer afraid of, for

in those years I had been in touch with several thousand Chinese and aborigines, most of them going barefooted as I did, and in all that time I had only heard of one man being bitten by a snake (while he was pulling up tapioca roots) and one man treading on a centipede. And neither of them died.

5. For me the jungle now seemed a very friendly place. How glad I always was to get back to its welcome shade after a day in the open, perhaps picking sweet-potato leaves in the oppressive heat of an abandoned clearing. With a firearm of some sort, a jungle knife, and flint and steel and piece of rubber to make a fire, I knew I could keep alive for weeks. I had learnt how to cut the leaves of certain palms and to plait them to make a rainproof shelter, and I knew how to kindle a fire of dry bamboo even in a rainstorm.

6. There is actually very little you can eat in the jungle; sometimes I hunted day after day without even seeing an animal, but there is an unlimited supply of good drinking water, and I knew that a man can exist for weeks as long as he has plenty of water. On one occasion when I had escaped from the Japs after being a prisoner for one evening and half a night, I did in fact go for six days with nothing whatsoever to eat, and travelling hard all day too, and I could have gone another six days if it had been necessary. Unfortunately, I could not take my jungle knife or flint and steel with me, but I hacked down wild banana leaves with a stone to make a shelter at night, and really quite enjoyed myself. Keeping direction was always a problem, but I studied it as a science; indeed, when I got too bored living with the Chinese, I used to go and deliberately get lost, just for the fun of finding my way back to camp, which I always did eventually, though once or twice I had to spend the night out. As long as I could picture the lie of the land and which way the rivers ran, I could

eventually find my way down to some place I could recognise, and at last get back to camp. Even the animals ceased to be a source of fear. I knew that very few wild animals would attack unless provoked; but I never lost my respect for elephants.

7. My two greatest enemies were sickness and boredom— both of them far more dangerous than the Japanese. At one time or another I had all the jungle fevers, including tick typhus and even blackwater. My first attack of malaria was so severe that I was unconscious for seventeen days. For the first two years I had practically no quinine and had to rely on various herbs collected by the Chinese in the jungle. I remember once when I was shot right through the arm, and had nothing except one First Field Dressing, they put on a poultice of chopped leaves and told me it would be better in ten days; and sure enough, it was. And for fevers they would boil up various leaves in a four-gallon paraffin tin and make me sit over it underneath a rug until I was almost asphyxiated and pouring with sweat. The fact that they used different leaves for different maladies made it much more convincing! But even leaves failed to cure the jungle ulcers which we would get on our legs and feet as the result of leech bites and scratches. These would get larger and deeper until one was completely immobilised; then suddenly they would start to get better of their own accord. With most of these things all one could do was to hope for the best: either one died or one did not.

8. For me the worst thing of all was the frustration. It was stupid, once Singapore fell, to go on annoying the Japs. It was obviously in our interest to lie low and concentrate on keeping our food lines open. Once we were on the run we were pretty well done for, as we depended on the outside for food. I was not a Communist, so my Chinese friends never really took me into their con-

fidence. The whole direction and organisation of the guerrillas was in the hands of the Malayan Communist Party (not that there were any Malays in it), though most of the rank and file had simply taken to the jungle as the only possible way to have a crack at the Japs. The most they would let me do was to teach them how to use their weapons, and to hunt pigs and monkeys for them. I knew I could help them so much, yet they just did not want my help. I did not succeed in learning Chinese, largely because the leaders did not want me to know all that was going on, but I learnt Malay, which most of them could understand, and a few of the Chinese spoke a little English. Certainly I missed human companionship, but the lack of reading material was even worse.

9. Another source of frustration was that I had the most wonderful opportunities of studying the animals, birds and plant life of the jungle, but not having lived in Malaya before the war, I had no idea what was rare and what was common, and any notes and collections I did make were always taken by the Japs sooner or later. Nothing would have given me greater pleasure than to have gone and lived with the aborigines in the hills, and studied their way of life; but my job in Malaya was to organise resistance against the Japs and not to play at being an anthropologist.

10. There are, I think, two schools of thought about the jungle; one that it is teeming with pig and deer and wild fowl, as well as breadfruit, yams, papayas, bananas, and other luscious fruit. The other school of thought holds that everything is predominantly hostile: the animals attack one at sight; venomous snakes lie in wait for you; natives attack you with spears and arrows; the very thorns are poisonous, and if you do not die of fever you will starve to death. The fact is, of course, that the jungle is neither friendly nor hostile. The animals are there, but they abound only in clearings or near the

edge of the jungle, and considerable skill is needed to kill them. A few plants and fruits are edible but they are local and seasonal, and it needs an expert both to find them and to distinguish them from similar varieties which may be poisonous. The fierce animals, venomous reptiles and deadly plants are there all right, but they will not harm you if left to themselves. In war-time the jungle provides unlimited cover for both friend and foe and, above all, unlimited fresh water. As with most things in this world, it is the attitude of mind that matters.

F. SPENCER CHAPMAN, *Living Dangerously*

Précis and Comprehension

1. Make an analysis of the chapter quoted above, giving a heading to each paragraph; you should start

   Introduction—(title of para. 1)

   and end

   Conclusion—(title of final paragraph).

2. Write a clear summary of paragraphs 5 and 6 in not more than 80 words.

3. How does Colonel Chapman describe his two attitudes towards the jungle, and what accounted for the change?

4. What were more dangerous enemies than the Japanese, and why?

5. Explain briefly an important point that is made both in the first and last paragraphs of the chapter.

Vocabulary, Punctuation, Grammar

1. Find single words in paragraphs 7 to 10 above that mean much the same as

   suffocated

   fixed in one place

   a state of not being able to do anything effective

   individuals or small bodies of men acting independently in irregular warfare

   to be found only in certain places

   available only at certain times of the year.

2. Choose eight of the following and give words or phrases with as nearly as possible the same meaning:

symmetrical (para. 2)   reaction (para. 4)
festooned (para. 2)   oppressive (para. 5)
revulsion (para. 2)   deliberately (para. 6)
replete (para. 2)   eventually (para. 6)
aborigine (para. 3)   predominantly (para. 10)

3. (a)
   (i) What is the meaning of the termination "-logy"? Think of three words with this ending.
   (ii) What is the meaning of the termination "-ist"? Give an example and explain.
   (iii) Think of the meaning of "anthrop-" in mis-*anthrope*, *anthrop*oid ape, phil*anthrop*ist.
   (iv) Explain the meaning of the word "anthropologist".

   (b) Look up in a good dictionary:
         accord, concord, discord, record, cordial
      and show how the syllable that they share contributes to the meaning of each word.

4. Rewrite the following passage with correct punctuation and capital letters where necessary:

   ... it is not until 1936 that we hear of the abominable snowman again mr ronald caulback travelling in the upper salween reported having seen at 16000 feet five sets of tracks which in his words looked exactly as though made by a bare footed man he added and this is important that in those parts there were no bears more evidence was tendered by wing commander beauman who reported similar tracks from the central himalayas

   On the Air (O.U.P.)

5. In the morning, William, who was quite recovered, confessed that as the gentleman had taken home a bit of the crocodile to eat he did not see why he should not have some also, so he had a bit for supper. He found it so good that he made a meal of it. He declared, I

believe in all honesty, that he would never again eat crocodile for supper.

F. BUCKLAND, *Curiosities of Natural History*

From the above passage quote:

(a) an adjectival subordinate clause and the word it qualifies

(b) noun subordinate clauses and the verbs of which they are the objects

(c) adverbial subordinate clauses and the words they modify

(d) a clause in parenthesis.

6. Combine the following into one complex sentence:

Cats are fond of hunting at night. They see the shrew. It is also a nocturnal animal. They kill it. They will not eat it. It has a peculiarly nasty smell about it. This makes it an unpleasant subject for dissection.

7. Turn the following passage into Reported Speech. Your version should read smoothly and intelligibly. It might start "When they were at supper Patsy said that Father Ryan had lost . . ."

"Father Ryan has lost his wee bantam hen," said Patsy when they were at supper. "Old Rosie was looking for it when I came past the Presbytery."

"Somebody has stole it," said Honeybird. Mick challenged this statement. "Well, it's just like what somebody would do," Honeybird replied.

"I'm going to help old Rosie to look for it to-morrow," said Patsy.

Honeybird looked up from her plate of porridge.

"You'll never find it. Somebody that lives at the other side of the town took it. I saw him going away with it under his arm."

The others stopped scraping their plates to look at her.

"Why didn't you tell us before?" Jane asked.

"Because I was afraid," said Honeybird. "He told

me that if I told anybody he'd come back and cut my throat."

K. FITZPATRICK, *They Lived in County Down*

8. Explain in your own words the meaning of five of the following proverbs:
   (a) People who live in glass-houses shouldn't throw stones.
   (b) You can't make a silk purse out of a sow's ear.
   (c) The proof of the pudding is in the eating.
   (d) All work and no play makes Jack a dull boy.
   (e) Distance lends enchantment to the view.
   (f) Procrastination is the thief of time.

C. *Subjects for Essay or Discussion*

1. Describe a place that you knew as a small child and your impressions on seeing it again for the first time for five or six years.

2. Describe the "spirit" of two of:
   (a) A lonely heath.
   (b) A cathedral or large church.
   (c) A sports ground or swimming-pool closed after the season.
   (d) The centre of any town or village you know well.
   (e) The house you live in.
   (f) The school you go to.
   (g) Your favourite station (harbour, or airport).
   (h) A hospital.
   (i) A factory.
   (j) A fun-fair.

3. Write a reply to the following advertisement:
   Required in three months from the date of this advertisement a young man or woman with G.C.E. and some knowledge of cars, or cookery, or biology, to join an expedition that will study and combat the tsetse fly. One year contract, with possible extension. Detailed application in candidate's own handwriting should be sent in the first place to the Manager of the local office of the Ministry of Labour and National Service (from

whom further details can be obtained), quoting ref. EAM/5701/56.

4. Would you prefer a career that offers security, or one that involves risk? Give your reasons.

5. The problem and prevention of noise.

Books Recommended

F. SPENCER CHAPMAN, *The Jungle is Neutral*.

WINSTON CHURCHILL, *My Early Life*.

JIM CORBETT, *The Man-eating Leopard of Rudraprayag*.

JULIAN DUGUID, *Green Hell* (Pan Books). A very highly coloured account which should be read with the next book.

PETER FLEMING, *Brazilian Adventure*. Armed with a rook-rifle, the author searched for the remains of Colonel Fawcett, lost in the Brazilian jungle.

S. C. GEORGE, *Burma Story*.

H. HASLUND, *Tents in Mongolia*.

ALBERT SCHWEITZER, *On the Edge of the Primeval Forest*.

Chapter 9

A NIGHT AT AN INN

[SPENCER CHAPMAN found the excitement and action of *Moby Dick* the best kind of reading for the long Polar winter. The book relates the long hunt of a sea-captain for a white whale, Moby Dick, which had injured him in a harpooning encounter, their meeting, and the events that followed. The story is told by a young sailor, who describes in the passage below how he put up for a night at a water-side inn while looking for a ship. It is full, and the only room available is one that has to be shared with a harpooneer, who is very late in returning at night.]

1. Though the other boarders kept coming in by ones, twos, and threes, and going to bed, yet no sign of my harpooneer.

"Landlord!" said I, "what sort of a chap is he—does he always keep such late hours?" It was now hard upon twelve o'clock.

The landlord chuckled again with his lean chuckle, and seemed to be mightily tickled at something beyond my comprehension. "No," he answered, "generally he's an early bird—airley to bed and airley to rise—yes, he's the bird what catches the worm.—But to-night he went out a-peddling, you see, and I don't see what on airth keeps him so late, unless, may be can't sell his head."

"Can't sell his head?—What sort of a bamboozingly story is this you are telling me?" getting into a towering rage. "Do you pretend to say, landlord, that this harpooneer is actually engaged this blessed Saturday night, or rather Sunday morning, in peddling his head around this town?"

2. "That's precisely it," said the landlord, "and I told him he couldn't sell it here, the market's overstocked."

"With what?" shouted I.

"With heads, to be sure; ain't there too many heads in the world?"

"I tell you what it is, landlord," said I quite calmly, "you'd better stop spinning that yarn to me—I'm not green."

"Maybe not," taking out a stick and whittling a toothpick, "but I rayther guess you'll be done brown if that ere harpooneer hears you a-slanderin' his head."

"I'll break it for him," said I, now flying into a passion again at this unaccountable farrago of the landlord's.

"It's broke a'ready," said he.

"Broke," said I—"broke, do you mean?"

"Sartain, and that's the very reason he can't sell it, I guess."

3. "Landlord," said I, going up to him as cool as Mount Hecla in a snowstorm,—"landlord, stop whittling. You and I must understand one another, and that too without delay. I come to your house and want a bed; you tell me you can only give me half a one; that the other half belongs to a certain harpooneer. And about this harpooneer, whom I have not yet seen, you persist in telling me the most mystifying and exasperating stories, tending to beget in me an uncomfortable feeling towards the man whom you design for my bedfellow—a sort of connection, landlord, which is an intimate and confidential one in the highest degree. I now demand of you to speak out and tell me who and what this harpooneer is, and whether I shall be in all respects safe to spend the night with him. And in the first place, you will be so good as to unsay that story about selling his head, which if true I take to be good evidence that this harpooneer is stark mad, and I've no idea of sleeping

with a madman; and you, sir, you I mean, landlord, you, sir, by trying to induce me to do so knowingly, would thereby render yourself liable to a criminal prosecution."

4. "Wall," said the landlord, fetching a long breath, "that's a purty long sarmon for a chap that rips a little now and then. But be easy, be easy, this here harpooneer I have been tellin' you of has just arrived from the South Seas, where he brought up a lot of 'balmed New Zealand heads (great curios, you know), and he's sold all on 'em but one, and that one he's trying to sell to-night, 'cause to-morrow's Sunday, and it would not do to be sellin' human heads about the streets when folks is goin' to churches. He wanted to, last Sunday, but I stopped him just as he was goin' out of the door with four heads strung on a string, for all the airth like a string of onions."

5. This account cleared up the otherwise unaccountable mystery, and showed that the landlord, after all, had had no idea of fooling me—but at the same time what could I think of a harpooneer who stayed out of a Saturday night clean into the holy Sabbath, engaged in such a cannibal business as selling the heads of dead idolaters?

"Depend upon it, landlord, that harpooneer is a dangerous man."

"He pays reg'lar," was the rejoinder. "But come, it's getting dreadful late, you had better be turning flukes —it's a nice bed. There's plenty room for two to kick about in that bed; it's an almighty big bed that. Why, afore we give it up, Sal used to put our Sam and little Johnny in the foot of it. But I got a-dreaming and sprawling about one night, and somehow Sam got pitched on the floor, and came near breaking his arm. Arter that, Sal said it wouldn't do. Come along here, I'll give ye a glim in a jiffy"; and so saying he lighted a candle and held it towards me, offering to lead the way. But I stood irresolute; when looking at a clock in the corner, he exclaimed "I vum it's Sunday—you won't see that harpooneer to-night; he's come to anchor somewhere—come along then; do come; won't ye come?"

6. I considered the matter a moment, and then upstairs we went, and I was ushered into a small room, cold as a clam, and furnished, sure enough, with a prodigious bed, almost big enough indeed for any four harpooneers to sleep abreast.

"There," said the landlord, placing the candle on a crazy old sea-chest that did double duty as a washstand and centre-table; "there, make yourself comfortable now, and good-night to ye." I turned round from eyeing the bed, but he had disappeared.

Folding back the counterpane, I stooped over the bed. Though none of the most elegant, it yet stood the scrutiny tolerably well. I then glanced round the room; and besides the bedstead and centre table, could see no other furniture belonging to the place, but a rude shelf, the four walls, and a papered fireboard representing a man striking a whale. Of things not properly belonging to the room, there was a hammock lashed up, and thrown upon the floor in one corner; also a large seaman's bag, containing the harpooneer's wardrobe, no doubt in lieu of a land trunk. Likewise, there was a parcel of outlandish bone fish-hooks on the shelf over the fireplace, and a tall harpoon standing at the head of the bed.

7. But what is this on the chest? I took it up, and held it close to the light, and felt it, and smelt it, and tried every way possible to arrive at some satisfactory conclusion concerning it. I can compare it to nothing but a large door mat, ornamented at the edges with little tinkling tags something like the stained porcupine quills

round an Indian moccasin. There was a hole or slit in the middle of this mat, the same as in South American ponchos. But could it be possible that any sober harpooneer would get into a door mat, and parade the streets of any Christian town in that sort of guise? I put it on, to try it, and it weighed me down like a hamper, being uncommonly shaggy and thick, and I thought a little damp, as though this mysterious harpooneer had been wearing it of a rainy day. I went up in it to a bit of glass stuck against the wall, and I never saw such a sight in my life. I tore myself out of it in such a hurry that I gave myself a kink in the neck.

8. I sat down on the side of the bed, and commenced thinking about this head-peddling harpooneer, and his door mat. After thinking some time on the bedside, I got up and took off my monkey-jacket, and then stood in the middle of the room thinking. I then took off my coat, and thought a little more in my shirt-sleeves. But beginning to feel very cold now, half undressed as I was, and remembering what the landlord said about the harpooneer's not coming home at all that night, it being so very late, I made no more ado, but jumped out of my pantaloons and boots, and then blowing out the light tumbled into bed, and commended myself to the care of heaven.

Whether that mattress was stuffed with corn-cobs or broken crockery, there is no telling, but I rolled about a good deal, and could not sleep for a long time. At last I slid off into a light doze, and had pretty nearly made a good offing towards the land of Nod, when I heard a heavy footfall in the passage, and saw a glimmer of light come into the room from under the door.

9. "Lord save me," thinks I, "that must be the harpooneer, the infernal head-peddler." But I lay perfectly still, and resolved not to say a word till spoken to. Holding a light in one hand, and that identical New Zealand head

in the other, the stranger entered the room and, without looking towards the bed, placed his candle a good way off from me on the floor in one corner, and then began working away at the knotted cords of the large bag I before spoke of as being in the room. I was all eagerness to see his face, but he kept it averted for some time while employed in unlacing the bag's mouth. This accomplished, however, he turned round—when, good heavens! what a sight! Such a face! It was of a dark, purplish, yellow colour, here and there stuck over with large, blackish looking squares. Yes, it's just as I thought, he's a terrible bedfellow; he's been in a fight, got dreadfully cut, and here he is, just from the surgeon. But at that moment he chanced to turn his face so towards the light, that I plainly saw they could not be sticking-plasters at all, those black squares on his cheeks. They were stains of some sort or other. At first I knew not what to make of this; but soon an inkling of the truth occurred to me. I remembered a story of a white man—a whaleman too—who, falling among the cannibals, had been tattooed by them. I concluded that this harpooneer, in the course of his distant voyages, must have met with a similar adventure. And what is it, thought I, after all! It's only his outside; a man can be honest in any sort of skin. But then, what to make of his unearthly complexion, that part of it, I mean, lying round about, and completely independent of the squares of tattooing? To be sure, it might be nothing but a good coat of tropical tanning; but I never heard of a hot sun's tanning a white man into a purplish yellow one. However, I had never been in the South Seas; and perhaps the sun there produced these extraordinary effects upon the skin. Now, while all these ideas were passing through me like lightning, this harpooneer never noticed me at all. But, after some difficulty having opened his bag, he commenced fumbling in it, and presently pulled out a sort of tomahawk, and a sealskin wallet with the hair on. Placing these on the old chest in the middle of the room, he then took the New Zealand head—a ghastly thing enough—and crammed it down into the bag. He now took off his hat—a new beaver hat—when I came nigh singing out with fresh surprise. There was no hair on his head—none to speak of at least—nothing but a small scalp-knot twisted up on his forehead. His bald purplish head now looked for all the world like a mildewed skull. Had not the stranger stood between me and the door, I would have bolted out of it quicker than ever I bolted a dinner.

10. Even as it was, I thought something of slipping out of the window, but it was the second floor back. I am no coward, but what to make of this head-peddling purple rascal altogether passed my comprehension. Ignorance is the parent of fear, and being completely nonplussed and confounded about the stranger, I confess I was now as much afraid of him as if it was the devil himself who had thus broken into my room at the dead of night. In fact, I was so afraid of him that I was not game enough just then to address him, and demand a satisfactory answer concerning what seemed inexplicable in him.

11. Meanwhile, he continued the business of undressing, and at last showed his chest and arms. As I live, these covered parts of him were checkered with the same squares as his face; his back, too, was all over the same dark squares; he seemed to have been in a Thirty Years' War, and just escaped from it with a sticking-plaster shirt. Still more, his very legs were marked, as if a parcel of dark green frogs were running up the trunks of young palms. It was now quite plain that he must be some abominable savage or other shipped aboard of a whaleman in the South Seas, and so landed in this Christian country. I quaked to think of it. A peddler of heads too—perhaps the heads of his own brothers. He

might take a fancy to mine—heavens! look at that tomahawk!

12. But there was no time for shuddering, for now the savage went about something that completely fascinated my attention, and convinced me that he must indeed be a heathen. Going to his heavy grego, or wrapall, or dreadnought, which he had previously hung on a chair, he fumbled in the pockets, and produced at length a curious little deformed image with a hunch on its back, and exactly the colour of a three days' old Congo baby. Remembering the embalmed head, at first I almost thought that this black manikin was a real baby preserved in some similar manner. But seeing that it was not at all limber, and that it glistened a good deal like polished ebony, I concluded that it must be nothing but a wooden idol, which indeed it proved to be. For now the savage goes up to the empty fireplace, and removing the papered fireboard, sets up this little hunchbacked image, like a tenpin, between the andirons. The chimney jambs and all the bricks inside were very sooty, so that I thought this fireplace made a very appropriate little shrine or chapel for his Congo idol.

13. I now screwed my eyes hard towards the half-ridden image, feeling but ill at ease meantime—to see what was next to follow. First he takes about a double handful of shavings out of his grego pocket, and places them carefully before the idol; then laying a bit of ship biscuit on top and applying the flame from the lamp, he kindled the shavings into a sacrificial blaze. Presently, after many hasty snatches into the fire, and still hastier withdrawals of his fingers (whereby he seemed to be scorching them badly), he at last succeeded in drawing out the biscuit; then blowing off the head and ashes a little, he made a polite offer of it to the little negro. But the little devil did not seem to fancy such dry sort of fare at all; he never moved his lips. All these strange antics

were accompanied by still stranger guttural noises from the devotee, who seemed to be praying in a sing-song or else singing some pagan psalmody or other, during which his face twitched about in the most unnatural manner. At last extinguishing the fire, he took the idol up very unceremoniously, and bagged it again in his grego pocket as carelessly as if he were a sportsman bagging a dead woodcock.

14. All these queer proceedings increased my uncomfortableness, and seeing him now exhibiting strong symptoms of concluding his business operations, and jumping into bed with me, I thought it was high time, now or never, before the light was put out, to break the spell in which I had so long been bound.

But the interval I spent in deliberating what to say, was a fatal one. Taking up his tomahawk from the table, he examined the head of it for an instant, and then holding it to the light, with his mouth at the handle, he puffed out great clouds of tobacco smoke. The next moment the light was extinguished, and this wild cannibal, tomahawk between his teeth, sprang into bed with me. I sang out, I could not help it now; and giving a sudden grunt of astonishment he began feeling me.

Stammering out something, I knew not what, I rolled away from him against the wall, and then conjured him, whoever or whatever he might be, to keep quiet, and let me get up and light the lamp again. But his guttural responses satisfied me at once that he but ill comprehended my meaning.

15. "Who-e debel you?"—he at last said—"You no speak-e, dam-me, I kill-e." And so saying the lighted tomahawk began flourishing about me in the dark.

"Landlord, for God's sake, Peter Coffin!" shouted I. "Landlord! Watch! Coffin! Angels! Save me!"

"Speake-e! Tell-ee me who-ee be, or dam-me, I kill-e!" again growled the cannibal, while his horrid flourishings of the tomahawk scattered the hot tobacco ashes about me till I thought my linen would get on fire. But thank heaven, at that moment the landlord came into the room light in hand, and leaping from the bed I ran up to him.

"Don't be afraid now," said he, grinning again. "Queequeg here wouldn't harm a hair of your head."

"Stop your grinning," shouted I, "and why didn't you tell me that infernal harpooneer was a cannibal?"

"I thought ye know'd it;—didn't I tell ye, he was a peddlin' heads around town?—But turn flukes again and go to sleep. Queequeg, look here—you sabbee me, I sabbee you—this man sleepe you—you sabbee?"

"Me sabbee plenty"—grunted Queequeg, puffing away at his pipe and sitting up in bed.

16. "You gettee in," he added, motioning to me with his tomahawk, and throwing the clothes to one side. He really did this in not only a civil but a really kind and charitable way. I stood looking at him a moment. For all his tattooings he was on the whole a clean, comely looking cannibal. "What's all this fuss I have been making about," thought I to myself—"the man's a human being just as I am: he has just as much reason to fear me as I have to be afraid of him. Better sleep with a sober cannibal than a drunken Christian."

"Landlord," said I, "tell him to stash his tomahawk there, or pipe, or whatever you call it; tell him to stop smoking, in short, and I will turn in with him. But I don't fancy having a man smoking in bed with me. It's dangerous. Besides, I ain't insured."

This being told to Queequeg, he at once complied, and again politely motioned me to get into bed—rolling over to one side as much as to say—"I won't touch a leg of ye."

"Good-night, landlord," said I; "you may go."

I turned in, and never slept better in my life.

HERMANN MELVILLE, *Moby Dick*

Précis and Comprehension

1. Read carefully the speeches of the narrator and the landlord, and note down how what they say and the way they say it help to describe the character of each.

2. (*a*) Show by what stages curiosity about the harpooneer is built up. List the points in the order in which they occur, up to the moment when the narrator says "I . . . tumbled into bed" (sect. 8).

or

(*b*) Quote sentences which show the further stages whereby interest in and curiosity about the harpooneer are developed, from his entry (sect. 9) up to "look at that tomahawk" (sect. 11).

3. List the points at which the narrator is almost on the point of speaking (after the harpooneer's entry), but refrains from doing so.

4. Tell the whole story in not more than 100 words.

5. Such expressions as "kink in the neck" and "stuffed with broken crockery" (sect. 8) suggest by their exaggeration that this is a comic scene not to be taken too seriously. Do you think that the narrator was really afraid of the harpooneer? Quote any evidence you can.

6. In section 16 the narrator says "He has just as much reason to fear me as I have to be afraid of him." Give the reasons.

7. There are a number of similes ("as cool as Mount Hecla", "like a string of onions") in the passage. Find two similes—or a simile and a metaphor—which show that a sailor is speaking.

Vocabulary, Punctuation, Grammar

1. Below are listed a number of words used by Melville, and against each of them is an alternative, in brackets. Say in each case why you think Melville chose the word he did, and not the one in the bracket.

working away at (sect. 9: untying).
fumbling (sect. 9: searching)
pulled out (sect. 9: took out)
crammed (sect. 9: placed)
screwed (sect. 13: turned)
snatches (sect. 13: gropings)
antics (sect. 13: movements)
bagged (sect. 13: placed)

2. Give words or phrases that could replace the following
words in their contexts:

farrago (sect. 2)   exasperating (sect. 3)
irresolute (sect. 5)   prodigious (sect. 6)
scrutiny (sect. 6)   tolerably (sect. 6)
inexplicable (sect. 10)   unceremoniously (sect. 13)
limber (sect. 12)   civil (sect. 16).

3. Think of a substitute for each of the expressions "good
job", "bad job", etc., in the passage that follows. Your
substitute can be more than one word.

Good job (1) the road was clear—the car skidded
backwards into the wall. If a cyclist had been there,
it would have been a bad job (2) for him. The ambu-
lance men had a job (3) getting the driver out—they
did a clever job (4) with his broken arm. But the car's a
bad job (5)—nice job (6) for the repairers. Wilson's'll
make a neat job (7) of the repair—Tompkins
wouldn't touch a job (8) like that. The borough
surveyor ought to have made a better job (9) of that
corner, though; we'll be having more jobs (10) like
this one till it's cleared up. Well, I've got a job (11)
to see to—I'll be losing my job (12) if I hang about
like this.

4. Add the punctuation, capital letters and quotation
marks that are needed in the following passages:

(a) Andersen asked Mitchell to go through the cargo
of a boat manned by chicago toughs you may get
hurt he said theyre a dangerous bunch thats all
right with me said mitchell you understand that

youre acting officially as my deputy andersen went
on sure are you armed oh yes said mitchell ive heard
all this stuff before lets go

(b) i stood up and said my friend its time to say good-
bye but francis never winked an eye he just asked
why i explained that the captain said hed got to
leave right off but all francis did was to look round
calmly and say tell him to leave when he wants to

ANGUS GRAHAM *The Golden Grindstone*

5. (a) In section 9 of the extract from *Moby Dick*, starting
at the words "But at that moment", find two adverbial
clauses, one adjectival clause and one noun clause. State
if you can the word in the main sentence to which the
clause concerned is related.

(b) Turn each of the following groups of sentences into
a complex sentence:

(i) One morning I sat there. I watched. I made notes.
One of the young birds came to the entrance. He
pushed his body out. This was further than he had
ever done before. He set up a fearful chirping.

(ii) My owl has never yet shown anger. He has shown
only a kind of resentment. He expresses this with a
sound. The sound mixes a whistle and a warble.
It is in a high key. His wings are outspread. His
head is held low.

6. Correct any mistakes (including errors in grammar
and style) that you find in these sentences:

(a) Its a pity there is no chance of them winning this year.
(b) None of the swimmers have arrived in time; they
prefer a walk than a drive.
(c) Knowing the route well, the coach stopped at all
towns unless Ashford to pick up the passengers who
had booked.
(d) Well anyway personally I couldn't care less if we
do run into a spot of bother with the customs blokes
over a coupla bottles of booze, so long as they leave
the grub OK.

(e) Of the three or four alternatives proposed, re-roofing with felt will do equally as well.

(f) He's quite good, but never has he sang anything like you do.

7. Briefly define the meaning of five of the following expressions:

(a) To be a wet blanket.
(b) To sow the seeds of discord.
(c) Don't make two bites at a cherry.
(d) That's putting all your eggs in one basket.
(e) To have one's back to the wall.
(f) To smell a rat.

Subjects for Essay or Discussion

1. Would you rather read novels or books of travel? Give your reasons and some examples from your own reading.

2. Describe the first occasion you were away from home for a night or more.

3. If you have been abroad, say what you learned and what you gained from the experience; if not, say what trip abroad you would like to make when you start earning your own living.

4. A hundred and fifty years ago, no journey could be made at a pace faster than that of a horse. What difference to our lives has been brought about by the great increase in speed of communication?

5. Compare the pros and cons of travel by sea and air.

6. Outline the plot of a novel that you yourself would like to write or read.

Books Recommended

DAVID W. BONE, *The Brassbounder* (Penguin). A boy's account of a voyage on a windjammer round Cape Horn.

F. T. BULLEN, *The Cruise of the Cachalot.*

JOSEPH CONRAD, *Typhoon.*

RICHARD HUGHES, *In Hazard.*

H. MELVILLE, *Moby Dick.*

F. D. OMMANEY, *This Way Southward.*

J. SLOCUM, *Sailing Alone Around the World.*

VEEDAM and WALL, *Sailing to Freedom.*

Chapter 10

SONG

[DAVID LACK's book on the robin is one of the classics of natural history. In it he tells the life story of the robin, based on his observations of birds which he ringed and got to know as individuals. One of the most interesting features is the account of the robin's habit of establishing itself in a clearly defined territory of about one and a half acres, which it defends against other robins. Chapter II of Dr. Lack's book is reprinted below, with a few omissions.]

1. The spring song of the robin starts near the end of December and continues until about the middle of June. The autumn song, which is thinner and less rich, is first heard in late July from some of the young birds, the adult robins starting about a fortnight later. It is continued throughout the autumn, but is rather feeble in the early winter, until the spring song suddenly starts again in late December. Thus robins sing throughout the year except for a gap between mid-June and mid-July, but an occasional late adult or early youngster can sometimes be heard even in the latter period, and once on 13 July I heard an early juvenile singing the autumn song against a late adult singing the spring song. The above dates refer to South Devon and are rather different in other parts of England.

2. The song of the robin is one of the most characteristic sounds of the English countryside in autumn, and the robin is the only British bird to sing persistently then. At this season not only the cocks but also about half of the hen robins sing, their song being indistinguishable from that of the cocks. Other hens sing poorly and some

are not heard at all. After a hen has paired with a cock in spring it very rarely sings.

3. The robin's song shows considerable individual variations. There are good and poor singers. Some start earlier in the season than others, or continue later. In spring unmated cocks usually sing better than mated ones, but a few mated males have sung very well. Robins have occasionally been heard to sing at night.

4. The robin's spring song can be heard on a gramophone record made by Ludwig Koch. Analysis of the soundtracks of bird song has shown that most small birds include in their songs notes of a frequency well above the limits to which the human ear is sensitive, so that a bird's song probably does not sound the same to another bird as it does to us. Nor does it sound the same to every ornithologist, since the sensitivity of the human ear to these frequencies varies markedly with the individual, and declines with increasing age.

5. Why do birds sing? The most popular answer is because they are happy. From which it could be concluded that whereas cock robins are happy most of the year the hens are happy only in autumn, that cock robins are happier before than after obtaining mates, and that they are happiest of all when fighting. "Premises assumed without evidence or in spite of it; and conclusions drawn from them so logically, that they must necessarily be false," as Peacock puts it. A bird's happiness is unobservable and the question "Is a bird happy?" is impossible to answer and perhaps meaningless. The other popular view, that the cock bird sings in courtship to please the hen, was finally disproved by Eliot Howard, who showed that the chief function of bird song is to advertise the cock in his territory, both to other cocks which may intrude and to hens in search of mates.

6. Observation soon establishes that each colour-ringed

male robin sings only in its own territory, and by noting on a map every place in which each bird is seen singing, the boundaries of the different territories are quickly determined. It is impossible to drive a singing robin from its territory. As the observer approaches the bird retreats, but on reaching the edge of its territory it does not proceed further, and if chivied it unexpectedly flies back over the observer's head to the middle of its ground.

7. The aviary experiments showed the connexion between ownership of territory and song, since in each aviary there were two pairs of robins, and in each case one of the two cocks became the owner of the whole aviary and it was this bird which did nearly all the singing. In each aviary for a short time near the beginning of the experiment the second male temporarily became the owner, and then it was this second male which sang and the other was silent. While ownership was in dispute, both cocks sang.

8. The occurrence of autumn song also shows the connexion between song and territory, for at this season courtship does not occur, but each cock robin holds a territory, while those hens which sing in autumn are, like cocks, defending individual territories. Only two hen robins were heard to sing strongly in spring after pairing up, in one case when a pair moved into and claimed a new territory, and in the other case when a pair were defending their territory against a rival pair. The correlation between song and territory is again clear.

9. The fact that hen robins sing has found its way into ornithological works only since Burkitt proved it in 1924 with his colour-ringed birds in Ireland, though actually this possibility was mentioned in 1831, and was stated more definitely by Charles Darwin in 1871. Female song is uncommon in birds. Among European species it has been recorded in the starling and in the dipper. Perhaps some of the autumn song of skylarks comes from hen

birds, since these, like the female robin, have been recorded as singing in captivity. An occasional hen blackbird or chaffinch also sings in a wild state, but only as an abnormality, and the females of a few other species have been heard in captivity. Possibly future observations will show that there are other British birds in which the female sings, for there are many birds in which, like the robin, the sexes cannot be distinguished by plumage, and most observers assume that a singing bird is necessarily a male. Female song also occurs in various North American species. The hen mocking-bird sings regularly in the fall, as does the loggerhead shrike. The mocking-bird is one of America's most famous song-birds, and at the present time the song is frequently heard in England, as it is the thrush-like song regularly introduced into Hollywood films for sentimental occasions. In both mocking-bird and logger-head shrike the hen holds an individual autumn terri-tory, thus providing further confirmation of the connexion between song and territory.

10. The most important use of song to the robin in its territory is to advertise possession to rivals and to warn them off. When an intruding robin comes close to the boundary or actually trespasses, the owner's song be-comes specially loud, the intruder often retreats at once, and in this way song saves many fights. To cite an example: on 27 May 1937, an unringed newcomer robin, evidently wandering without territory, started to sing in a corner of the territory owned by a long-established resident male. The latter, then in a distant part of its territory, promptly sang in reply. The new-comer, which could not, of course, yet know that it was trespassing, sang again. The owner, having flown rather closer in the interval, sang again in reply. The new-comer again sang, the owner again approached and replied, now more vigorously, and this procedure was

repeated twice more, the owner finally uttering a violent song-phrase from only some fifteen yards away, but still hidden from sight by thick bushes. At this point the newcomer fled, from an opponent it never saw, nor did it appear again.

11. With the above incident, compare the following from H. G. Wells' *Outline of History*: "It was at three o'clock on 14 August 1431, that the crusaders, who were encamped in the plain between Domazlice and Horsuv Tyn, received the news that the Hussites, under the leadership of Prokop the Great, were approaching. Though the Bohemians were still four miles off, the rattle of their war-wagons and the song 'All ye warriors of God' which their whole host was chanting, could already be heard. The enthusiasm of the crusaders evaporated with astounding rapidity. Lützow describes how the papal representative and the Duke of Saxony ascended a convenient hill to inspect the battlefield. It was, they discovered, not going to be a battlefield. The German camp was in utter confusion. Horsemen were streaming off in every direction, and the clatter of empty wagons being driven off almost drowned the sound of that terrible singing. . . . So ended the Bohemian crusade."

12. The influence of song in the fighting of the robin was also shown in connexion with the aviaries. When captive robins were put in one of the aviaries, the wild owners of the ground outside perched on the aviary roof and sang and displayed at the birds inside. After a few days one of the captive male robins came into full song, singing particularly whenever the wild male approached the aviary, and after a few days the latter retired, leaving the captive male in undisputed possession not only of the aviary but of the ground immediately around it. A similar series of events occurred at the other aviary. This result can be attributed only in part to the singing

of the captive robins, since a wild robin gradually ceases to attack an intruding robin which will not retreat out of its territory. But song can be given full credit for subsequent victories. During April the territory in the copse outside one of the aviaries fell vacant. A cock robin soon arrived, claiming the vacant ground with loud song. The aviary male, which had been rather quiet for some time, promptly came into full song, and so vigorously that the newcomer made no serious attempt to acquire the ground immediately round the aviary. A similar incident occurred outside the other aviary a month later. Hence through singing the aviary males were victorious against wild rivals which they could never attack directly, and conquered territory on which they could never settle.

13. Not only does the song of the robin serve as a warning prelude to a fight, but robins actually sing while fighting, interpolating vigorous song-phrases between their attacks on intruders, while the finest singing of the year is heard when one cock is trying to establish itself in the territory of another. At least in the robin, the chorus of song early on a spring morning—often called the birds' Hymn to the Dawn—is a hymn of battle rather than of love.

14. Similarly war-whoops, gongs, trumpets, and the pibroch have played no inconsiderable part in human battles. Marco Polo's description of one of Kublai Khan's engagements is typical: "As soon as the order of battle was arranged, an infinite number of wind instruments of various kinds were sounded, and these were succeeded by songs, according to the custom of the Tartars before they engage in fight, which commences upon the signal given by the cymbals and drums, and there was such a beating of cymbals and drums, and such singing, that it was wonderful to hear . . . and then a fierce and bloody conflict began." The value of such

methods is demonstrated by the account of the Bohemian crusade already given.

15. Warning to rivals is not the sole use of song in the robin, though it is the most important. In the early spring the song also serves to advertise the unmated cock in possession of a territory to hens in search of mates. "Ful loude he sang—Com hider, love, to me"— like the Pardoner of Rouncivale. Song is the chief way in which the hen robin can locate an unmated cock, and almost immediately after the cock has obtained a mate its song declines to a rather moderate intensity and remains so, except during fights, unless the mate is lost, in which case the cock again comes into loud song. In the late spring nearly all the robin song comes from cocks which are unmated.

16. In some other species of birds the song of the male is loud until pair-formation, and thereafter becomes extremely poor. Thus Mrs. Nice writes of the American song-sparrow: "I often say to myself on nearing a territory where silence reigns over night, 'Such and such a male must be either dead or married,' and upon careful search I find either two birds or none." Evidently in such species advertisement for a female is a much more important function of song than is the warning off of a rival male from the territory.

17. It need hardly be stressed that this second function of song is to advertise for, and not to please, a hen. So soon as a hen is obtained the song declines, and in most birds it plays no part in the subsequent courtship. There are, however, a few birds, but not including the robin, in which the cock sings while courting the hen. I have observed this in one of the American goldfinches, and it is true of other finches in the linnet group. In some of these finches, also in barbets, American wrens, and others, the hen may sing antiphonally with the cock, another example of female song in birds.

18. Once when I was trying to catch an elusive robin in the house-trap the bird burst into song as it ran about the ground, and it continued to sing for a little after I had caught it and was holding it on its back in my hand. It is well known that other birds will occasionally sing or display when alarmed. A sudden thunder-clap or bomb often starts them off. As a more spectacular example, when in an Imperial Airways machine over the Kenya Game Reserve, we on several occasions flew close to a male ostrich, at which the latter would go down in the sand, spread its white plumes, and rock gently from side to side in display at the aircraft.

19. Occasionally robins will sing in answer to the song of other species of birds, but usually only when no other robins are singing. One hen robin in autumn used to get particularly excited by the singing of a tame canary in a room bordering her territory, and she would come down to the cage and sing in answer. More curious, a correspondent wrote to me of a robin which used to sing whenever he used a double-handed cross-cut saw. The latter has a characteristic note, and the robin regularly sang back at it, stopping as soon as the sawing stopped.

20. A puzzling feature of robin singing is the subdued song sometimes heard in autumn. A robin may utter quiet phrases, audible at only a few yards, continuously for several minutes. Several other species sometimes sing in this apparently purposeless way in autumn.

21. The song of each species of bird is distinctive from that of every other found in the same region with it. This arrangement, so convenient for the ornithologist, is no accident. To quote Montagu again: "The peculiar note of each is an unerring mark for each to discover its own species." It is essential that the female should recognize a male of its own species. Such recognition has survival value since hybrids between species are rarely fertile and may also be less efficient in other ways.

22. A few of the South Devon robins, though not many, incorporated the notes of other species into their songs. Thus one used a phrase reminiscent of the song of the chaffinch, and another of the spring "teacher" call of the great tit. Witchell has listed the songs and calls of other species of birds which he states that he has heard in different robins' songs. More extraordinary is the report by John Morton in 1712. "Besides the common Sort of Singing Birds . . . the Ingenious Mr Mansel has had . . . a Robinredbreast that not only learnt some Flagelet Tunes, but spoke distinctly several short Sentences." This account I at first rejected as incredible, but since then have read Gesner who quotes Porphyry (*De Abstinentia ab Animatis, lib*. 3, third century A.D.) to the effect that crows, magpies, and robins imitate man and remember what they hear; and in 1823 there was a lady in Edinburgh whose tame robin very distinctly pronounced "How do ye do?" and several other words. Other song-birds can also be trained to speak. Pliny noted that "Agrippina the Empresse, wife to Claudius Caesar, had a Blackbird or a Throstle, at what time I compiled this book, which could counterfeit man's speech. The two Caesars also, the yong Princes (to wit Germanicus and Drusus) had one Stare and sundry Nightingales taught to parle Greek and Latin." Barrington knew of a linnet which sang "pretty boy".

23. Such occurrences raise the question of whether bird song is inherited or learnt. Aristotle already knew the answer. "Of little birds, some give a different note from the parent birds, if they have been removed from the nest and have heard other birds singing." It is rather surprising that almost the only experiments on this subject in British birds were made in the late eighteenth century by Daines Barrington, best known as one of Gilbert White's correspondents. Of the robin Barrington wrote: "I educated a young robin under a very fine

nightingale; which, however, began already to be out of song, and was perfectly mute in less than a fortnight. The robin afterwards sung three parts in four nightingale; and the rest of his song was what the bird-catchers call rubbish, or no particular note whatsoever." Barrington got another captive robin to sing like a "skylark-linnet", i.e. like a linnet which has been raised under a skylark, and so sings like the latter. His experiments show with admirable clearness that in the species with which he worked the specific characteristics of the song are learnt by the young bird from the birds which it hears during and shortly after fledging. This suggests that those wild robins which imitate the songs of other species may have heard the latter along with the song of their parent when they were young birds.

24. Experiments in the United States fully confirm Barrington's results for a large number of other song-birds, and show also that, when such birds are raised without hearing any other birds sing, they sing an original type of song quite unrecognizable as that of their own kind, i.e. "what the bird-catchers call rubbish". Even the chirping house-sparrow can be made to sing—how excellent if Britain's cities could be filled with "nightingale-sparrows".

25. For long I was puzzled to account for the sudden marked increase in the cock robin's song just after the young leave the nest and while they are still under his care. This happened both in the wild and in the aviaries. I suggest that song at this period may have survival value because it is at this stage that the young robins learn the song of their species, though they do not themselves sing then. The young robins start to sing in late July, before the adults, so they get no other chance to learn their song. Observations by Burkitt and others show that in other song-birds there is a similar revival of song about the time that the young leave the

nest, and perhaps it has the same function as that suggested here for the robin. In all those species in which the song is not inherited but is acquired by the young bird, it is clear that the young must get such an opportunity as this to hear the song before they leave their parents' charge.

DAVID LACK, *The Life of the Robin*

Précis and Comprehension

1. Write a summary of paragraphs 1–6 inclusive; your version should contain between 170 and 200 words.

2. State clearly, for the benefit of someone who has not read the chapter, the fact about robins for which paragraphs 7 and 8 are evidence.

3. What likeness in the behaviour of men and robins is suggested by paragraph 11?
   A metaphor can be explained thus: 'His voice thundered across the field' means that his voice sounded as loud as thunder. Find three metaphors in paragraph 11, and explain them.

4. What words link each of paragraphs 13, 14, 15, 16 and 17 to the preceding paragraph?

5. (a) What word or words link paragraph 23 to the preceding paragraph; and to what information in paragraph 22 is the link effected?
   (b) "Those features of a bird's song which distinguish it from other birds." This is a paraphrase of half a dozen words in paragraph 23; what are the words?
   (c) What does "rubbish" mean as applied to the song of a bird?
   (d) If a robin is heard singing like another bird, how may it have learned to do so?
   (e) What is the meaning of "survival value" in paragraph 25?

Vocabulary, Punctuation, Grammar

1. (a) Give one word meaning "a person who studies

birds" and an adjective meaning "connected with the study of birds".

(b) Give the nouns connected with "interpolate" and "reminiscent" and then give the meaning of each noun.

(c) Give the verbs that are connected with "characteristic" and with "elusive" and then give the meaning of each verb.

(d) In what connection are you most likely to hear the words "antiphonally" (para. 17) and "counterfeit" (para. 22) used again?

2. Substitute a better word for "nice", "nicer" and "nicely" in the passage below. You need not write it all out; set out the numbers in column form.

We had a very nice (1) time on holiday. The place we stayed at was nice (2) and clean; the view was nice (3), and the ginger ices were rather nice (4) too. It might have been nicer (5) if we had had a car to take us to some of the nice (6) places, but even so we managed quite nicely (7). A very nice (8) man lent us a nice (9) boat, and after some nice (10) rows on the lake we were nice and (11) tired. But it was nice (12) to be home again.

3. Punctuate each of the following passages; in the case of dialogue start a fresh line for each speaker.

(a) Come aboard come aboard cried the gay *Bachelor's* commander lifting a glass and bottle in the air Hast seen the White Whale gritted Ahab in reply No only hear of him but don't believe in him at all said the other good-humouredly Come aboard

(b) Ye havent seen him yet have ye said the stranger No we havent Hes sick they say but is getting better and will be all right again before long All right again before long laughed the stranger with a solemnly derisive sort of laugh Look ye when Captain Ahab is all right then this left arm of mine will be all right not before

4. (a) From paragraphs 4 and 5 find one example each of:
a noun subordinate clause
an adverbial subordinate clause
an adjectival subordinate clause.

(b) State what parts of speech are the words in the sentence below, and describe the grammatical connection of each word with the rest of the sentence.

The most popular answer is that they are happy.

(c) Combine the following sentences into one complex sentence:

We were in a hurry. We departed. We had no time to organise our ten brakesmen. They were all confined in the guard's van. They should have been dispersed along the train. Thus they could operate the brakes on individual goods wagons.

5. Recast the following extract from a speech in the House of Lords in Direct Speech: remember to alter tenses and person where necessary.

Lord Sempill said that some of the fruit that went into jam was mixed with fruit pulp, put into barrels containing sulphur dioxide, and might be kept there for up to six months. This process in the "witches' brew" bleached the fruit white and hardened it. As much as possible of the sulphur dioxide was removed by boiling, then sugar and colouring were added in an endeavour to imitate the natural colour. If any of their lordships had been present at this rite, it was a memory that would be with them for all time, since the stench emanating from the barrels containing the fruit before boiling would never be forgotten. It even out-Heroded smog.

The Times report, 4th December 1953

6. Explain four of the following proverbs and invent an incident to illustrate each proverb of your choice:
(a) Empty vessels make the most noise.
(b) A rolling stone gathers no moss.
(c) Birds of a feather flock together.

(*d*) Never swap horses in mid-stream.
(*e*) Half a loaf is better than no bread.
(*f*) Rome was not built in a day.

Subjects for Essay or Discussion

1. Write an article for a school magazine on bird-watching as a hobby.

2. Compare the flight of aircraft (including gliders) with that of birds; what has man learned from the flight of birds?

3. Read Coleridge's *Ancient Mariner* and write the story of it in prose as if it had happened in this century.

4. Describe the battery system of keeping hens and compare it with other systems. Say what would happen if the battery system were applied to human beings in order to make industry more productive.

5. Describe the plan, furnishing and equipment of the bed-sitting room you would like when eventually you leave home.

6. Which season of the year do you prefer, and why?

Books Recommended

JAMES FISHER, *Watching Birds* (Penguin—there are several other books on birds on their list).

VISCOUNT GREY, *The Charm of Birds*.

D. LACK, *The Life of the Robin* (Penguin).

D. H. LAWRENCE, *Phoenix*. The essay "Man is a Hunter" is suitable for reading aloud to older forms.

K. LORENZ, *King Solomon's Ring*. A remarkable and exceptionally interesting book on the study of birds and animals.

H. J. PENROSE, *I Flew with the Birds*. The author was recently chief test pilot to Westland Aircraft.

A. H. VERRILL, *Strange Birds and their Stories*.

Chapter 11

ADRIFT ON AN ICE-FLOE

[The Worst Journey in the World was a six-week sledge trip over frozen seas, in darkness, by three members of Captain Scott's expedition to the South Pole. The account of it can be found in pages 255 to 313 in the Penguin edition; pages 293 to 299 describe their most terrible experience, and if one of them had not survived to write the book it would be difficult to believe that men could endure what they did. The whole account needs to be read, and I shall not attempt to quote from it.

The story told below happened during the preparations for the attempt on the Pole; Scott had sent three men and four ponies over sea ice in an attempt to reach Hut Point. In a letter home, Lt. Bowers describes how it turned out.]

1. I plugged on in the dog-tracks till we came to the seal crack which was an old pressure-ridge running many miles S.W. from Pram Point. We considered the ice behind this crack—over which we had just come—fast ice; it was older ice than that beyond, as it had undoubtedly frozen over first. Having crossed the crack we streaked on for Cape Armitage. The animals were going badly, owing to the effects of the blizzard, and frequent stoppages were necessary. On coming to some shaky ice we headed farther west as there were always some bad places off the cape, and I thought it better to make a good circuit. Crean, who had been over the ice recently, told me it was all right farther round. However, about a mile farther on I began to have misgivings; the cracks became too frequent to be pleasant, and although the ice was from five to ten feet thick, one does not like to see water squelching between them, as

we did later. It spells motion, and motion on sea-ice means breakage. I shoved on in the hope of getting on better ice round the cape, but at last came a moving crack, and that decided me to turn back. We could see nothing owing to the black mist, everything looked solid as ever, but I knew enough to mistrust moving ice, however solid it seemed. It was a beastly march back: dark, gloomy and depressing. The beasts got more and more down in their spirits and stopped so frequently that I thought we would never reach the seal crack. I said to Cherry, however, that I would take no risks, and camp well over the other side on the old sound ice if we could get there. This we managed to do eventually. Here there was soft snow, whereas on the sea side of the crack it was hard; that is the reason we lost the dogs' tracks at once on crossing. Even over this crack I thought it best to march as far in as possible. We got well into the bay, as far as our exhausted ponies would drag, before I camped and threw up the walls, fed the beasts, and retired to feed ourselves. We had only the primus with the missing cap, and it took over $1\frac{1}{2}$ hours to heat up the water; however, we had a cup of pemmican. It was very dark, and I mistook a small bag of curry powder for the cocoa bag, and made cocoa with that, mixed with sugar; Crean drank it right down before discovering anything was wrong. It was 2 p.m. before we were ready to turn in. I went out and saw everything quiet; the mist still hung to the west, but you could see a good mile and all was still. The sky was very dark over the Strait, though, the unmistakable sign of open water. I turned in. Two and a half hours later I awoke, hearing a noise. Both my companions were snoring; I thought it was that, and was on the point of turning in again, having seen that it was only 4.30, when I heard the noise again. I thought —"my pony is at the oats!" and went out.

2. I cannot describe either the scene or my feelings. I must

leave those to your imagination. We were in the middle of a floating pack of broken-up ice. The tops of the hills were visible, but all below was thin mist and as far as I could see there was nothing solid; it was all broken up, and heaving up and down with the swell. Long black tongues of water were everywhere. The floe on which we were had split right under our picketing line, and cut poor Guts' wall in half. Guts himself had gone, and a dark streak of water alone showed the place where the ice had opened under him. The two sledges securing the other end of the line were on the next floe and had been pulled right to the edge. Our camp was on a floe not more than 30 yards across. I shouted to Cherry and Crean, and rushed out in my socks to save the two sledges; the two floes were touching farther on and I dragged them to this place and got them on to our floe. At that moment our own floe split in two, but we were all together on one piece. I then got my finnesko on, remarking that we had been in a few tight places, but this was about the limit. I have been told since that I was quixotic not to leave everything and make for safety. You will understand, however, that I never for one moment considered the abandonment of anything.

3. We packed up camp and harnessed up our ponies in remarkably quick time. When ready to move I had to decide which way to go. Obviously towards Cape Armitage was impossible, and to the eastward also, as the wind was from that direction, and we were already floating west towards the open sound. Our only hope lay to the south, and thither I went. We found the ponies would jump the intervals well. At least Punch would and the other two would follow him. My idea was never to separate, but to get everything on to one floe at a time, and then wait till it touched or nearly touched another in the right direction, and then jump the

ponies over and drag the four sledges across ourselves. In this way we made slow but sure progress. While one was acting all was well; the waiting for a lead to close was the worst trial. Sometimes it would take ten minutes or more, but there was so much motion in the ice that sooner or later bump you would go against another piece, and then it was up and over. Sometimes they split, sometimes they bounced back so quickly that only one horse could get over, and then we had to wait again. We had to make frequent detours and were moving west all the time with the pack, still we were getting south, too.

4. Very little was said. Crean, like most bluejackets, behaved as if he had done this sort of thing often before. Cherry, the practical, after an hour or two dug out some chocolate and biscuit, during one of our enforced waits, and distributed it. I felt at that time that food was the last thing on earth I wanted, and put it in my pocket; in less than half an hour, though, I had eaten the lot. The ponies behaved as well as my companions, and jumped the floes in great style. After getting them on a new floe we simply left them, and there they stood chewing at each other's head ropes or harness till we were over with the sledges and ready to take them on again. Their implicit trust in us was touching to behold. A 12-feet sledge makes an excellent bridge if an opening is too wide to jump. After some hours we saw fast ice ahead, and thanked God for it. Meanwhile a further unpleasantness occurred in the arrival of a host of the terrible "killer" whales. These were reaping a harvest of seal in the broken-up ice, and cruised among the floes with their immense black fins sticking up, and blowing with a terrific roar. The Killer is scientifically known as the Orca and, though far smaller than the sperm and other large whales, is a much more dangerous animal. He is armed with a huge iron jaw and great

blunt socket teeth. Killers act in concert, too, and, as you may remember, nearly got Ponting when we were unloading the ship, by pressing up the thin ice from beneath and splitting it in all directions.

5. It took us over six hours to get close to the fast ice, which proved to be the Barrier, some immense chunks of which we actually saw break off and join the pack. Close in, the motion was less owing to the jamming up of the ice somewhere farther west. We had only just cleared the Strait in time, though, as all the ice in the centre, released beyond Cape Armitage, headed off into the middle of the Strait, and thence to the Ross Sea. Our spirits rose as we neared the Barrier edge, and I made for a big sloping floe which I expected would be touching; at any rate I anticipated no difficulty. We rushed up the slope towards safety, and were little prepared for the scene that met our eyes at the top. All along the Barrier face a broad lane of water from thirty to forty feet wide extended. This was filled with smashed-up brash ice, which was heaving up and down to the swell like the contents of a cauldron. Killers were cruising there with fiendish activity, and the Barrier edge was a sheer cliff of ice on the other side fifteen to twenty feet high. It was a case of so near and yet so far. Suddenly our great sloping floe calved in two, so we beat a hasty retreat. I selected a sound-looking floe just clear of this turmoil, that was at least ten feet thick, and fairly rounded, with a flat surface. Here we collected everything and having done all that men could do, we fed the beasts and took counsel.

6. Cherry and Crean both volunteered to do anything, in the spirit they had shown right through. It appeared of first necessity to communicate with Captain Scott. I guessed his anxiety on our behalf, and, as we could do nothing more, we wanted help of some sort. It occurred to me that a man working up to windward along the

Barrier face might happen upon a floe touching the Barrier. It was obviously impossible to take ponies up there anywhere, but an active man might wait his opportunity. Going to windward, too, he could always retreat on to our floes, as the ice was being pushed together in our direction. The next consideration was whom to send. To go myself was out of the question. The problem was whether to send one, or both, my companions. As my object was to save the animals and gear, it appeared to me that one man remaining would be helpless in the event of the floe splitting up, as he would be busy saving himself. I therefore decided to send one only. This would have to be Crean, as Cherry, who wears glasses, could not see so well. Both volunteered, but, as I say, I thought out all the pros and cons and sent Crean, knowing that, at the worst, he could get back to us at any time. I sent a note to Captain Scott, and, stuffing Crean's pockets with food, we saw him depart.

7. Practical Cherry suggested pitching the tent as a mark of our whereabouts, and having done this I mounted the theodolite to watch Crean through the telescope. The rise and fall of the floe made this difficult, especially as a number of Emperor penguins came up and looked just like men in the distance. Fortunately the sunlight cleared the frost smoke, and as it fell calm our westerly motion began to decrease. The swell started to go down. Outside us, in the centre of the Strait, all the ice had gone out, and open water remained. We were one of a line of loose floes floating near the Barrier edge. Crean was hours moving to and fro before I had the satisfaction of seeing him up on the Barrier. I said: "Thank God one of us is out of the wood, anyhow."

8. It was not a pleasant day that Cherry and I spent all alone there, knowing as we did that it only wanted a zephyr from the south to send us irretrievably out to

sea; still there is satisfaction in knowing that one has done one's utmost, and I felt that, having been delivered so wonderfully so far, the same Hand would not forsake us at the last. We gave the ponies all they could eat that day. The Killers were too interested in us to be pleasant. They had a habit of bobbing up and down perpendicularly, so as to see over the edge of a floe, in looking for seals. The huge black and yellow heads with sickening pig eyes only a few yards from us at times, and always around us, are among the most disconcerting recollections I have of that day. The immense fins were bad enough, but when they started a perpendicular dodge they were positively beastly. As the day wore on skua gulls, looking upon us as certain carrion, settled down comfortably near us to await developments. The swell, however, was getting less and less and it resolved itself into a question of speed, as to whether the wind or Captain Scott would reach us first.

9. Crean had got up into the Barrier at great risks to himself as I gathered afterwards from his very modest account. He had reached Captain Scott some time after his (Scott's) meeting with Wilson.[1] I heard that at the time Captain Scott was very angry with me for not abandoning everything and getting away safely myself. For my own part I must say that the abandoning of the ponies was the one thing that had never entered my head. It was a long way round, but at 7 p.m. he arrived at the edge of the Barrier opposite us with Oates and Crean. Everything was still, and Cherry and I could have got on safe ice at any time during the last half hour by using the sledge as a ladder. A big overturned fragment had jammed in the lane, between a high floe and the Barrier edge, and, there being no wind, it

[1] Wilson camped with the two dog-teams on the land, and in the morning saw us floating on the ice-floes through his field-glasses. He made his way along the peninsula until he could descend to the Barrier, where he joined Scott.

remained there. However, there was the consideration of the ponies, so we waited.

10. Scott, instead of blowing me up, was too relieved at our safety to be anything but pleased. I said: "What about the ponies and the sledges?" He said: "I don't care a damn about the ponies and sledges. It's you I want, and I am going to see you safe here on the Barrier before I do anything else." Cherry and I had got everything ready, so, dragging up two sledges, we dumped the gear off them, and using them as ladders, one down from the berg on to the buffer piece of ice, and the other up to the top of the Barrier, we got up without difficulty. Captain Scott was so pleased that I realized the feeling he must have had all day. He had been blaming himself for our deaths, and here we were very much alive. He said: "My dear chaps, you can't think how glad I am to see you safe—Cherry likewise."

11. I was all for saving the beasts and sledges, however, so he let us go back and haul the sledges on to the nearest floe. We did this one by one and brought the ponies along, while Titus dug down a slope from the Barrier edge in the hope of getting the ponies up it. Scott knew more about ice than any of us, and realizing the danger we didn't, still wanted to abandon things. I fought for my point tooth and nail, and got him to concede one article and then another, and still the ice did not move till we had thrown and hauled up every article on to the Barrier except the two ladders and the ponies.

APSLEY CHERRY-GARRARD, *The Worst Journey in the World*

(In the end one pony and all the sledges were recovered.)

Guts, one of the ponies. *Finnesko*, boots made of fur. *Lead*, a big crack. *Brash*, pieces of loose ice.

Précis and Comprehension

1. There are about three points in the story at which the fortunes of the explorers take a turn for good or bad;

each turning-point ends a phase of the narrative. Write down a title for each of these phases, and mention the incident which brings it to a climax.

2. How long do the events take? They start on the *night* of 28th February; another book on the same expedition (*South with Scott*) states that "at 4.30 *the next morning* Bowers awoke hearing a strange noise". Assuming that this is correct, either Lt. Bowers made a mistake over describing the time, or else there is a misprint. Find the mistake.

3. (*a*) Note any evidence of good leadership in the extract above.

(*b*) What do you learn of the characters of the three men?

4. Give in your own words the reasons why each of the three was either rejected or chosen as the messenger to return to Capt. Scott.

5. Can you find any passages where the writer expresses his feelings about what is going on, or what may happen?

Vocabulary, Punctuation, Grammar

1. Fill in the blanks with words to be found in the paragraphs mentioned:

(*a*) A person who neglects his own interests for some worthy cause may be called . . . (para. 2)

(*b*) A complete though not necessarily spoken belief in someone or something could be described as . . . (para. 4)

(*c*) Something that upsets one's self-possession is . . . (para. 8)

(*d*) Dead flesh, usually going bad, is called . . . (para. 8)

(*e*) Something to be taken into account is . . . (para. 9)

(*f*) To give way on a point is to . . . it (para. 11)

2. Write down the correct prepositions to follow:

associate (verb)	oblivious	acquiesce	unconscious
impervious	responsible	yearn	indifferent
deter	exposed	triumph (verb)	deputise

3. Add punctuation, capital letters and inverted commas to the following, and set it out as two verses of a poem.

ill tell thee everything i can theres little to relate i saw an aged aged man a-sitting on a gate who are you aged man i said and how is it you live and his answer tricked through my head like water through a sieve he said i look for butterflies that sleep among the wheat i make them into mutton-pies and sell them in the street i sell them unto men he said who sail the stormy seas and thats the way i get my bread— a trifle if you please

4. (a) In the first paragraph of "Adrift on an Ice-floe" find

> three adverbial subordinate clauses
> two adjectival subordinate clauses
> one noun subordinate clause

and mention in each case the word or words in the main clause to which it is related.

(b) Combine into one complex sentence:

The temperature seemed to fall. We advanced into the barrier. This night it fell to 62 degrees below zero. This meant more shivering. It meant more discomfort. There was moisture from our bodies and our breath. It formed ice in the fur of our sleeping bags. It did so especially at the head, hips and feet.

5. Correct any mistakes of grammar or expression that you can find in the following sentences. You need write down only your correction.

(a) Arriving rather late the meeting had already started; it was very unanimous that something should be done.

(b) The opera house with the theatre, ferroconcrete buildings and which had survived the earthquake, were in the centre of the town.

(c) I should have liked to have gone to a school different to this one.

(d) The youngest of my two brothers is as tall or taller than you.

(e) My father, whom everyone knows is very punctual, for once arrived later than me.

6. Explain the meaning of the following italicised expressions:

(a) He'll soon *meet his Waterloo*.

(b) I fear Smith is *a broken reed*.

(c) Counsel for the defence *out-heroded Herod*.

(d) He adopted a *Pharisaic* attitude.

(e) She has *too many irons in the fire*.

(f) The child behaved like *a dog in a manger*.

Subjects for Essay or Discussion

1. Why is it that books and films about life and exploration in the far north and south are so popular? Use your own reading and observation.

2. The climate of England has varied greatly in the past. Describe this country and the life in it after the climate has become very much warmer, or very much colder.

3. Climate and Character.

4. Write a short story entitled "How I stowed away".

5. You are secretary of a school society which meets for talks and discussions, and you wish to invite to it a well-known explorer who lives in the same district as you. Write the letter, complete with all necessary details.

6. Should all day schools have a boarding-house attached which all pupils can attend for two years from fourteen to sixteen?

Books Recommended

APSLEY CHERRY-GARRARD, *The Worst Journey in the World*.

DAVID GARNETT, *Pocahontas*. The true story of an Indian princess who married an English adventurer.

ANGUS GRAHAM, *The Golden Grindstone*. Another true story—of a Yukon gold-rush in the '90s.

T. HEYERDAHL, *The Kon-Tiki Expedition*. The famous
story of a drift across the Pacific to prove a theory.

LORD MOUNTEVANS, *South with Scott*.

F. NANSEN, *Farthest North*. Another drift to prove a
theory—in a specially built ice-ship to a point near the
North Pole. One of the most original, well-planned
and exciting polar expeditions.

Chapter 12

DARK SATANIC MILLS

[THE passage below comes from Arthur Bryant's *English Saga*, a popular history of the past hundred years, and forms part of the chapter which describes the horrors of the Industrial Revolution—the employment of children and women, treated worse than animals, for long hours in mines and factories, unemployment, starvation wages and actual starvation as machinery displaced men, the crippling and maiming of workers by machinery, the filthy slums that clotted round the factories. In 1837 the People's Charter had been put forward by a group of radical M.P.s and others, and in 1842 came a specially bad depression. Thousands of unemployed in the north were starving and were talking of burning down the mills to enforce a nation-wide strike.]

1. The first rumblings of the storm came from Staffordshire. Here towards the end of July the colliers, following a reduction of their wages to 2s. 6d. a day, turned out and, marching on every works in the neighbourhood, compelled their comrades to do likewise. Those who refused were flung into the canals, plugs were hammered out of the boilers and furnaces extinguished. The word went round that all labour was to cease until the Charter had become the law of the land. The markets in the towns of the western midlands were deserted and every workhouse besieged by vast queues of gaunt women and children and idle men.

2. The Lord Lieutenant, sitting with the magistrates at the Dartmouth Hotel, West Bromwich, called out the county yeomanry. The 3rd Dragoon Guards, stationed in Walsall, endeavoured to restore order. Shopkeepers

and farmers were enrolled as special constables, and the old England was pitted against the new. But in the industrial areas the dispossessed had the advantage of numbers and they were desperate. At Wolverhampton strikers surrounded the workhouse and established virtual mob-law. Farther north a procession of 6,000 workmen surged down on collieries, iron-works and potteries until every chimney in the district had ceased to smoke. There was little physical violence for only in a few places was there any resistance. Under threat of crowbar and torch, the owners of bakeries, groceries and public houses distributed provisions with the best face they could. Bills appeared on the walls calling the "Toiling Slaves" to monster demonstrations: others, issued by alarmed authorities, threatened transportation to those who destroyed machinery or used intimidation.

3. Such was the position as the parliamentary session of 1842 drew to a close and Ministers, who doubted the ability to keep the peace for more than a few days longer, prepared after the imperturbable manner of England for the customary Cabinet fish dinner at the Crown and Sceptre tavern, Greenwich. In the seaports there were signs of a slight improvement in trade. But the reports that poured in from every manufacturing district continued menacing. The whole population was in a state of intense excitement. It was difficult to say whether the cause was hunger, wage reductions, Chartism or the popular demand for cheap bread and repeal of the Corn Laws.

4. The explosion came on 4th August at Stalybridge, where the employees of Messrs. Bayley's mill had received notice of a further reduction in wages. The strikers, as though acting on prearranged orders, turned out the workers at every factory in Ashton and Oldham. Next morning they marched on Manchester. For a few

noisy hours the main body was held up by a small detachment of police and troops at Holt Town. But other rioters swarming out from the streets on either flank, the authorities were forced to fall back, leaving factories and provision shops at their mercy. At Messrs. Birley's mill, where momentary resistance was encountered, the roof was stormed, every window broken, and two policemen and an onlooker killed. On Saturday, 6th, while Sir Robert and his fellow Ministers were embarking at Hungerford Pier on the *Prince of Wales* steam packet for their outing at Greenwich, riots were raging in every district of Manchester. Police stations were demolished and more officers killed.

5. The great "Turn Out," long threatened by heady orators and whispered among the people, had come at last. The workers were on the march. On Sunday the rioting spread to Stockport and other parts of Cheshire. Mills were attacked, bakeries looted and the police pelted with stones. At Preston the mob attacked the military, and several lost their lives. In the Potteries some colliers arrested by the police were rescued by their fellow miners who subsequently stormed the Burslem Town Hall, burnt its records and rate books, and sacked the George Inn and the principal shops. Afterwards the town looked as though an invading army had passed through it.

6. The scene of the insurrection would not have been England had its grim and starving landscape not been lightened by flashes of humour. At one place where a band of marauding Amazons from the cotton mills threatened to burn down a farm, the farmer turned the tables by loosing his bull. In another—it was at Wigan —the local miners insisted on keeping guard round Lord Crawford's park against their fellow strikers so that, as one of them put it, the old Lord could drink his port in peace.

7. Work throughout the industrial north was now at a complete standstill. In Manchester all the shops were shuttered and the streets thronged with thousands of workmen who besieged the sidewalks demanding money and food from passers-by. Similar scenes were enacted in almost every industrial town from Leicester to Tyneside, and in western Scotland. At Stoke-on-Trent the mob gutted the Court of Requests, the Police Station and the larger houses; at Leeds the Chief of Police was seriously wounded, and fatal casualties occurred at Salford, Blackburn and Halifax. The wildest rumours circulated: that in Manchester the police had been cut to pieces with volleys of brickbats; that the redcoats, welcomed by the hungry populace as brothers, had risen against their officers; that the Queen who had "set her face against gals working in mills" was ready to grant the Charter and open the ports to cheap corn.

8. The alarm of the well-to-do classes in the adjacent rural areas was by now intense. In the factory towns of Lancashire 6,000 millowners and shopkeepers enrolled as special constables to defend their menaced interests. The Government decided to act with vigour. In every northern and midland county the yeomanry were called out, and farmers' sons sharpened sabres on the grindstone at the village smithy before riding off to patrol the grimy streets of a world they did not understand. Tall-hatted magistrates rode beside them ready to mumble through the Riot Act and loose the forces that had triumphed at Peterloo over the urban savagery their own neglect had created.

9. On Saturday, 13th August, there was fierce rioting in Rochdale, Todmorden, Bury, Macclesfield, Bolton, Stockport, Burslem and Hanley. At the latter place 5,000 strikers marched on a neighbouring country mansion and left it blazing. Hordes of rough-looking men in fur caps, carrying clubs and faggots, patrolled the

squalid unpaved roads around the idle mills; others attempted to hold up the mail and tear up the permanent way on the Manchester–Leeds railway. Next morning, though Sunday, the Cabinet met and issued urgent orders to the Guards and the Artillery at Woolwich to hold themselves in readiness for Manchester. That evening as the 3rd battalion of the Grenadiers debouched with band playing through the gates of St. George's Barracks into Trafalgar Square, vast numbers of working men and boys closed in and tried to obstruct its progress. In Regent Street the crowd became so menacing that the order was given to fix bayonets; all the way to Euston Square Station, which was packed with police, hisses and groans continued. The 34th Foot, summoned in haste from Portsmouth, was also continuously hooted on its march across London.

10. By the evening of the 16th, Manchester was held by three regular infantry battalions, the 1st Royal Dragoons and artillery detachments with howitzers and six-pounders. A few miles away the streets of Bolton were patrolled by companies of the 72nd Highlanders. Other troops poured in by the new railroads with such rapidity that the rebellion quickly began to lose its dangerous appearance. All that week the magistrates and police, protected by the military, were busy arresting ringleaders and detachments of rioters, and every main road and railway was watched by mounted constables and dragoons.

11. After that the insurrection crumbled. Further resort to force was useless. Hunger did the rest. Anger and hectic excitement gave place to weakness and despair. The shops were guarded and, with the mills closed, even the miserable wages of the past year of want ceased. The poor rates in every Lancashire town soared as pale, famished multitudes besieged the workhouses, and ruined householders, unable to pay their rent, aban-

doned their homes. In November Engels saw gaunt, listless men at every street corner in Manchester, and whole streets of houses in Stockport standing empty.

. . . .

12. Gradually the factories reopened and a defeated people crept back to work. The insurrection had failed. Yet, like the Report on the employment of children in coal mines, it had done something to awaken the conscience of England. It had added to pity fear, and, as is the way with the English in times of trial, a sober resolve to remove the cause of the evil. So long as the rioting continued, worthy and peace-loving folk set their faces resolutely against the rioters. But when it was over they took counsel of their consciences.

13. Many, particularly the manufacturers and the new middle-class, who had nothing to gain by the protection of agriculture and much by the cheapening of provisions, laid the blame on the Corn Laws. Others, like the country landowners, condemned the inhumanity of the millowners, who retaliated by pointing to the low wages and neglected hovels of the agricultural workers in the southern counties. As Ashley, the factory reformer, knew to his misery, none were worse than those on the Dorset estate of his father, Lord Shaftesbury. The economists and the statesmen who subscribed to their theories continued to reiterate the importance of non-interference with the laws of supply and demand.

14. But with the general thinking public the view gained ground that there were limits to the efficacy of *laissez-faire*, where public health and the employment of children were concerned. Sanitary reform and factory regulation began for the first time to be taken seriously. Early in 1843 Ashley was able to carry without opposition an address to the Crown for the diffusion of moral and religious education among the working

classes. In the following year a new Factory Bill became law limiting the hours of children under sixteen to six and a half a day, and establishing further regulations for the fencing of machinery and the inspection of industrial premises. In the same year a commission on the Health of Towns was appointed. Its Report examined, only six had a good water supply and not one an adequate drainage system.

15. Public opinion was by now far ahead of Parliamentary action. During the middle and later 'forties the novels of Dickens, Disraeli and Charles Kingsley, the pamphlets of Carlyle and the poems of Elizabeth Barrett Browning educated the reading classes in the Condition of the People question and stimulated their desire for social reform. Intelligent England had become conscious of the new towns. Even Tennyson turned from his dreams of a remote chivalry to confront the inescapable problem of his age:

"Slowly comes a hungry people, as a lion creeping nigher,
       Glares at one that nods and winks behind a slowly dying fire."

The thought of a new generation was crystallised in Ashley's unanswerable question, "Let me ask the House, what was it gave birth to Jack Cade? Was it not that the people were writhing under oppressions which they were not able to bear? It was because the Government refused to redress their grievances that the people took the law into their own hands."

16. So inspired by pity and purged by the fear of some new and more terrible arising, the conscience and common sense of England addressed themselves to the redress of great wrongs. They received little direction from the responsible rulers of the nation who were

blinded by a theory.[1] The urge for social reform was spontaneous and its first fruits were mainly voluntary and unofficial. It took the form of numberless remedial activities of a private or only semi-public nature, from feverish church building and the foundation of industrial schools for the waifs and strays of the urban slums to the "poor peopling" which became so fashionable an occupation for well-to-do young ladies in the late 'forties: it was in this work that Florence Nightingale began her life of voluntary service. All over England and Scotland isolated individuals began to tackle self-imposed tasks, each striving to cleanse his or her own small local corner of the Augean stable. Such were provincial doctors who faced fever and vested interest in a tireless campaign against insanitary conditions, devoted clergymen and non-conformist ministers, city missionaries and temperance workers, and young men and women of comfortable circumstances—often evangelicals or quakers—who gave up their leisure hours to teach in ragged schools or to organise clubs, sports and benefit societies for their poorer neighbours. In this way, not for the first time in England's history, the destruction wrought by her own tumultuous vitality was redeemed in part by the operation of her own generous conscience.

17. But the evil was deeply rooted, and the remedy, for all the energy and enthusiasm behind it, so ill-co-ordinated and tardy that those who prophesied revolution and social chaos might have been proved right had it not been for one over-riding factor. The social maladies that provoked revolt were not destroyed though they were henceforward slowly but steadily mitigated. On the other hand, while diminishing in intensity, they con-

---

[1] In later years men like Sir James Graham, the Home Secretary, and John Roebuck, the Radical Economist, admitted that they had been wrong in their fear that the limitation of hours of labour would ruin the country.

tinued to grow in extent through further urbanisation. Revolution was avoided by extending the area of exploitation. But the very factor which most hastened that process ended the isolation of the industrial areas from the rest of the community. The railways had already been decisive in the suppression of the rebellion: an express train had brought a critical appeal for help from Preston to Manchester, and the Guards had been transferred from London to Lancashire in the course of a single night. Rapid internal communication and a new habit of travel, born of cheap transport, was within a few years to transform England and give her a new unity and orientation.

ARTHUR BRYANT, *English Saga*

Précis and Comprehension

1. Write a clear and connected summary of paragraphs 16 and 17. Your summary should so far as possible be in your own words, and should be between 120 and 140 words in length. State at the end the number of words you have used.

2. Re-read paragraphs 12 and 13 and then answer these questions:
   (a) Who pitied whom, and why? (para. 12).
   (b) Why were they now afraid? (para. 12).
   (c) Express "a sober resolve" (para. 12) in a sentence beginning "They now began . . ."
   (d) Similarly explain "they took counsel of their consciences".
   (e) What is meant by "the protection of agriculture"? What was the intention of the Corn Laws? (para. 13).
   (f) Express more simply "who subscribed to their theories".
   (g) What three groups of men are mentioned in paragraph 13?
   ("The laws of supply and demand" meant in effect that if men were unemployed through the closing

of a factory they would have to wait until demand for another product gave them work in another factory; governments were not expected to help with the provision of work or to relieve the distress that followed unemployment.)

3. Give in your own words the meaning of:

mob-law (para. 2)	adjacent rural areas
best face they could	(para. 8)
(para. 2)	urban savagery (para. 8)
heady orators (para. 5)	Public opinion was ahead of
marauding Amazons	Parliamentary action
(para. 6)	(para. 15)
	Augean stable (para. 16)

Vocabulary, Punctuation, Grammar

1. Provide dictionary definitions of the meanings of six of the following words in their contexts; remember that if you are defining an adjective you must give an adjective or a phrase that is the equivalent of an adjective, and so on.

transportation (para. 2)	imperturbable (para. 3)
intimidation (para. 2)	loot (para. 5)
menace (para. 8)	reiterate (para. 13)
debouched (para. 9)	redress (para. 15)
retaliate (para. 13)	mitigated (para. 17)

2. In the following passage find alternative expressions for the phrases in which "get" or "got" occur.

We got up (1) in good time, got a hasty breakfast ready (2) and got to (3) the station in good time. Mr. Barry had got the tickets beforehand (4). When we got past (5) the first station, John got teased (6) a little for the smile he got (7) from a lady whose suitcase he got down (8) from the rack—it was ungetatable (9) she said. John rightly gave as good as he got (10); in fact he got (11) the best of the argument, and the others got (12) confused. When we got out (13) at Southampton we got (14) some fruit and got into (15) the harbour in plenty of time. By the time we got (16) on board it was getting near (17) sailing time. One of the stewards got quite excited (18) over a kitten which got over (19) the gangway just before we got off (20).

3. Find single words for six of the phrases in italics:
   (a) The seals of the chest were *not interfered with.*
   (b) The story was *one which could not be believed.*
   (c) I read it in a recent *article on new books* in a magazine.
   (d) Before the days of gunpowder the keep was *not one that could be stormed.*
   (e) No, you are *not qualified to enter* for this event.
   (f) We were entertained *in a manner fit for a king or queen.*
   (g) The ship was well known for her *capacity to keep an even keel.*
   (h) Selling books was now his only *means of earning a living.*

4. Punctuate the following passages; direct speech should start on a fresh line.
   (a) it was wilfred who doling cigarettes out to the crew after supper suggested a game of poker we dont know how to play said nanette youll soon learn said wilfred the rules are easy so with hatches shut tight and the curtains drawn across the porthole and the stove a furnace we took our first lessons in poker
   (b) how much money said nanette hours later has wilfred won all of it said emma turning the cocoa tin where we kept it upside down hell have to lend us some tomorrow to buy the food he did play well didnt he i dont remember said nanette

5. (a) Expand into subordinate clauses the phrases in italics in each of the following sentences. State the kind of each clause, and its connection with the main clause.
       (i) The surveyor ordered *the widening of the road.*
       (ii) The new road, *without any side turnings* for two miles, was a success.
       (iii) We went slowly *on account of the heavy traffic.*
       (iv) We had reached halfway *at sunset.*

(b) Keeping the same meaning, reduce each of the following to a simple sentence.

  (i) He was given a warm welcome when he arrived.

  (ii) Though two tugs assisted, she could not be moved off the rocks.

  (iii) The peace treaty required that all the forts should be demolished.

  (iv) They will do it if they are well paid.

6. Correct anything that you find wrong with the grammar or expression of the following sentences:

(a) If you don't mind me saying so, I'd rather you did the stitches like I do.

(b) Going into the nearest restaurant, there was no room, so a pub. was the only alternative.

(c) Smith and his wife collaborated together in a book which was superior than any they had written before.

(d) Between you and I, his daughter is suffering with german measles.

(e) "Get from hence very quickly," he said, "or I'll go in search for a policeman."

7. Explain the meaning of five of the following proverbs:

(a) When the cat's away, the mice will play.

(b) A little learning is a dangerous thing.

(c) There's no smoke without fire.

(d) You can't teach an old dog new tricks.

(e) It's the last straw that breaks the camel's back.

(f) Least said, soonest mended.

Subjects for Essay or Discussion

1. So far as your knowledge goes, describe what the welfare state does to help an individual throughout the whole of his or her life.

2. Give an account of any man or woman whose life and work you specially admire.

3. The making of a newspaper.

4. Should we preserve the countryside?

5. What has science done for mankind?

6. Should schools be equipped with T.V.?

Books Recommended

S. R. BADMIN, *Village and Town* (Penguin). How houses, villages and towns have developed.

ARTHUR BRYANT, *English Saga* (Collins—Fontana Books).

CHARLES DICKENS, *David Copperfield, Barnaby Rudge, Hard Times.*

IAN NAIRN, *Outrage, Counter-Attack* (Architectural Press).

OSBERT LANCASTER, *Homes, Sweet Homes.*

J. M. RICHARDS, *An Introduction to Modern Architecture* (Penguin).

RALPH TUBBS, *The Englishman Builds* (Penguin).

H. G. WELLS, *A Short History of the World* (Penguin).

JANET WHITNEY, *Elizabeth Fry.*

C. WOODHAM-SMITH, *Lady-in-Chief.* The Story of Florence Nightingale.

Chapter 13

THE RIGHTS OF ANIMALS

[THE hero of *Erewhon* strays into an undiscovered country, where he is at once arrested for possessing a watch. Later he finds that all machinery has been abolished, except for specimens in museums, and that the Erewhonians are much happier without it. He learns too that disease is treated as a crime, and crime as a disease. When he wrote *Erewhon*, Samuel Butler was far ahead of his time in presenting new ideas, many of which are now widely accepted; some criminals are now given treatment by doctors, instead of prison, and if disease itself is not yet regarded as punishable the neglect of disease can be a serious offence. Bernard Shaw and others borrowed much from Butler.

The extract that follows sums up the views of one of their philosophers on the rights of animals.]

1. "You know," he said, "how wicked it is of you to kill one another. Once upon a time your forefathers made no scruple about not only killing, but also eating their relations. No one would now go back to such detestable practices, for it is notorious that we have lived much more happily since they were abandoned. From this increased prosperity we may confidently deduce the maxim that we should not kill and eat our fellow-creatures. I have consulted the higher power by whom you know that I am inspired, and he has assured me that this conclusion is irrefragable.

2. "Now it cannot be denied that sheep, cattle, deer, birds and fishes are our fellow-creatures. They differ from us in some respects, but those in which they differ are few and secondary, while those that they have in common with us are many and essential. My friends, if

it was wrong of you to kill and eat your fellow-men, it is wrong also to kill and eat fish, flesh, and fowl. Birds, beasts and fishes have as full a right to live as long as they can unmolested by man, as man has to live unmolested by his neighbours. These words, let me again assure you, are not mine, but those of the higher power which inspires me.

3. "I grant," he continued, "that animals molest one another, and that some of them go so far as to molest man, but I have yet to learn that we should model our conduct on that of the lower animals. We should endeavour, rather, to instruct them, and bring them to a better mind. To kill a tiger, for example, who has lived on the flesh of men and women whom he has killed, is to reduce ourselves to the level of the tiger, and is unworthy of people who seek to be guided by the highest principles in all, both their thoughts and actions.

4. "The unseen power who has revealed himself to me alone among you, has told me to tell you that you ought by this time to have outgrown the barbarous habits of your ancestors. If, as you believe, you know better than they, you should do better. He commands you, therefore, to refrain from killing any living being for the sake of eating it. The only animal food that you may eat, is the flesh of any birds, beasts, or fishes, that you may come upon as having died a natural death, or any that may have been born prematurely, or so deformed that it is a mercy to put them out of their pain; you may also eat all such animals as have committed suicide. As regards vegetables you may eat all those that will let you eat them with impunity."

5. So wisely and so well did the old prophet argue, and so terrible were the threats he hurled at those who should disobey him, that in the end he carried the more highly educated part of the people with him, and presently the poorer classes followed suit, or professed to do so.

Having seen the triumph of his principles, he was gathered to his fathers, and no doubt entered at once into full communion with that unseen power whose favour he had already so pre-eminently enjoyed.

6. He had not, however, been dead very long, before some of his more ardent disciples took it upon them to better the instruction of their master. The old prophet had allowed the use of eggs and milk, but his disciples decided that to eat a fresh egg was to destroy a potential chicken, and that this came to much the same as murdering a live one. Stale eggs, if it was quite certain that they were too far gone to be able to be hatched, were grudgingly permitted; but all eggs offered for sale had to be submitted to an inspector, who, on being satisfied that they were addled, would label them "Laid not less than three months" from the date, whatever it might happen to be. These eggs, I need hardly say, were only used in puddings, and as a medicine in certain cases where an emetic was urgently required. Milk was forbidden inasmuch as it could not be obtained without robbing some calf of its natural sustenance, and thus endangering its life.

7. It will be easily believed that at first there were many who gave the new rules outward observance, but embraced every opportunity of indulging secretly in those flesh-pots to which they had been accustomed. It was found that animals were continually dying natural deaths under more or less suspicious circumstances. Suicidal mania, again, which had hitherto been confined exclusively to donkeys, became alarmingly prevalent even among such for the most part self-respecting creatures as sheep and cattle. It was astonishing how some of these unfortunate animals would scent out a butcher's knife if there was one within a mile of them, and run right up against it if the butcher did not get it out of their way in time.

8. Dogs, again, that had been quite law-abiding as regards domestic poultry, tame rabbits, sucking pigs, or sheep and lambs, suddenly took to breaking beyond the control of their masters, and killing anything that they were told not to touch. It was held that any animal killed by a dog had died a natural death, for it was the dog's nature to kill things, and he had only refrained from molesting farmyard creatures hitherto because his nature had been tampered with. Unfortunately, the more these unruly tendencies became developed, the more the common people seemed to delight in breeding the very animals that would put temptation in the dog's way. There is little doubt, in fact, that they were deliberately evading the law; but whether this was so or no they sold or ate everything their dogs had killed.

9. Evasion was more difficult in the case of the larger animals, for the magistrates could not wink at all the pretended suicides of pigs, sheep, and cattle that were brought before them. Sometimes they had to convict, and a few convictions had a very terrorising effect— whereas in the case of animals killed by a dog, the marks of the dog's tooth could be seen, and it was practically impossible to prove malice on the part of the owner of the dog.

10. Another fertile source of disobedience to the law was furnished by a decision of one of the judges that raised a great outcry among the more fervent disciples of the old prophet. The judge held that it was lawful to kill any animal in self-defence, and that such conduct was so natural on the part of a man who found himself attacked, that the attacking creature should be held to have died a natural death. The High Vegetarians had indeed good reason to be alarmed, for hardly had this decision become generally known before a number of animals hitherto harmless, took to attacking their owners with such ferocity, that it became necessary to

put them to a natural death. Again, it was quite common at that time to see the carcase of a calf, lamb, or kid exposed for sale with a label from the inspector certifying that it had been killed in self-defence. Sometimes even the carcase of a lamb or calf was exposed as "warranted still-born", when it presented every appearance of having enjoyed at least a month of life.

11. As for the flesh of animals that had *bona fide* died a natural death, the permission to eat it was nugatory, for it was generally eaten by some other animal before man got hold of it; or failing this it was often poisonous, so that practically people were forced to evade the law by some of the means above spoken of, or to become vegetarians. This last alternative was so little to the taste of the Erewhonians that the laws against killing animals were falling into desuetude, and would very likely have been repealed, but for the breaking out of a pestilence, which was ascribed by the priests and prophets of the day to the lawlessness of the people in the matter of eating forbidden flesh. On this, there was a reaction; stringent laws were passed, forbidding the use of meat in any form or shape, and permitting no food but grain, fruits, and vegetables to be sold in shops and markets. These laws were enacted about two hundred years after the death of the old prophet who had first unsettled people's minds about the rights of animals; but they had hardly been passed before people again began to break them.

12. I was told that the most painful consequence of all this folly did not lie in the fact that law-abiding people had to go without animal food—many nations do this and seem none the worse, and even in flesh-eating countries such as Italy, Spain, and Greece, the poor seldom see meat from year's end to year's end. The mischief lay in the jar which undue prohibition gave to the consciences of all but those who were strong enough

to know that though conscience as a rule boons, it can also bane. The awakened conscience of an individual will often lead him to do things in haste that he had better have left undone, but the conscience of a nation awakened by a respectable old gentleman who has an unseen power up his sleeve will pave hell with a vengeance.

13. Young people were told that it was a sin to do what their fathers had done unhurt for centuries; those, moreover, who preached to them about the enormity of eating meat, were an unattractive academic folk; and though they overawed all but the bolder youths, there were few who did not in their hearts dislike them. However much the young person might be shielded, he soon got to know that men and women of the world— often far nicer people than the prophets who preached abstention—continually spoke sneeringly of the new doctrinaire laws, and were believed to set them aside in secret, though they dared not do so openly. Small wonder, then, that the more human among the student classes were provoked by the touch-not, taste-not, handle-not precepts of their rulers, into questioning much that they would otherwise have unhesitatingly accepted.

SAMUEL BUTLER, Erewhon

Précis and Comprehension

1. Write out the substance of paragraphs 1–4 inclusive in about 120 words. Your summary should be clear, simple and logically connected; it should be in your own words.

   Write at the end of your answer the exact number of words you have used. You will lose marks if your version is over ten words more or less than 120.

2. Say very briefly what you think there is to be said for and against the old philosopher's view.

3. On paragraphs 10 and 11:

    (a) What caused the law to be broken more frequently?

    (b) Why were the High Vegetarians alarmed?

    (c) What made worthless the permission to eat the flesh of animals which had died a natural death?

    (d) What effect did enforced vegetarianism nearly have on the law against killing animals, and why did it not in the end affect the law?

    (e) What caused a tightening up of the law?

4. Is there any sign in the extract that Samuel Butler himself agrees or disagrees with the views of the old philosopher? (This is best discussed orally.)

5. What words or phrases in the paragraphs mentioned have nearly the same meaning as:

    (a) had no qualms of conscience (para. 1)

    (b) try to behave in the same way as (para. 3)

    (c) without fear of punishment (para. 4)

    (d) that the plan of things he believed in had come about (para. 5)

    (e) obedience on the surface (para. 7)

    (f) luxurious habits of eating (para. 7)

    (g) to show that there was wrongful intention (para. 9)

    (h) generally does good, but can also do harm (para. 12)

6. Rewrite in your own words, without abbreviating, the last sentence of paragraph 13.

Vocabulary, Punctuation, Grammar

1. Find synonyms for eight of:

    unmolested, professed, ardent, exclusively, prevalent, evasion, practically, ascribed, stringent, academic.

2. (a) Form adjectives from:

    evade, scruple, mischief, explain, prosperity.

    (b) Give the nouns connected with:

    ardent, potential, profess, detestable, deduce.

3. Find in this list words to fit into each of the numbered gaps in the passage below:

ensued, attempt, discussion, ceremony, glanced, stocked, unprofitable, intended, companion, protested, nervously, bargaining.

The clergyman, without any (1), asked the price of the crystal egg. Mr. Cave (2) (3) towards the door leading into the parlour, and said five pounds. The clergyman (4) that the price was high, to his (5) as well as to Mr. Cave—it was, indeed, very much more than Mr. Cave had (6) to ask when he had (7) the article—and an (8) at (9) (10). Mr. Cave stepped to the shop-door, and held it open. "Five pounds is my price," he said, as though he wished to save himself the trouble of (11) (12).

4. Punctuate and where necessary add capital letters to the passage below; start a fresh line where the sense requires it. There are two speakers only.

you read my thoughts sir do my eyes deceive me or is that object up there a pie it cant be a pie yes its a pie wegg said mr boffin have i lost my smell for fruits or is it an apple pie sir asked wegg its a veal and ham pie said mr boffin

5. (a) In paragraph 1 of the extract from *Erewhon* find
    three noun subordinate clauses
    one adverbial subordinate clause
    one adjectival subordinate clause
    and state in each case how they are related to the main clause.

  (b) Turn into subordinate clauses the phrases in italics, and state the kind of each clause:

    I realised *the truth of what he said.*

    Despite slight lameness, she covered the 100 yards in 11 seconds.

    You can rely on me, *a resident for so long in* this country.

    I could not discover *the reason for his nervousness.*

6. Turn the following passage into Reported Speech after the opening "Major urged his comrades . . ."

And remember, comrades, your resolution must never falter. No argument must lead you astray. Never listen when they tell you that Man and the animals have a common interest, that the prosperity of the one is the prosperity of the others. It is all lies. Man serves the interests of no creature except himself. And among us animals let there be perfect unity, perfect comradeship in the struggle. All men are enemies. All animals are comrades.

GEORGE ORWELL, *Animal Farm*

7. Explain five of the following expressions:
   - (*a*) to preach to the converted
   - (*b*) to tilt at windmills
   - (*c*) to go on a wild goose chase
   - (*d*) to cry for the moon
   - (*e*) to carry coals to Newcastle
   - (*f*) to cast pearls before swine

Subjects for Essay or Discussion

1. *Either*, Do animals get a square deal? *or* An account of the R.S.P.C.A.
2. Consider the various forms of captivity in which animals are kept—agricultural, domestic, in cages on wheels, and so on—and decide which can be justified.
3. "Men as I see them" by a Pig.
4. An old house, or Castles.
5. Imagine that a person, either from abroad or from a remotely different part of the country, comes to your town or village for the first time. Describe it as it would appear to him.
6. Should membership of a cadet organisation for three years exempt young men from a year's national service?

Books Recommended

SAMUEL BUTLER, *Erewhon* (Penguin).

LORD DUNSANY, "The Use of Man" in *Plays for Earth and Air*.

Rowena Farre, *Seal Morning*.

Margaret Shaw and J. Fisher, *Animals as Friends*. One of the best general books on the keeping of animals.

H. Munro Fox, *The Personality of Animals* (Penguin).

George Orwell, *Animal Farm* (Penguin).

Jonathan Swift, *Gulliver's Travels*. Especially "A Voyage to the Houyhnhnms".

Chapter 14

AFTER LONDON

[IN the novel from which the extract below is taken, Richard Jefferies tells the story of a man who lived in England after some catastrophe had destroyed civilisation and altered the shape of the land. The centre of England is occupied by a great lake, round the banks of which clumsy barges and the canoes of hunters make their careful way. The people are barbarous, and divided into quarrelsome tribes. The opening chapters, from which comes the passage below, describe with magnificent vividness the savagery of men and animals and the country's relapse into a wilderness.]

1. At the eastern extremity the Lake narrows, and finally is lost in the vast marshes which cover the site of the ancient London. Through these, no doubt, in the days of the old world there flowed the river Thames. By the changes of the sea level and the sand that was brought up there must have grown great banks, which obstructed the stream. I have formerly mentioned the vast quantities of timber, the wreckage of towns and bridges, which was carried down by the various rivers, and by none more so than by the Thames. These added to the accumulation, which increased the faster because the foundations of the ancient bridges held it like piles driven in for the purpose. And before this the river had become partially choked from the cloacae of the ancient city, which poured into it through enormous subterranean aqueducts and drains.

2. After a time all these shallows and banks became well matted together by the growth of weeds, of willows, and flags, while the tide, ebbing lower at each drawing back,

left still more mud and sand. Now it is believed that,
when this had gone on for a time, the waters of the
river, unable to find a channel, began to overflow up
into the deserted streets, and especially to fill the under-
ground passages and drains, of which the number and
extent was beyond all the power of words to describe.
These, by the force of the water, were burst up, and the
houses fell in.

3. For this marvellous city, of which such legends are
related, was after all only of brick, and when the ivy
grew over and trees and shrubs sprang up, and lastly
the waters underneath burst in, the huge metropolis
was soon overthrown. At this day all those parts which
were built upon low ground are marshes and swamps.
Those houses that were upon high ground were, of
course, like the other towns, ransacked of all they contained by the remnant that was left; the iron, too, was
extracted. Trees growing up by them in time cracked
the walls, and they fell in. Trees and bushes covered
them; ivy and nettles concealed the crumbling masses
of brick.

4. The same was the case with the lesser cities and towns
whose sites are known in the woods. For though many
of our present towns bear the ancient names, they do not
stand upon the ancient sites, but are two or three, and
sometimes ten miles distant. The founders carried with
them the name of their original residence.

5. Thus the low-lying parts of the mighty city of London
became swamps, and the higher grounds were clad with
bushes. The very largest of the buildings fell in, and
there was nothing visible but trees and hawthorns on
the upper lands, and willows, flags, reeds, and rushes on
the lower. These crumbling ruins still more choked the
stream, and almost, if not quite, turned it back. If any
water ooze past, it is not perceptible, and there is no
channel through to the salt ocean. It is a vast stagnant

swamp, which no man dare enter, since death would be his inevitable fate.

6. There exhales from this oozy mass so fatal a vapour that no animal can endure it. The black water bears a greenish-brown floating scum, which for ever bubbles up from the putrid mud of the bottom. When the wind collects the miasma, and, as it were, presses it together, it becomes visible as a low cloud which hangs over the place. The cloud does not advance beyond the limits of the marsh, seeming to stay there by some constant attraction; and well it is for us that it does not, since at such times when the vapour is thickest, the very wild-fowl leave the reeds, and fly from the poison. There are no fishes, neither can eels exist in the mud, nor even newts. It is dead.

7. The flags and reeds are coated with slime and noisome to the touch; there is one place where even these do not grow, and where there is nothing but an oily liquid, green and rank. It is plain there are no fishes in the water, for herons do not go thither, nor the kingfishers, not one of which approaches the spot. They say the sun is sometimes hidden by the vapour when it is thickest, but I do not see how any can tell this, since they could not enter the cloud, as to breathe it when collected by the wind is immediately fatal. For all the rottenness of a thousand years and of many hundred millions of human beings is there festering under the stagnant water, which has sunk down into and penetrated the earth, and floated up to the surface the contents of the buried cloacae.

8. Many scores of men have, I fear, perished in the attempt to enter this fearful place, carried on by their desire of gain. For it can scarcely be disputed that un-told treasure lies hidden therein, but guarded by terrors greater than fiery serpents. These have usually made their endeavours to enter in severe and continued frost,

or in the height of a drought. Frost diminishes the power of the vapour, and the marshes can then, too, be partially traversed, for there is no channel for a boat. But the moment anything be moved, whether it be a bush, or a willow, even a flag, if the ice be broken, the pestilence rises yet stronger. Besides which, there are portions which never freeze, and which may be approached unawares, or a turn of the wind may drift the gas towards the explorer.

9. In the midst of the summer, after long heat, the vapour rises, and is in a degree dissipated into the sky, and then by following devious ways an entrance may be effected, but always at the cost of illness. If the explorer be unable to quit the spot before night, whether in summer or winter, his death is certain. In the earlier times some bold and adventurous men did indeed succeed in getting a few jewels, but since then the marsh has become more dangerous, and its pestilent character, indeed, increases year by year, as the stagnant water penetrates deeper. So that now for very many years no such attempts have been made.

10. The extent of these foul swamps is not known with certainty, but it is generally believed that they are, at the widest, twenty miles across, and that they reach in a winding line for nearly forty. But the outside parts are much less fatal; it is only the interior which is avoided.

11. Towards the Lake the sand thrown up by the waves has long since formed a partial barrier between the sweet water and the stagnant, rising up to within a few feet of the surface. This barrier is overgrown with flags and reeds, where it is shallow. Here it is possible to sail along the sweet water within an arrow-shot of the swamp. Nor, indeed, would the stagnant mingle with the sweet, as is evident at other parts of the swamp, where streams flow side by side with the dark or reddish water; and there are pools upon one side of which the

deer drink, while the other is not frequented even by rats.

12. The common people aver that demons reside in these swamps; and, indeed, at night fiery shapes are seen, which, to the ignorant, are sufficient confirmation of such tales. The vapour, where it is most dense, takes fire, like a blue flame of spirits, and these flaming clouds float to and fro, and yet do not burn the reeds. The superstitious trace in them the forms of demons and winged fiery serpents, and say that white spectres haunt the margin of the marsh after dusk. In a lesser degree, the same thing has taken place with other ancient cities. It is true that there are not always swamps, but the sites are uninhabitable because of the emanations from the ruins. Therefore they are avoided. Even the spot where a single house has been known to have existed is avoided by the hunters in the woods.

13. They say, when they are stricken with ague or fever, that they must have unwittingly slept on the site of an ancient habitation. Nor can the ground be cultivated near the ancient towns, because it causes fever; and thus it is that, as I have already stated, the present places of the same name are often miles distant from the former locality. No sooner does the plough or the spade turn up an ancient site than those who work there are attacked with illness. And thus the cities of the old world, and their houses and habitations, are deserted and lost in the forest. If the hunters, about to pitch their camp for the night, should stumble on so much as a crumbling brick or a fragment of hewn stone, they at once remove at least a bowshot away.

14. The eastward flow of the Thames being at first checked, and finally almost or quite stopped by the formation of these banks, the water turned backwards as it were, and began to cover the hitherto dry land. And this, with the other lesser rivers and brooks that

no longer had any ultimate outlet, accounts for the Lake, so far as this side of the country is concerned.

15. At the western extremity the waters also contract between the steep cliffs called the Red Rocks, near to which once existed the city of Bristol. Now the Welsh say, and the tradition of those who dwell in that part of the country bears them out, that in the time of the old world the river Severn flowed past the same spot, but not between these cliffs. The great river Severn coming down from the north, with England on one bank and Wales upon the other, entered the sea, widening out as it did so. Just before it reached the sea, another lesser river, called the Avon, the upper part of which is still there, joined it, passing through this cleft in the rocks.

16. But when the days of the old world ended in the twilight of the ancients, as the salt ocean fell back and its level became lower, vast sandbanks were disclosed, which presently extended across the most part of the Severn River. Others, indeed, think that the salt ocean did not sink, but that the land instead was lifted higher. Then they say that the waves threw up an immense quantity of shingle and sand, and that thus these banks were formed. All that we know with certainty, however, is, that across the estuary of the Severn there rose a broad barrier of beach, which grew wider with the years, and still increases westwards. It is as if the ocean churned up its floor and cast it forth upon the strand.

17. Now when the Severn was thus stayed yet more effectually than the Thames, in the first place it also flowed backwards, as it were, till its overflow and that of the lesser rivers which ran into it met and mingled with the reflux of the Thames. Thus the inland sea of fresh water was formed; though Silvester hints (what is most improbable) that the level of the land sank and formed a basin. After a time, when the waters had risen

high enough, since all water must have an outlet some-where, the Lake, passing over the green country behind the Red Rocks, came pouring through the channel of the Avon.

18. Then, farther down, it rose over the banks which were lowest there, and thus found its way over a dam into the sea. Now when the tide of the ocean is at its ebb, the waters of the Lake rush over these banks with so furious a current that no vessel can either go down or come up. If ships attempted to go down, they would be swamped by the meeting of the waves; if they attempted to come up, the strongest gale that blows could not force them against the stream. As the tide gradually returns, however, the level of the ocean rises to the level of the Lake, the outward flow of the water ceases, and there is even a partial inward flow of the tide, which, at its highest, reaches to the Red Rocks. At this state of the tide, which happens twice in a day and night, vessels can enter or go forth.

19. The Irish ships, of which I have spoken, thus come into the Lake, waiting outside the bar till the tide lifts them over. Being built to traverse the ocean from their country, they are large and stout and well manned, carrying from thirty to fifty men. The Welsh ships, which come down from that inlet of the Lake which follows the ancient course of the Severn, are much smaller and lighter, as not being required to withstand the heavy seas. They carry but fifteen or twenty men each, but then they are more numerous. The Irish ships, on account of their size and draught, in sailing about the sweet waters, cannot always haul on shore at night, nor follow the course of the ships of burden be-tween the fringe of islands and the strand.

20. They have often to stay in the outer and deeper waters; but the Welsh boats come in easily at all parts of the coast, so that no place is safe against them. The

Welsh have ever been most jealous as to that part of the Lake which we suppose to follow the course of the Severn, and will on no account permit so much as a canoe to enter it. So that whether it be a narrow creek, or whether there be wide reaches, or what the shores may be like, we are ignorant. And this is all that is with certainty known concerning the origin of the inland sea of sweet water, excluding all that superstition and speculation have advanced, and setting down nothing but ascertained facts.

21. A beautiful sea it is, clear as crystal, exquisite to drink, abounding with fishes of every kind, and adorned with green islands. There is nothing more lovely in the world than when, upon a calm evening, the sun goes down across the level and gleaming water, where it is so wide that the eye can but just distinguish a low and dark cloud, as it were, resting upon the horizon, or perhaps looking lengthways, cannot distinguish any ending to the expanse. Sometimes it is blue, reflecting the noon-day sky; sometimes white from the clouds; again green and dark as the wind rises and the waves roll.

22. Storms, indeed, come up with extraordinary swiftness, for which reason the ships, whenever possible, follow the trade route, as it is called, behind the islands, which shelter them like a protecting reef. They drop equally quickly, and thus it is not uncommon for the morning to be calm, the midday raging in waves dashing resistlessly upon the beach, and the evening still again. The Irish, who are accustomed to the salt ocean, say, in the suddenness of its storms and the shifting winds, it is more dangerous than the sea itself. But then there are almost always islands, behind which a vessel can be sheltered.

23. Beneath the surface of the Lake there must be concealed very many ancient towns and cities, of which the

names are lost. Sometimes the anchors bring up even now fragments of rusty iron and old metal, or black beams of timber. It is said, and with probability, that when the remnant of the ancients found the water gradually encroaching (for it rose very slowly), as they were driven back year by year, they considered that in time they would be all swept away and drowned. But after extending to its present limits the Lake rose no farther, not even in the wettest seasons, but always remains the same. From the position of certain quays we know that it has thus remained for the last hundred years at least.

24. Never, as I observed before, was there so beautiful an expanse of water. How much must we sorrow that it has so often proved only the easiest mode of bringing the miseries of war to the doors of the unoffending! Yet men are never weary of sailing to and fro upon it, and most of the cities of the present time are upon its shore. And in the evening we walk by the beach, and from the rising grounds look over the waters, as if to gaze upon their loveliness were reward to us for the labour of the day.

RICHARD JEFFERIES, *After London*

Précis and Comprehension

1. Summarise the first three paragraphs in eighty to ninety words. State at the end the number you have used.

2. Describe the site of London in about fifty to sixty words, after re-reading paragraphs 6 and 7.

3. *Either* give an account in about eighty words of how the Lake came to be formed,

   Or show how and where ships from the salt sea could enter and leave the Lake.

4. State the difference between the Irish and Welsh ships and mention the reason for the difference.

5. Has the history of the world in the last half century increased or diminished the possibility of Jefferies' vision coming true?

6. Briefly describe the contrast mentioned in paragraph 24.

Vocabulary, Punctuation, Grammar

1. Choose six of the following words; think of six other words with similar prefixes (e.g. if you were given *premeditate* you might set *prepare* next to it); and explain the meaning of the prefix, referring to both words of the pair.

   obstruct, subterranean, exhale, perceptible, inevitable, attraction, disclose, reflux, traverse.

2. Find synonyms for six of:

   metropolis (para. 3), constant (para. 6), dissipate (para. 9), aver (para. 12), ultimate (para. 14), speculation (para. 20), and encroach (para. 23).

3. (*a*) Mention nouns connected with:

   constant, penetrate, stagnant, diminish, dissipate, sufficient.

   (*b*) Mention adjectives derived from:

   metropolis, pestilence, effect, extent, swamp, fragment.

4. Punctuate the following:

   (*a*) ghmason esq bsc 110 queen besss way rockingham london ne 15

   (*b*) up rode the squatter mounted on his thoroughbred up rode the troopers one two three wheres that jolly jumbuck youve got in your tucker bag youll come a waltzing matilda with me

   (*c*) its a pity isnt it that the cat cant have its supper without mrs joness permission.

5. (*a*) Analyse the second sentence of paragraph 2 of the extract from *After London* (from "Now it is . . ." to ". . . to describe") into clauses; state the kind of each clause, and its exact grammatical function.

(b) Make up four separate sentences including the sentence "The river began to overflow" unaltered, on these lines:

    (i) Make it a noun clause in a sentence.
    (ii) Add to it an adjectival clause.
    (iii) Add to an adverbial clause of result.
    (iv) Insert within it a phrase in apposition.

6. Correct the style, grammar or expression of the following:

(a) Dear Sir, We are in receipt of your favour of the 11th inst. We beg to assure you that the matter is receiving immediate attention, and we trust that your good self will accept the assurance. Meanwhile, we beg to remain, dear sir, yours faithfully, Josiah Jones, Ltd.

(b) The innkeeper and his wife where we are going to-morrow is expecting us early.

(c) Yes, I getting a puncture was the reason because John and I were late.

(d) We were literally thunderstruck by the news which was better than anyone would of thought possible.

(e) We inferred from the speaker that everyone these days must think for themselves.

7. Explain five of the following proverbs:

(a) When in Rome do as Rome does.
(b) Handsome is as handsome does.
(c) He might as well be hanged for a sheep as a lamb.
(d) Beauty is in the eye of the beholder.
(e) Beauty is skin-deep.
(f) As you sow, so shall you reap.

Subjects for Essay or Discussion

1. Write an account and criticism of any book or film of which the story is set in the future, or of any work of "science fiction" you have read.

2. If some catastrophe were likely to wipe out most of the population, and you had the chance of saving fifty

people (in addition to relatives), what kind of men and women would you try to include?

3. Describe the purpose and methods of any youth organisation with which you are acquainted.

4. Astronomy.

5. Write an account, suitable for foreigners, of what England has to offer as a place for a holiday.

6. Farming to-day.

Books Recommended

W. H. DAVIES, *Autobiography of a Super Tramp.*

J. B. S. HALDANE, *Possible Worlds.*

H. STAFFORD HATFIELD, *The Inventor and his World* (Penguin).

FRED HOYLE, *The Nature of the Universe.*

RICHARD JEFFERIES, *After London.*

GEORGE ORWELL, *Nineteen Eightyfour* (Penguin).

G. R. STEWART, *Earth Abides* (Corgi).

H. G. WELLS, *Tales of Space and Time, The Time Machine, The War of the Worlds* (Penguin).

Chapter 15

THE MACHINE STOPS

[THE extract that follows is the opening of a story in which
E. M. Forster imagines a future rather different from that
which H. G. Wells hoped would come about. People
dwell in their own rooms and rarely move from them,
because radio, television (two-way, of course) and other
devices bring to them all that they need. Kuno, the hero
of the story, revolts against conditions in which man is
losing the use of his senses and muscles, and eventually
the civilisation of his day collapses. The whole tale takes
over two periods to read aloud.]

1. Imagine, if you can, a small room, hexagonal in shape,
   like the cell of a bee. It is lighted neither by window nor
   by lamp, yet it is filled with a soft radiance. There are
   no apertures for ventilation, yet the air is fresh. There
   are no musical instruments, and yet, at the moment
   that my meditation opens, this room is throbbing with
   melodious sounds. An armchair is in the centre, by its
   side a reading-desk—that is all the furniture. And in the
   armchair there sits a swaddled lump of flesh—a woman,
   about five feet high, with a face as white as a fungus. It
   is to her that the little room belongs.

   An electric bell rang.

   The woman touched a switch and the music was
   silent.

   "I suppose I must see who it is," she thought, and set
   her chair in motion. The chair, like the music, was
   worked by machinery, and it rolled her to the other side
   of the room, where the bell still rang importunately.

2. "Who is it?" she called. Her voice was irritable, for she
   had been interrupted often since the music began. She

knew several thousand people; in certain directions human intercourse had advanced enormously.

But when she listened into the receiver, her white face wrinkled into smiles, and she said:

"Very well. Let us talk, I will isolate myself. I do not expect anything important will happen for the next five minutes—for I can give you fully five minutes, Kuno. Then I must deliver my lecture on 'Music during the Australian Period'."

She touched the isolation knob, so that no one else could speak to her. Then she touched the lighting apparatus, and the little room was plunged into darkness.

"Be quick!" she called, her irritation returning. "Be quick, Kuno; here I am in the dark wasting my time."

3. But it was fully fifteen seconds before the round plate that she held in her hands began to glow. A faint blue light shot across it, darkening to purple, and presently she could see the image of her son, who lived on the other side of the earth, and he could see her.

"I have called you before, mother, but you were always busy or isolated. I have something particular to say."

"What is it, dearest boy? Be quick. Why could you not send it by pneumatic post?"

"Because I prefer saying such a thing. I want——"

"Well?"

"I want you to come and see me."

Vashti watched his face in the blue plate.

"But I can see you!" she exclaimed. "What more do you want?"

"I want to see you not through the Machine," said Kuno. "I want to speak to you not through the wearisome Machine."

4. "Oh hush!" said his mother, vaguely shocked. "You mustn't say anything against the Machine."

"Why not?"

"One mustn't."

"You talk as if a god had made the Machine," cried the other. "I believe that you pray to it when you are unhappy. Men made it, do not forget that. Great men, but men. The Machine is much, but it is not everything. I see something like you in this plate, but I do not see you. I hear something like you through this telephone, but I do not hear you. That is why I want you to come. Come and stop with me. Pay me a visit, so that we can meet face to face, and talk about the hopes that are in my mind."

5. She replied that she could scarcely spare the time for a visit.

"The air-ship barely takes two days to fly between me and you."

"I dislike air-ships."

"Why?"

"I dislike seeing the horrible brown earth, and the sea, and the stars when it is dark. I get no ideas in an air-ship."

"I do not get them anywhere else."

"What kind of ideas can the air give you?"

He paused for an instant.

"Do you not know four big stars that form an oblong, and three stars close together in the middle of the oblong, and hanging from these stars, three other stars?"

"No, I do not. I dislike the stars. But did they give you an idea? How interesting; tell me."

"I had an idea that they were like a man."

"I do not understand."

6. "The four big stars are the man's shoulders and his knees. The three stars in the middle are like the belts that men wore once, and the three stars hanging are like a sword."

"A sword?"

"Men carried swords about with them, to kill animals and other men."

"It does not strike me as a very good idea, but it is certainly original. When did it come to you, first?"

"In the air-ship——" He broke off, and she fancied that he looked sad. She could not be sure, for the Machine did not transmit subtleties of expression. It gave only a general idea of people—an idea that was good enough for all practical purposes, Vashti thought. The imponderable bloom was rightly ignored by the Machine, just as the imponderable bloom of the grape was ignored by the manufacturers of artificial fruit. Something "good enough" had long since been accepted by our race.

7. "The truth is," he continued, "that I want to see these stars again. They are curious stars. I want to see them not from the air-ship, but from the surface of the earth, as our ancestors did, thousands of years ago. I want to visit the surface of the earth."

She was shocked again.

"The surface of the earth is only dust and mud, no life remains on it, and you would need a respirator, or the cold of the outer air would kill you. . . . And besides——"

"Well?"

"It is contrary to the spirit of the age," she asserted.

"Do you mean by that, contrary to the Machine?"

"In a sense, but——"

His image in the blue plate faded.

"Kuno!"

He had isolated himself.

For a moment Vashti felt lonely.

8. Then she generated the light, and the sight of her room, flooded with radiance and studded with electric buttons, revived her. There were buttons and switches every-

where—buttons to call for food, for music, for clothing. There was the hot-bath button, by pressure of which a basin of (imitation) marble rose out of the floor, filled to the brim with a warm deodorised liquid. There was the cold-bath button. There was the button that produced literature. And there were of course the buttons by which she communicated with her friends. The room, though it contained nothing, was in touch with all that she cared for in the world.

Vashti's next move was to turn off the isolation switch, and all the accumulations of the last three minutes burst upon her. The room was filled with the noise of bells, and speaking-tubes. What was the new food like? Could she recommend it? Had she any ideas lately? Would she make an engagement to visit the public nurseries at an early date?—say this day month.
9. To most of these questions she replied with irritation—a growing quality in that accelerated age. She said that the new food was horrible. That she could not visit the public nurseries through press of engagements. That she had no ideas of her own but had just been told one —that four stars and three in the middle were like a man: she doubted there was much in it. Then she switched off her correspondents, for it was time to deliver her lecture on Australian music.

The clumsy system of public gatherings had been long since abandoned; neither Vashti nor her audience stirred from their rooms. Seated in her armchair she spoke, while they in their armchairs heard her, fairly well, and saw her, fairly well. . . . Her lecture, which lasted ten minutes, was well received, and at its conclusion she and many of her audience listened to a lecture on the sea; there were ideas to be got from the sea; the speaker had donned a respirator and visited it lately. Then she fed, talked to many friends, had a bath, talked again, and summoned her bed.

10. The bed was not to her liking. It was too large, and she had a feeling for a small bed. Complaint was useless, for beds were of the same dimension all over the world, and to have had an alternative size would have involved vast alterations in the Machine. Vashti isolated herself—it was necessary, for neither day nor night existed under the ground—and reviewed all that had happened since she summoned the bed last. Ideas? Scarcely any. Events—was Kuno's invitation an event?

By her side, on the little reading-desk, was a survival from the ages of litter—one book. This was the Book of the Machine. In it were instructions for every possible contingency. If she was hot or cold or dyspeptic or at a loss for a word, she went to the book, and it told her which button to press. The Central Committee published it. In accordance with a growing habit, it was richly bound.

11. Sitting up in the bed, she took it reverently in her hands. She glanced round the glowing room as if someone might be watching her. Then, half ashamed, half joyful, she murmured "O Machine! O Machine!" and raised the volume to her lips. Thrice she kissed it, thrice inclined her head, thrice she felt the delirium of acquiescence. Her ritual performed, she turned to page 1376, which gave the times of the departure of the airships from the island in the southern hemisphere, under whose soil she lived, to the island in the northern hemisphere, whereunder lived her son.

She thought, "I have not the time."

12. She made the room dark and slept; she awoke and made the room light; she ate and exchanged ideas with her friends, and listened to music and attended lectures; she made the room dark and slept. Above her, beneath her, and around her, the Machine hummed eternally; she did not notice the noise, for she had been

born with it in her ears. The earth, carrying her, hummed as it sped through silence, turning her now to the invisible sun, now to the invisible stars. She awoke and made the room light. . . .

Again she consulted the book. She became very nervous and lay back in her chair palpitating. Think of her as without teeth or hair. Presently she directed the chair to the wall, and pressed an unfamiliar button. The wall swung apart slowly. Through the opening she saw a tunnel that curved slightly, so that its goal was not visible. Should she go to see her son, here was the beginning of the journey.

13. Of course she knew all about the communication-system. There was nothing mysterious in it. She would summon a car and it would fly with her down the tunnel until it reached the lift that communicated with the air-ship station: the system had been in use for many, many years, long before the universal establishment of the Machine. And of course she had studied the civilisation that had immediately preceded her own—the civilisation that had mistaken the functions of the system, and had used it for bringing people to things, instead of bringing things to people. Those funny old days, when men went for change of air instead of changing the air in their rooms! And yet—she was frightened of the tunnel: she had not seen it since her last child was born. It curved—but not quite as she remembered; it was brilliant—but not quite as brilliant as a lecturer had suggested. Vashti was seized with the terrors of direct experience. She shrank back into the room, and the wall closed up again.

"Kuno," she said, "I cannot come to see you. I am not well."

Immediately an enormous apparatus fell on to her out of the ceiling, a thermometer was automatically inserted between her lips, a stethoscope was automatically laid upon her heart. She lay powerless. Cool pads soothed her forehead. Kuno had telegraphed to her doctor.

E. M. FORSTER, *Collected Short Stories*

Précis and Comprehension

1. In section 1:
   (*a*) What does the simile of the cell suggest to you about the life of the people of Vashti's time?
   (*b*) What meaning is conveyed by the word "swaddled"? (Think why "clothed" or "wrapped" would not do as well.)
   (*c*) What does the word "fungus" convey that "chalk" would not?
   In section 2, try to find an example of irony, and explain in what way it is ironical.

2. "I see something like you" (section 4). Look through the whole extract and see if you can find other remarks which also suggest that there is a great deal of "second-handness" about the civilisation E. M. Forster describes.

3. (*a*) "The ages of litter" (section 10): what is meant by this?
   (*b*) "It was richly bound" (section 10): what attitude towards the book is suggested by "the growing habit"? What book of our age does the Book of the Machine replace?
   (*c*) "Bringing things to people" (section 13): remembering that this story was written about fifty years ago, say if you think we have in this respect ("bringing things to people") moved in the direction of E. M. Forster's future.

4. What do you learn about the two characters, Vashti and Kuno?

Vocabulary, Punctuation, Grammar

1. Explain the meaning in their contexts of:
   importunately (section 1), imponderable (section 6), contingency (section 10), dyspeptic (section 10),

delirium (section 11), acquiescence (section 11) and ritual (section 11).

2. Give abstract nouns connected with:

attend, friend, familiar, importunate, woman, white, irritable, curious.

3. Choose eight of the following words and explain the meaning of the prefixes in those you have chosen:

interrupt, prefer, dislike, transmit, expression, imponderable, surface, respirator, produce, communicate, deodorised, accumulate.

4. Find from the list that follows words to fill in the numbered blanks in the passage below:

Few have (1) Frank Buckland in the power of (2) at once (3) and amusement. He (4) from his father the (5) of (6) a subject, dry in other hands (and how dry lectures often are), with a (7) and picturesque interest, and to this he added a (8) of subject and a fund of droll yet (9) illustration (10) his own. His (11) was (12), yet was always informing; while his (13) earnestness, and (14) of the serious with the (15), never failed to (16) attention.

vehement, drollery, vivid, conveying, arrest, humorous, inherited, excelled, peculiarly, variety, faculty, information, alternation, irresistible, apt, investing.

5. Punctuate:

(a) It is now thirty-three years ago he wrote in the temple bar magazine since a frightened and trembling lad i found myself standing underneath the gateway of william of wykehams noble college at winchester duly entered by the nomination of dr shuttleworth then warden of new college oxford afterwards bishop of chichester

(b) this is the third clever operation in dentistry that mr bartlett has performed first removing a big tooth from the hippopotamus second operating on the base of the tusk of the big elephant third taking a horses leg-bone out of the lions mouth

6. (a) Analyse the following sentence into clauses, writing out each clause in full. Give the grammatical description of each clause, and state its grammatical function in the sentence.

> If you take the longest street in New York, and travel up and down it, *conning* its features patiently until you know every house and window and door and lamp-post and big and little sign by heart, and know them so accurately that you can *instantly* name the one you are abreast of when you are set down at random in that street *in* the middle of an inky black night, then you will have a tolerable notion of the amount and the exactness of a pilot's knowledge who carries the Mississippi River in his head.

(b) Name the part of speech and its function in its clause of each of the three words in italics.

7. Put section 4 of the extract from *The Machine Stops* into Reported Speech after a verb of saying in the past tense.

8. Explain the meaning of five of the following figurative expressions:
   (a) a finger in many pies
   (b) trying to run before one can walk
   (c) to hold all the cards
   (d) to spoil the ship for a ha'porth of tar
   (e) to burn one's fingers
   (f) to turn over a new leaf

Subjects for Essay or Discussion

1. Are we tending through things like films, broadcasting, television and tinned food to accept things at second-hand?

2. Is life becoming too easy?

3. Are we becoming too standardised?

4. What is the litter problem, and in what ways might it be dealt with?

5. Describe the educational system of the country to an American friend of your father's, settling in England with two children, a girl of four and a boy of seven.

6. The Roads of Britain.

Books Recommended

G. C. BOMPAS, *Life of Frank Buckland*.

FRANK BUCKLAND, *Curiosities of Natural History*.

CONAN DOYLE, *The Lost World*.

E. M. FORSTER, *Short Stories* (Penguin).

JAMES HILTON, *Lost Horizon*.

C. NIEDER, *Man Against Nature* (Corgi).

The Oxford Junior Encyclopædia.

A. F. TSCHIFFELY, *Tschiffely's Ride*.

H. W. VAN LOON, *The Arts of Mankind*.

Chapter 16

ELEPHANTS IN WAR-TIME

[IN the first half of *Elephant Bill*, Col. Williams describes how as a young man he learned the job of managing teams of elephants and their "oozies". In the second half, from which the extract below is taken, he describes his adventures in organising elephants for all sorts of war-time tasks in the struggle against the Japanese in Burma.]

1. Considerable information had been gathered from the Burmans and former employees of the timber firms on the use the Japanese had made of elephants during their occupation of Burma.

2. During their advance of 1942 the Japanese used elephants to transport mortars and ammunition over the Caukeraik Pass from Siam into Burma. It is probable that this had been planned in advance, and the operation was successful. It seems very unlikely, however, that the Japanese had intended to make other military use of elephants in Burma before their invasion. For we know that they had made preparations for an organisation to work the forests under military control. A Japanese company, called the Nipponese Burmese Timber Union, was formed soon after the fall of Burma. The company did round up a considerable number of elephants and their oozies, who remained inseparable from their animals. They appointed as many of the Anglo-Burman assistants of the timber firms as they could find, as officers. But these Anglo-Burmans were never trusted by the Japanese. Such suspicions did not make for efficiency, even if the men had been trying to work. No British firm would have ever paid a dividend, unless it had done the same work in less than a third of

the time that the Nipponese Burmese Company took over it. As a matter of fact, though they made an effort to show that they intended to develop the forests, they did very little extraction of timber from the forests, and relied almost entirely on what had already been hauled to the waterways or rafted to the depots. This may have partly been due to the fact that the Japanese military had a prior claim on elephants, and would send for working parties of a hundred elephants whenever occasion arose for their use. No Anglo-Burman was ever appointed to command these columns of elephants for military purposes, and the Japanese had to rely on the small number of Burmese-speaking officers in their army to coerce the oozies. There were many causes of difficulty and trouble. The Japanese soldiers' rations were inferior to what the oozie was accustomed to, and this was undoubtedly a principal cause of discontent.

3. The Japanese also insisted on elephants being tied up after a day's work, and being hand-fed by the oozies. This meant more work for the men, who had to cut fodder, and less food for the elephants, which always do best when they can pick their own food. After feeding their animals, the oozies were themselves kept penned in camp under guard. I found that most of the oozies who had worked under the Japanese hated them so much that they preferred not to discuss them. "They lived like dogs; they ate like dogs; and they died like dogs," one of the oozies said to me, in summing up the invaders.

4. The elephants and their oozies were of the greatest military use to the Japanese. The big Japanese offensive to break into India via Imphal, Ukhrul, Kohima and Jesami from the Upper Chindwin, depended largely on elephant transport. This accounted for their rapid movement over jungle paths in very difficult country.

5. On 13 March, 1944, the Japanese crossed the Chind-

win by night, with a column of three hundred and fifty elephants, which they marched direct to the Chin hills. A Japanese N.C.O. was in charge of every thirty animals. The elephants were used over precipitous and impassable country, linking up with motor transport and bullock-carts when they reached roads once more. Their transport system was improvised *ad hoc* from all available means and, though it did not look smart, it functioned and moved fast.

6. The Japanese did not ill-treat elephants in the sense of being cruel to the animals, as their management was left entirely to the oozies. But they pushed them hard, and never gave them opportunities to get the full amount of fodder they needed. I have already referred to the careless indifference which led to injuries from [battery] acid spilt on elephants' backs.

7. The Japanese had, however, a passion for ivory, and practically every tusker elephant which had been in Japanese hands had his tusks sawn off, as near to the nerve as possible. This work could not have been done by the Japanese themselves, as it demanded expert knowledge. It was no doubt done by Burmans of the toughest type, who wished to curry favour with Japanese officers, who were mad about ivory. No serious damage was done to the health of the elephants by this. I did not see a single case in which the nerve had been exposed. But, nevertheless, it was criminal, as it greatly reduced the value of a tusker for timber work, since the tusks left were not long enough for him to get under a log in order to move it. The Japanese, however, were more concerned with using elephants for transport than they were with timber extraction. Perhaps they thought the elephants looked less dangerous without their tusks. Early in 1943 I was present at the examination of a full pack, dropped by a Japanese soldier, when avoiding a patrol of ours on the east bank of the

Chindwin. The pack weighed approximately seventy-five pounds, and contained two tips of tusks weighing six pounds in all. The soldier obviously valued his souvenir, to add it to such a heavy load. I don't think, however, that the Japanese got all the ivory obtained in this way, as the Burman also has a passion for it.

8. "Four thousand elephants used for hauling timber have disappeared in Burma." This statement appeared in the *Daily Mail*, and was quoted in *Punch* with the query: "Have you looked everywhere?" Well, the answer is that we had not, and nobody ever will. The statement appeared before we had completely cleared the Japanese out, and a few more may have come to light. I can, however, claim to have discovered the whereabouts of one of the missing four thousand. He is the Regimental Mascot of a famous Indian regiment, which captured him, and would not surrender him to me. On their return from the Burma Campaign he was marched across India to the Regimental Depot. Unfortunately, there is on his behind a capital C branded on with white phosphorous paint when he was seven years old. This proclaims his real ownership—the Bombay Burma Trading Corporation—and all the dhobies in the Punjab can never erase it. The Quartermaster is advised to get busy with the regimental tailor and fit him with cloth of gold trappings to cover it up. When the Regiment reached Assam a language difficulty arose. The Burman oozie wished to return home, and it was decided that an Indian mahout must be found among the ranks of the battalion. Not one could be found, so it became a Brigade request, and eventually a sepoy, who claimed to have been employed in a Rajah's elephant stable, was appointed.

9. The handing over of the Regimental Mascot by the Burmese oozie to the Indian mahout was planned to be a ceremony of importance. Many officers were present,

including three Battalion Commanders and the Brigadier. There was considerable speculation on the parade-ground as to how the elephant would react to orders spoken in Hindustani, for the animal's understanding of Burmese words of command had become a by-word in the regiment.

10. The new Indian mahout arrived on the parade-ground in bottle-green battle-dress, wearing boots, belt and side-arms. The Burmese oozie sat on the elephant's head, dressed as usual in his lungyi shirt and a Japanese cotton vest. The Indian wore a look of immense self-importance, the Burman one of complete indifference. Not a word was exchanged between the pair as the oozie ordered the elephant to sit down on all fours. As the Burman slipped off the elephant's head, the Indian mounted and the animal stood up. The Burman walked off the parade-ground, and then came the great test, as the Indian was left to prove himself. Drawing his bayonet from its scabbard with a flourish, he first held it at the sword present arms. Then he gave the elephant a probe with it behind the right ear, and to the astonishment of everyone, exclaimed in English: "Now, Mr. B——, come on!"—and off they marched.

11. In all, one thousand six hundred and fifty-two other elephants were recaptured from the Japanese between November 1942 and the date of unconditional surrender. They went back to their working lives. Before I left Burma I visited and said good-bye to four hundred and seventeen of them, working in the Kabaw Valley in Upper Burma, where they were still being employed in pulling out the tail of the XIVth Army. They were all that was left of Elephant Companies Nos. 1 and 2. The rest had gone back to their pre-war work of timber extraction, and were soon happily scattered through the teak forests of Burma where they belong. Some were war-weary, some were battle-scarred, but they were in

good hands, and would be nursed back to good health and good condition. Of the lost host of three thousand nine hundred and ninety-nine (according to the *Daily Mail*), many hundreds lost their lives owing to the folly and ruthlessness of man. There can be no roll call of the survivors. But there were numbers of wounded who, though they may have had a hard fight for existence to gather their food, would recover after they had treated their wounds in the traditional elephant fashion, by sealing them with mud two or three times a day. When they recovered they would set forth to leave the valleys which had become hells in the jungle during the war, for peaceful areas. But many must have escaped unhurt.

12. Those that had stampeded and those that survived their wounds must greatly outnumber those that lost their lives, and I know well enough where they are now. For the herds of wild elephants show no resentment when domesticated animals join them. They have none of that herd instinct directed against the stranger that one finds in cattle, in small boys and among grown-up men. This tolerance is just one of the things about elephants which makes one realise they are big in more ways than one. No doubt some attempts will be made by the jungle Burmans to recapture branded elephants from the wild herds. The only successful way to do this is for two very daring oozies to ride a really trustworthy animal into the wild herd as it is grazing in open kaing grass and edge it alongside the animal they are trying to recapture. One of the oozies will then begin to talk to it, very quietly, and if it listens without alarm, he will slip across from the animal he is riding on to its back. A short stampede is almost certain to follow, but a good oozie will soon gain control as the wild herd disappears. But those that will be recaptured in this way are few indeed, and with Burma in its present condition I like to think

of the hundreds that will remain leading their happy wild life, undisturbed by the restless demands of man.

13. Elephants have recently been nationalised in Burma, which means that they will lose their best friends in captivity, the European assistants, many of whom would never have gone on with their work in the jungle but for their interest in the most lovable and sagacious of all beasts.

J. H. WILLIAMS, *Elephant Bill*

Précis and Comprehension

1. For what reasons was the Nipponese Burmese Timber Union only a partial success?

2. How did the attitudes of the oozies and of the Japanese towards elephants differ?

3. Why did the oozies dislike working for the Japanese?

4. What is the writer's attitude towards the transfer ceremony? (paras. 8, 9, 10)

5. What qualities does the writer ascribe to elephants?

6. Explain the meaning of the following:

prior claim (para. 2), occasion arose (para. 2), *ad hoc* (para. 5), curry favour (para. 7), considerable speculation (para. 9), herd instinct (para. 12).

Vocabulary, Punctuation, Grammar

1. Find words in the paragraphs mentioned which mean much the same as:

to force a person to do as he is told (para. 2)

constructed to meet an emergency from materials ready to hand (para. 5)

lack of interest (para. 6)

without any terms being specified (para. 11)

a complete lack of regret for action which may cause harm (para. 11)

feeling of anger in response to the action of another (para. 12)

2. (a) What is the force of the prefix in these words:
transport, invasion, preparations, extraction, reduce, recapture, survivor.

(b) Give adjectives connected with:
information, occasion, custom, precipice, resentment, instinct, tolerance.

(c) Give nouns connected with:
occupy, pay, develop, rely, know, realise, prefer.

(d) Find four different negative prefixes in the passage from *Elephant Bill*. (*a* in *a*pathy—lack of feeling or interest—is a negative prefix.)

3. Add punctuation and capitals where necessary to each of these passages:

(a) the co at blackdown raoc camp near aldershot sent for officer cadet j n marshall for your initiative test get yourself into a film he said and you have 36 hours to do it

(b) sun rises 610 am sets 749 pm moon 1054 am to 833 pm lights 848 pm to 511 am tomorrow high water at london bridge 509 pm 529 am tomorrow

4. Combine the following sentences so as to form three complex sentences:

There was a mansion house in the south of Scotland. It had gardens. One year the squirrels were very destructive to the song birds. It was decided to shoot down the squirrels. The decision was not carried out. A squirrel was caught red-handed. It was devouring a nestling. It was shot on the spot. The killing of birds ceased. The individual squirrel was the only sinner. The whole race had been condemned for the crime. Only one was guilty.

5. (a) Analyse the following sentence into clauses, writing out each clause in full. State the grammatical function of each clause in the sentence:

The caribou's huge, spreading hoofs are their snowshoes, by which they can skim the swamps and drifts where any but themselves sink and become exhausted, while, as the animal treads, the hoof clicks *loudly*, a sound which helps to keep the herds together *during* darkness and blizzard, just as the *twittering* of small birds, heard in the heavens during autumn nights, helps to keep the migrating flocks together.

(b) Parse each of the three words italicised in the passage above.

6. Correct any mistakes of style, grammar and sense that you find in the following sentences:

(a) Each of the kinds of tree you mention are too big for a garden like you have.

(b) To entirely complete this paper is a task beyond you and I.

(c) Suffering with mumps, the match between the two schools was cancelled.

(d) In the event of my proceeding to London, I shall endeavour to assist you by purchasing approximately three shirts, which I anticipate will be sufficient.

(e) There are only two alternatives if you really prefer cycling than walking.

7. Explain four of the following proverbs by describing briefly a situation to which each might apply:

(a) Out of sight, out of mind.
(b) Where there's a will, there's a way.
(c) An ounce of practice is worth a pound of precept.
(d) Still waters run deep.
(e) The burnt child fears the fire.
(f) Every dog has his day.
(g) You can't make bricks without straw.

Subjects for Essay or Discussion

1. Write three letters (from different people) to show the development of a correspondence in a newspaper on ONE of these subjects:

(a) The use of ponies in mines.
(b) The battery system of keeping hens.

    (c) Stag-hunting.

    (d) The training of performing animals.

2. Kindness to animals.

3. What—apart from scientific data—can be learned from studying animals?

4. "My opinion of *Elephant Bill*", by an elephant.

5. What is soil erosion, and how can it be dealt with?

6. What is to be said for and against the keeping of pets by young children?

7. Give instructions for keeping any bird or animal or fish, or for growing any particular plant, that you are interested in.

Books Recommended

    A. BOMBARD, *The Bombard Story*.

    MAURICE O'SULLIVAN, *Twenty Years A-growing*.

    V. PENIAKOV, *Private Army*. His peace-time hobby of navigating the North African sands in an old car enabled "Popski" to lead his private army in war.

    D. REITZ, *Commando*. A Boer journal of the South African War.

    SIEGFRIED SASSOON, *Sherston's Progress* (Penguin).

    J. H. WILLIAMS, *Elephant Bill*.

    J. H. WILLIAMS, *Bandoola*.

Chapter 17

PAPERS ACTUALLY SET

THIS chapter consists of the English Language papers set in the summer examinations of 1953, with some exceptions.

Essays set as a separate paper have not usually been reprinted. Three of the papers are composite, for certain examining bodies do not permit the reproduction of a complete paper. Thus the Cambridge paper printed here is made up of questions from the December Examination 1952 and questions from the July Examination 1953. Again, the Oxford paper consists of two questions (Nos. 3 and 4) that were actually set, and two that were made up to match; in the Oxford and Cambridge paper only Nos. 2 and 3 were actually set, the others being made up on lines very similar to those of the actual questions set. The Associated Examining Board's papers are specimens issued for the guidance of schools.

UNIVERSITY OF BRISTOL

ENGLISH LANGUAGE

2½ HOURS

[*Answer* **Questions 1** *and* **2.** *You are advised to spend approximately half the time on each question.*]

1. Read the following passage very carefully, and then answer question (*a*) and three of the questions (*b*)—(*f*).

Do we realize the extent to which the modern world relies on public utterances and the Press? Do we realize how completely we are all in the power of report? Any

little lie or exaggerated sentiment uttered by one with a
5 bee in his bonnet, with a principle, or an end to serve,
can, if cleverly expressed and distributed, distort the
views of thousands, sometimes of millions. Any wilful
suppression of truth for Party or personal ends can so
falsify our vision of things as to plunge us into endless
10 cruelties and follies. Honesty of thought and speech and
written word is a jewel, and they who curb prejudice
and seek honourably to know and speak the truth are
the only true builders of a better life.

But what a dull world it will be if we cannot chatter
15 and write irresponsibly, cannot explode with hatred, or
pursue our own ends without scruple! To be tied to the
apron-strings of truth, or coiffed with the nightcap of
silence—who in this age of cheap ink and oratory will
submit to such a fate? And yet, if we do not want
20 another seven million violent deaths, another eight
million maimed and halt and blind, and if we do not
want anarchy, our tongues must be sober, and we must
tell the truth. Report, I would almost say, now rules the
world and holds the fate of man on the sayings of its
25 many tongues. If the good sense of mankind cannot somehow restrain utterance and cleanse report,
Democracy, so highly vaunted, will not save us; and
all the glib words of promise spoken might as well have
lain unuttered in the throats of orators.

30 Under Democracy we are always in peril of taking
the line of least resistance and immediate material
profit. The gentleman, for instance, whoever he was,
who first discovered that he could sell his papers better
by undercutting the standard of his rivals, and appeal-
35 ing to the lower tastes of the Public under the flag of
that convenient expression "what the Public wants,"
made a most evil discovery. The Press is for the most
part in the hands of men who know what is good and
right. It can be a great agency for levelling up. But
40 whether it is so or not is a debatable point. There ought
to be no room for doubt in any of our minds that the
Press is on the side of the angels. It can do as much as

any single agency to raise the level of honesty, intelligence, public spirit, and taste in the average citizen; in
45 other words, to build Democracy on a sure foundation.
This is truly a tremendous trust; for the safety of
civilization and the happiness of mankind hang thereby.
The saying about little children and the kingdom of
heaven was meant for the ears of all those who have it
50 in their power to influence simple folk. To be a good
and honest editor or a good and honest journalist is in
these days to be a veritable benefactor of mankind.

(*a*) In a passage of not more than seventy of your own
words, summarise the ways in which, according to the
author, the Press can misuse its power, and what the
consequences of such misuse might be.

(*b*) Answer the following questions, avoiding, as far
as possible, the words of the passage. Each answer should
not exceed thirty words.

> (i) What good, according to the writer, can an
> honest Press do?
> (ii) What objection does the author suggest might
> be brought against an honest Press?

(*c*) Give a word or short phrase of similar meaning to
each of the following words as used in the passage: distort
(line 6), suppression (line 8), prejudice (line 11), irresponsibly (line 15), scruple (line 16), oratory (line 18),
anarchy (line 22), vaunted (line 27), glib (line 28),
benefactor (line 52).

(*d*) Put the following expressions into your own
words, so as to bring out clearly the meaning of each:—

> (i) An exaggerated sentiment uttered by one with
> a bee in his bonnet.
> (ii) Honesty of thought and speech is a jewel.
> (iii) . . . to be tied to the apron-strings of truth.
> (iv) We are in peril of taking the line of least
> resistance.
> (v) The Press is on the side of the angels.

(*e*) Write out all the subordinate clauses in the
passage "The gentleman, for instance (line 32) . . . on a

sure foundation" (line 45). Give the kind and function of each clause.

(*f*) **Either:** Compose a speech of not more than a hundred words on the power of the cinema, for good **or** for evil;

Or: Write a paragraph of not more than a hundred words on the merits of your favourite newspaper or weekly journal, giving reasons for your preference.

2. Write about three pages on **one** of the following:—

(i) It is proposed to erect a large "sixpenny and shilling" store in your town. In the form of a letter to a newspaper, give your reasons why you agree **or** disagree with the project.
(ii) Pocket money.
(iii) An account of some craft or manufacturing process in which you are interested.
(iv) The fascination of a fair.
(v) Why try to break records?
(vi) Day-dreaming.
(vii) The attraction of thrillers.
(viii) Ships, old and new.

UNIVERSITY OF CAMBRIDGE

ENGLISH LANGUAGE

PAPER II

(One hour and a half)

Read the passage below, and answer Question **1.**
Then answer **any two** *of Questions* **2–4.**

Read the following passage carefully and answer Question **1.**

British mountaineering began as the sport of a few climbers who found in Britain agreeable practising grounds for their more serious annual expeditions to the Alps. Today, better wages, holidays with pay, accommodation in youth hostels—all these have brought the mountains within reach of many who had in the past neither the money nor the leisure to visit them. The natural desire to escape from the routine of the work-a-day world is leading more and more people to seek adventure on our British mountains.

The newspapers have in recent years reported a rapid rise in the number of climbing accidents. It is not only the increase in the numbers of climbers that has led to this rise; an even more serious factor has been the failure of the new generation to establish—as their more experienced predecessors established—a firm tradition of good and safe behaviour on the mountains.

Many climbers expose themselves to danger because they are ignorant of the elementary precautions which used to be observed by all mountaineers. It is frequently reported that a certain mountaineering party has come to grief through having set out with no equipment—not even a compass—and with totally inadequate clothing; at other times, disaster has occurred because there was no one in the party to whom the others could look for knowledge of the district and its peculiar difficulties; again, other climbing parties which set out over-confidently have lost one or more of their number through attempting difficult feats of ascent without previous training or experience. In short, these stories combine to make it clear that too many holiday-makers rush on to the wild and craggy spaces of the mountain sides with no more preparation than they would give to a trip to the beaches of their favourite seaside resort.

The remedy would seem to lie in some kind of publicity campaign to educate these would-be climbers. They should be persuaded to accept, in their own interests as well as in those of the whole community, a code of behaviour, the observance of which they would regard as a matter of honour.

Question 1

Make a summary of the whole passage, which contains 353 words, in **not more than 125 words**. Take care to give a continuous connexion of ideas, and use your own words as far as possible. **Failure to keep within the limit of 125 words will be penalised.**

You may write your summary with the main verbs in the present tense, as in the original; or you may use indirect (reported) speech, beginning with a phrase like: "The writer said (says) that. . . ." [If you adopt this latter method, the introductory phrase will not be included in the 125 words which you are allowed.]

Answer **any two** *of Questions 2–4.*

Question 2

Read the following passage carefully, and then answer (*a*) **and** (*b*).

Christopher Columbus faces difficulty with his crew during his voyage of discovery in 1492

As the seemingly interminable voyage wore on, Columbus observed with growing concern how ignorance and superstitious fear helped to foment disaffection among the crew of the *Santa Maria*. They had
5   been restless and insubordinate from the first; but at any moment he feared they might break into open mutiny. Sensible of his precarious situation, he disguised from them his natural anxiety. He affected ignorance of their intrigues, and appeared amongst
10 them serene and cheerful, as if well satisfied with the ship's progress and scornful of possible failure. Sometimes he tried to work upon their ambition or avarice by giving glowing descriptions of the fame and wealth that would attend their success. Only occasionally would he
15 assume the tone of authority or dwell upon the unpleasant consequences of treachery. It is a tribute to his tact and patience that he ultimately prevailed upon them to see the enterprise through.

(*a*) Choose **five** of the following words, which are taken from the above passage, and give for each another word, or phrase, of similar meaning, **which might be**

used to replace the word in the passage: interminable (l. 1); concern (l. 2); insubordinate (l. 5); disguised (ll. 7–8); serene (l. 10); scornful (l. 11); avarice (l. 12); glowing (l. 13).

(b) Choose **five** of the following phrases, which are taken from the same passage, and explain concisely the meaning of each: to foment disaffection (ll. 3–4); break into open mutiny (ll. 6–7); Sensible of his precarious situation (l. 7); He affected ignorance of their intrigues (ll. 8–9); assume the tone of authority (l. 15); to see the enterprise through (l. 18).

Question 3

The writer of each of the following passages (i), (ii) and (iii) has written in short sentences what would be better expressed in one sentence. Avoiding the use of "and," "but" and "so" as much as possible, rewrite each group of sentences to form one sentence that is clear, concise and readable. You may change the wording, but you must not omit any information or alter the general sense.

(i) The general was sitting in his tent. He was alone. He was studying a map. Suddenly a messenger arrived. He brought good news. The enemy were in full flight. They had left much booty behind.

(ii) There was a mysterious noise. It appeared to come from the room above. We mounted the stairs cautiously. We wanted to find out the cause. We opened the door. We saw a huge bird. It was flapping its wings against the window-pane. It was trying frantically to escape.

(iii) Henry's father died suddenly. Henry was in Australia. He had emigrated there ten years before. He was the only son. He had to return at once to England. No alternative was open to him. The family business needed attending to.

Question 4

Both parts of the question to be answered.

(a) Punctuate the following passages, inserting capital letters where necessary.

(i) oh dear ive lost my copy of hamlet wherever could i have put it

(ii) across the sahara desert is the title of my uncles latest book a best seller so they tell me

(iii) the procession passed the crowd dispersed and soon the street was silent and deserted life became normal once again

(*b*) Turn the following into direct speech:

He informed the chairman that only that morning he had received an urgent summons which meant that he would have to sail for his homeland the next day. He would always carry with him the liveliest memories of their kindness. If his country were not then on the brink of war, he would have been looking forward to staying among them a little longer in those delightful surroundings.

UNIVERSITY OF DURHAM

ENGLISH LANGUAGE

$2\frac{1}{2}$ HOURS

Candidates **must** *answer* **Questions 1, 2,** *and* **3** *and any* **one** *other question.*

Candidates are advised to spend not more than one hour on **Question 1.**

1. Write a composition on **one** of the following subjects:

(*a*) A happy (or an unhappy) experience in your life.

(*b*) Labour-saving devices that you consider should be in every home.

(*c*) Friends of your family, wishing their young son (or daughter), aged about twelve years, to enter your school as a pupil, have written to you for information and advice. Write a suitable letter in reply.

(*d*) The career that you are hoping to follow when you leave school, with the reasons for your choice.

(*e*) Give your views, as a member of a debating team, on any **two** of the following topics:

(i) That the increased use of television is a menace to the community.

(ii) That winter sports are preferable to those of summer.

(iii) That learning a foreign language is largely a waste of time for most people.

(*f*) Character sketches of two people personally known to you (one should be young and the other middle-aged).

(*g*) A composition suggested by the following lines:

The song of her whistle screaming at curves,
Of deafening tunnels, brakes, innumerable bolts;
And always light aerial, underneath
Goes the elate metre of her wheels.

2. Read the following passage carefully, and then write a summary of the whole in not more than 150 words, taking care to give a continuous connexion of ideas, and using your own words as far as possible. State the number of words you have used but note that *failure to keep within the limits of 150 words will be penalized*:

The death of Nelson was felt in England as something more than a public calamity: men started at the intelligence and turned pale, as if they had heard of the loss of a dear friend. An object of our admiration and
5 affection, of our pride and of our hopes, was suddenly taken from us; and it seemed as if we had never, till then, known how deeply we loved and reverenced him. What the country had lost in its great naval hero—the greatest of our own and of all former times—was
10 scarcely taken into the account of grief. So perfectly indeed had he performed his part that the maritime war, after the battle of Trafalgar, was considered at an end; the fleets of the enemy were not merely defeated, but destroyed; new navies must be built, and a new
15 race of seamen reared for them, before the possibility of their invading our shores could again be contem-

plated. It was not therefore from any selfish reflection upon the magnitude of our loss that we mourned for him: the general sorrow was of a higher character. The
20 people of England grieved that funeral ceremonies, public monuments and posthumous rewards were all that they could bestow upon him whom the king, the legislature, and the nation would have alike delighted to honour; whom every tongue would have blessed;
25 whose presence in every village through which he might have passed would have wakened the church-bells, have given schoolboys a holiday, have drawn children from their sports to gaze upon him, and "old men from the chimney corner" to look upon Nelson ere they died.
30 The victory of Trafalgar was celebrated indeed with the usual forms of rejoicing, but they were without joy. . . .

Yet he cannot be said to have fallen prematurely whose work was done; nor ought he to be lamented who died so full of honours and at the height of human fame.
35 The most triumphant death is that of the martyr; the most awful, that of the martyred patriot; the most splendid, that of the hero in the hour of victory; and if the chariot and the horses of fire had been vouchsafed for Nelson's translation, he could scarcely have de-
40 parted in a brighter blaze of glory. He has left us, not indeed his mantle of inspiration, but a name and an example which are at this hour inspiring thousands of the youth of England—a name which is our pride, and an example which will continue to be our shield and our
45 strength. Thus it is that the spirits of the great and the wise continue to live and to act after them.

3. Answer concisely, and as far as possible in your own words, the following questions, which are based on the passage in Question 2. Answers to the last four questions (*b* to *e*) should consist of a complete sentence or complete sentences:

(*a*) What is a suitable title for the extract?

(*b*) Why are the words, "old men from the chimney corner" (ll. 28–29) enclosed in inverted commas?

(*c*) What is the meaning of the following words: "A new race of seamen reared for them"? (ll. 14–15).

(*d*) Explain and briefly illustrate the meaning of the following sentence: "He has left us . . . and our strength" (ll. 40–45).

(*e*) What evidence do you find that the passage was written shortly after Nelson's death?

4. Explain the meaning in their context of—

(*a*) **six** of the following words: *calamity* (l. 2); *intelligence* (ll. 3–4); *reverenced* (l. 7); *maritime* (l. 11); *legislature* (l. 23); *wakened* (l. 26); *prematurely* (l. 32); *martyred* (l. 36); *blaze* (l. 40);

(*b*) **two** of the following phrases: *an object of our pride and of our hopes* (l. 5); *public monuments and posthumous rewards* (l. 21); *if the chariot and the horses of fire had been vouchsafed for Nelson's translation* (ll. 38–9).

5. The following questions are based on the passage for Question 2:

(*a*) What picture does each of the following metaphors convey to your mind, and how does such a picture throw light upon the meaning of the phrase as used in the passage: "his mantle of inspiration" (l. 41); "continue to be our shield and our strength" (ll. 44–5)?

(*b*) Select any extract (of not more than about twenty words) that particularly appeals to you and briefly give the reasons for your choice.

(*c*) The passage has been selected from what is generally regarded as one of the best English biographies. Judging from the extract, do you think that the opinion is justified? Give a brief, considered reply.

6. (*a*) Analyse the following passage into clauses and state the function of each clause:

It seemed as if we had never, till then, *known how* deeply we loved and reverenced him. What the country had lost in its great naval hero—the *greatest* of our *own* and of all former times—*was* scarcely taken *into* the account of grief.

(*b*) Name the part of speech and state the grammatical function of each of the six words italicized in (*a*).

7. (*a*) Punctuate and paragraph the following passage, inserting all the necessary capitals:

come quickly shouted my guide from a platform near the bells i ran down and stood leaning over an iron fence watching the great nest of five bells startling hair raising sounds broke suddenly from the four little bens and ran round them again before every hour they say all through this hour lord be my guide and by thy power no foot shall slide then they stop to let big ben do his gigantic bit

(*b*) Give a brief dictionary definition of any **four** of the following: ballot; cashiered; cold war; lair; speedway; tenor.

UNIVERSITY OF LONDON

ENGLISH LANGUAGE

2½ Hours

[*Answer* QUESTION 1 *and* QUESTION 2 *and* TWO *other questions.*]

1. Do *two* of the following exercises, *one* from Group A and *one* from Group B, allowing about half an hour for each:

A

(i) Describe any *one* special room in your school, *e.g.*, library, art room, workshop, laboratory.

(ii) Write a letter to a friend describing *one* of the following events which has happened re-recently in your family: a birthday, a family reunion, a wedding.

(iii) Explain, for the benefit of someone quite unfamiliar with the game, all you think it necessary to know about *one* of the following games in order to play or understand it: hockey, table-tennis, badminton.

(iv) Describe a typical evening spent at your favourite hobby or spare-time occupation.

B

(v) Which kind of summer holiday do you prefer, and why?

(vi) "The application of science to entertainment has made us lazy." Do you agree or disagree?

(vii) Does it matter how well England does in the Olympic Games?

(viii) Write a short composition on "Building castles in the air".

2. Summarise, *in your own words* as far as possible, the argument of the following passage (which contains about 500 words), reducing it to about 170 words. At the end of your *précis* state the *exact* number of words you have used.

From the earliest days of civilisation the lord of creation has been inclined to chafe at his inferiority to the meanest cabbage-white butterfly or house-sparrow in the matter of flight. Until the end of the nineteenth
5 century nothing practical had come of it, beyond the ability to drift precariously about in the cars of balloons. But in more than the literal sense it might have been said that flying was in the air. One of the commonest books about the future described how some man had
10 worked out the plans of a completely efficient airship and thereby achieved power to impose his own terms on the rest of the species. Meanwhile inventors were working out the design of flying-machines that never quite succeeded in flying. Even advanced thinkers were
15 inclined to be sceptical whether the final product of these activities was likely to be anything more than an ingenious toy, and there were still pious folk to deplore the presumption of those who invited the wrath of the Almighty by trying to improve upon his plan of creation.
20 It was the success of the brothers Wright in 1903 that at last manifested to the world that the age of flying had

actually dawned, and henceforth progress was astonish-
ingly rapid. So implicit was the faith in any sort of
mechanical improvement that nothing but delighted
25   applause was excited, in 1909, by what might well have
been regarded as one of the most ominous events in
British history. A Frenchman, M. Blériot, undeterred
by the failure of a compatriot a few days earlier, succeeded in piloting his monoplane across the Channel
30   and landing near Dover. Henceforth Britannia might
lord it as she would over the waves—her iron walls were
no protection against an enemy who could fly over them.
War had been transferred to a third dimension.

The conquest of the air was undoubtedly the most
35   spectacular feature of the early years of the reign of
George V. In an incredibly short space of time the
sight and sound of an aeroplane became familiar to
dwellers on the route from Croydon to the Continent.
Records for speed, height and distance were continually
40   being surpassed, while stunt flying began to be practised
and the loop was successfully looped. With construction
still in the experimental stage, the life of a leading air-
man was held on the most precarious tenure, although
the number of prominent casualties served only to in-
45   crease the thrills of this new chase after speed. The cult
of the thrill followed inevitably from this universal
speeding up, and answered the need for some stimulus
violent enough to impress itself upon nerves dulled by
long routine and absence of sensation. It was most un-
50   likely that a nice discrimination would be fostered under
such conditions, and the result was a sensational age,
one of crazes and panics in every department of life, in
politics and journalism, in art and the employment of
leisure.

3. The following questions relate to the passage in Question 2. Answer them as far as possible in complete statements *in your own words*.

(a) Explain the point of the reference to "the mean-

est cabbage-white butterfly or house-sparrow"
(l. 3).

(b) What is meant by "the literal sense" (l. 7), and
how does the writer show that "flying was in the
air" (l. 8) in another sense?

(c) Why might Blériot's flight across the Channel
have been regarded as "one of the most ominous
events in British history" (ll. 26–27), and why did
people nevertheless receive it with "delighted
applause" (ll. 24–25)?

(d) What were the conditions referred to in l. 51, and
why would they be unlikely to foster a "nice
discrimination" (l. 50)?

(e) Choose *three* of the four departments of life mentioned in ll. 53–54 and give examples (one for
each department) of the kind of craze or panic
the writer might have had in mind.

4. (a) Explain the meanings, in their contexts, of *five* of
the following words or phrases in the passage in Question
2:

chafe (l. 2), sceptical (l. 15), pious folk (l. 17), deplore
the presumption (l. 17), undeterred (l. 27), compatriot
(l. 28), precarious tenure (l. 43), cult (l. 45).

(b) The first word in each of the following pairs is
used in the passage in Question 2. Choose *four* of the pairs,
and show in any way you please that you understand the
difference in meaning between the two words in each pair.

century, centenary; practical, practicable; ingenious,
ingenuous; continually, continuously; successfully, successively; stimulus, stimulant.

5. (a) Analyse the following sentence into clauses,
writing out each clause in full. Give the grammatical
description of each clause, and state its grammatical
function in the sentence:

In *summing* up the case, the judge stated that he wished
to make it clear to the jury that unless they believed, *without* a shadow of doubt, that the prisoner was the man who,
shortly after midnight, had been seen leaving the house

where the crime was committed, it was their duty to acquit the accused, even though the rest of the evidence they had heard might have led them to a different verdict.

(*b*) Name the part of speech and state the grammatical function of each of the three italicised words in (*a*).

6. (*a*) Punctuate, supply the necessary capitals, and paragraph the following passage:

now then i said will you let me ask you duke what you think you will make of it he stopped and said by heaven i think blucher and myself can do the thing do you calculate on any desertions in bonapartes army i asked not upon a man he said from the colonel to the private we may pick up a marshal or two perhaps do you reckon i enquired on any support from the french kings troops oh he said dont mention such fellows no

(*b*) Express the meaning of *four* of the following expressions in your own words:

- (i) Discretion is the better part of valour.
- (ii) Every private has a baton in his knapsack.
- (iii) Fools rush in where angels fear to tread.
- (iv) Where ignorance is bliss, 'tis folly to be wise.
- (v) There's none so deaf as those that won't hear.
- (vi) A bird in the hand is worth two in the bush.

UNIVERSITIES OF MANCHESTER, LIVERPOOL, LEEDS, SHEFFIELD AND BIRMINGHAM

ENGLISH LANGUAGE

2½ Hours

Answer Questions 1 and 2 and in addition
 EITHER the whole of Question 3,
 OR two of Sections A, B, C, D in Question 3 and the whole of Question 4.
Candidates are recommended to spend not more

**than 50 minutes on Question 1 and not more than
60 minutes on Question 2.**
**Write legibly and pay great attention to spelling and
punctuation.**

1. Read the following passage carefully and then answer
the questions on it:

I will say a little about the value to the reader of history of discovering what life was like in various ages and
countries of old. It is a relief to escape from our
mechanical age into a world when the craftsman was
5   more and the machine less, when imagination was more
and science was less. Nor is this mere escapism. It en-
larges the mind and imagination, otherwise imprisoned
in the present. We get glimpses of other worlds, human
and faulty like ours, but different from our own, and
10   suggesting many things, some of great value, that man
has thought, experienced and forgotten. Indeed, I know
of no greater triumph of the modern intellect than the
truthful reconstruction of past states of society that have
been long forgotten or misunderstood, recovered now by
15   the patient work of antiquarians and historians. To discover in detail what the life of man on earth was like a
hundred, a thousand, ten thousand years ago is just as
great an achievement as to make ships sail under the
sea or through the air.
20   How wonderful a thing it is to look back into the past
as it actually was, to get a glimpse through the curtain of
old night into some brilliantly lighted scene of living
men and women, not mere creatures of fiction and
imagination, but warm-blooded realities even as we
25   are. In the matter of reality, there is no difference between past and present; every portion of our prosaic
present drops off and is swallowed up into the past. The
patient scholar, wearing out his life in scientific historical
research, and the reader idly turning the pages of his-
30   tory, are both enthralled by the mystery of time, by the
mutability of all things, by the succession of the ages
and generations.

(*a*) Summarize, **in about 70 of your own words,** what the writer says about the value and interest of reading history.

(*b*) What does he mean by (i) mere escapism (line 6), (ii) prosaic present (line 26)?

(*c*) Say whether you agree with the opinion expressed in lines 16–19. Give your reasons.

(*d*) Give the meaning, in a word or phrase, of each of the following words, as used in the text: creatures (line 23), enthralled (line 30), mutability (line 31).

(*e*) Examine the appropriateness in the context of the metaphor "the curtain of old night" (lines 21–22).

2. Write from **two** to **three** pages on **one** of the following subjects:

(*a*) A city by night.
(*b*) Your favourite periodical.
(*c*) On wearing uniform.
(*d*) The problem of litter.
(*e*) An agricultural *or* flower show.
(*f*) On being left to oneself.

3. **A.** (*a*) Expand into subordinate clauses the phrases in italics in each of the following sentences. State the kind and function of each subordinate clause and its relation to the main clause.

(i) They need a school *with more accommodation.*
(ii) The tyrant demanded *the punishment of the culprits.*
(iii) *In spite of his injury*, he entered the race.
(iv) *To make certain of reaching our destination early* we left home *at dawn.*

(*b*) Without altering the meaning, reduce each of the following to a simple sentence.

(i) They can do nothing unless we assist them.
(ii) Because the doctor was absent, the nurse attended the patient when she arrived.
(iii) It is evident that he is guilty.
(iv) I shall go if you permit me.

B. Combine the following simple sentences so as to form **three** complex sentences. The order of sentences need not be strictly kept.

It was a month later. A tramp strolled along the road. He was dusty. He had his hands in his pockets. The road led to Uppingham. Uppingham was his destination. The tramp was now leading a healthy life. It was the first time he had done so. He lived constantly in the open air. He walked every day for eight hours. He ate sparingly. He had done no real work at all. But he had mended a hole in his coat. He had made the hole. He had negotiated barbed wire. He had borrowed needle and thread from a lodging-house. He had stayed at the lodging-house for a night.

C. Supply a word for each of the numbered spaces in the passage below, choosing appropriately from the following list: gravity, felicity, incredibly, rude, practicable, foraging, bondage, menace, provincial, releases, assembling, revivals.

(Do **not** write out the passage. Write each word on a separate line in your answer-book, giving it the same number as that in the corresponding space below.)

When Easter (1) the child, in any (2) suburb, from his (3) to grammar and sums, you will see him enjoying himself with sportive (4) of one of the earliest concerns of man. (5) around like a magpie, he collects odd bits of tarpaulin and sacking and fragments of corrugated iron. (6) these buildings on some (7) patch of waste grass, he raises a simple dwelling. A small fire crowns these simple provisions for domestic (8), and numbers of children may be seen sitting round their (9) hearths, conversing with the (10) of Red Indian chiefs, or at the (11) of rain, packing themselves into (12) small spaces of wigwam.

D. Compose a short piece of narrative introducing the following correctly (in any order): question mark, quotation marks, semi-colon, comma, exclamation mark.

Give a brief explanation why, in the passage, you have

used the quotation marks, semi-colon, comma. (Illustrate from **one** example if you have used more than one of each.)

4. Read the following poem carefully and then answer the questions below:

To a Cat

Cat! who hast pass'd thy grand climacteric,
    How many mice and rats hast in thy days
    Destroy'd?—How many titbits stolen? Gaze
With those bright languid segments green, and prick
5 Those velvet ears—but pr'ythee do not stick
    Thy latent talons in me—and upraise
    Thy gentle mew—and tell me all thy frays
Of fish and mice, and rats and tender chick.
Nay, look not down, nor lick thy dainty wrists—
10   For all the wheezy asthma,—and for all
Thy tail's tip is nick'd off—and though the fists
    Of many a maid have given thee many a maul,
Still is that fur as soft as when the lists
    In youth thou enter'dst on glass bottled wall.

(*a*) Is the cat old or young? Give all the evidence you can find.

(*b*) "bright languid segments green": consider what each of these words adds to the description of that part of the cat they refer to.

(*c*) Give the meaning of "latent" (l. 6), "frays" (l. 7), and "maul" (l. 12).

(*d*) Give the meaning of the last two lines of the poem in your own words.

OXFORD LOCAL EXAMINATIONS
ENGLISH LANGUAGE
Paper II
1¾ Hours

Errors in spelling and punctuation, and in the construction of sentences, will cause you to lose marks.

Attempt ALL questions. Question 1 carries high marks and candidates are advised to allow plenty of time for it.

1. Summarize in continuous prose the following passage. **You will lose marks if your summary contains more than 100 words.** The passage contains 287 words:

I can imagine nothing better in theory or more successful in practice than private banks as they were in the beginning. A man of known wealth, known integrity, and known ability is largely entrusted with the money of his neighbours. The confidence is strictly personal. His neighbours know him, and trust him because they know him. They see daily his manner of life, and judge from it that their confidence is deserved. The bankers who for a long series of years passed successfully this strict and continual investigation became very wealthy and very powerful.

The name "London Banker" had especially a charmed value. He was supposed to represent, and often did represent, a certain union of pecuniary sagacity and educated refinement which was scarcely to be found in any other part of society. In a time when the trading classes were much ruder than they are now, many private bankers possessed a variety of knowledge and a delicacy of attainment which would even now be very rare. Such a position is indeed singularly favourable. The calling is hereditary; the credit of the bank descends from father to son; this inherited wealth soon brings inherited refinement. Banking is a watchful, but not a laborious trade. A banker, even in large business, can feel pretty sure that all his transactions are sound, and yet have much ʳspare time. A certain part of his time, and a considerable part of his thoughts, he can readily devote to other pursuits. And a London banker can also have the most intellectual society in the world if he chooses it. There has probably very rarely ever been so happy a position as that of a London private banker; and never perhaps a happier.

2. From the passage in Question 1 find and write out **in full**:

    (*a*) three adverbial clauses **of different types**;
    (*b*) three adjectival clauses;
    (*c*) two noun clauses.

3. Copy out the following passage, avoiding the use of the word *get* by replacing each of the words and phrases in italics by **a single word,** but making no other changes. Do not use any word twice as substitute. **Underline** the words you use as substitutes.

    Dick the poacher *got up* early that morning. It was *getting on for* three o'clock when he and his friends *got together*, *got hold of* the equipment they had *got ready* the night before, and *got off*. It was a difficult journey; they had to *get* over walls, *get* through hedges, and *get* under barbed wire in order to *get to* the wood before the sky *got* light. After twenty minutes they had *got* a dozen rabbits and were priding themselves on having *got the better of* the keeper. But he had *got wind of* their intentions and was already out, trying to prevent them from *getting away*. Soon one of the poachers, hearing a sound, *got on* a gate, saw the keeper, *got down*, and warned his friends to *get rid of* the rabbits and run. They *got back* home some hours later, glad to have *got out of* the danger so successfully.

4. Read the following passage carefully, and then answer **briefly** the questions printed after it. No more than four lines should be necessary for any answer, and most of the questions can be answered in fewer:

Samuel Pepys was the creator of three remarkable, and still surviving, things. The first, in order of their making, was his Diary. The second was the civil administration of the Admiralty—the rule and order that still give permanence to the material form, fighting traditions and transmitted knowledge of the Royal Navy. A century after Pepys' death, at a time when his achievement as a diarist was still unknown and his name almost forgotten, Lord Barham—the man who shares with him the honour of being England's greatest naval administrator—testified that there was not a department of the Admiralty that was not governed by the rules he had laid down in the seventeenth century. It was Pepys who made the scabbard for the sword that Nelson, and the heirs of Nelson, used.

Pepys' third creative achievement sprang from the second. He has been described as the father of the Civil Service. Here, too, his orders hold. The rules he laid down and the administrative principles he elucidated have become part of the continuing life of his country. His family may have grown somewhat large of late, but it is still governed by the moral standards, integrity and tradition of inflexible service on which in his lifetime he insisted. It has become in the course of generations what he strove to make it: a permanent watchdog against corruption.

Yet the work for which Pepys is best remembered and loved remains his Diary. It extends to over a million and a quarter words: the length of a dozen fair-sized novels. After three centuries, there is not a page in it that does not arrest the reader and quicken his perception of humanity. It is probably the most searching and honest record of a man's daily doings ever penned. It is also one of the most vivid. As historical material I know of nothing with such power to recreate the thought and daily *minutiae* of a vanished age. It is strange to reflect that this wonderful achievement should have been wrought at the end of crowded days of labour— the record of which is to be found not in the Diary but

40 in Pepys' vast collection of naval and administrative papers.

(From ARTHUR BRYANT'S *Samuel Pepys—the Man in the Making*)

(*a*) Of the three things of which Pepys was creator, which **two** were related to one another?

(*b*) When was the greatness of Pepys's work first recognized, according to this passage?

(*c*) What in fact is meant by *the scabbard* (line 14)?

(*d*) Write **two** words to give the meaning of *family* (line 21).

(*e*) Where, according to the author, is the record of Pepys's work to be found?

(*f*) What, according to the author, makes the *Diary* of special importance to the historian?

(*g*) What one word names a quality which the author indicates as being characteristic both of Pepys's administration and of his *Diary*?

(*h*) Find **single** words in the passage which mean the same as:

(i) *brought to light and explained* (second paragraph)
(ii) *not to be turned from its right form* (second paragraph)
(iii) *observation and understanding* (third paragraph)
(iv) *details* (third paragraph).

OXFORD AND CAMBRIDGE SCHOOLS EXAMINATION BOARD

ENGLISH LANGUAGE I

2½ HOURS

Candidates should answer **all** *the questions.*
Candidates are advised not to spend more than 1 hour on Question 1.

1. Summarize the following passage in not more than 200 words. Write, at the end of your version, the number of words you have used.

The development of the Press into a great industry coincided with an increase in the demands made upon the Press by the character of society. The extension of the franchise and the increasing complexity of public affairs have thrust upon the Press the responsibility for conveying and interpreting to the public a mass of information on subjects as complicated as they are important. Industrial development has not rendered the Press incapable of doing this: to the extent that it has facilitated the collection of news and the sale of newspapers at a low price it has enabled the Press to report and interpret more fully; but to the extent that it has given added importance to the commercial aspects of newspaper production, it has tended to divert the attention of newspapers to ends other than those to which the interests of society require them to attend. The problem is to limit this divergence of interest, to reconcile the claims of society and the claims of commerce.

The problem is not peculiar to the Press, but in this sphere it is particularly acute. If the Press is not aware of its responsibility to the public it cannot perform its functions adequately; but if it is not free it cannot perform them at all. Consequently the amount of direct pressure which society can afford to put on the Press is very limited. Except in certain well-recognised fields, responsibility cannot be enforced by prohibiting the publication of one type of material or enjoining the publication of another, because regulation of this kind in the long run dams the free flow of information and discussion and undermines the independence without which the Press cannot give the service required of it. Whereas it is a question of opinion whether state control should be extended in other directions, nearly everyone would agree that state control ought not to be extended to the Press. In our view, therefore, it is preferable to seek the means of maintaining the proper relationship between the Press and society not in Government action but in the Press itself. The sense of vocation to which we have referred leads us to believe that they will not be sought in vain.

So far, however, the Press has not developed the internal organisation necessary for the regulation of its own affairs. It is remarkable that although a number of organisations exist to represent sectional interests within the Press, there is none representing the Press as a whole. It is not that those engaged in newspaper production are unaware of the Press as an entity: they are on the contrary acutely aware of it and jealous for its independence and its reputation. It is the more surprising that there is no one body concerned to maintain either the freedom of the Press or the integrity on which its reputation depends: no single organisation expresses the common interest in these things of the men who share the responsibility for the character of the Press; and there is no means, other than *ad hoc* machinery created to deal with particular problems, by which this common interest can be translated into action. Indeed, the Press has taken fewer steps to safeguard its standards of performance than perhaps any other institution of comparable importance.

The Press is, in its modern form, a young institution, and a developing institution, and if it is to develop in the right direction—right, that is, from the point of view both of society and of those concerned for its own standing and reputation—it needs to consider where it is going and consciously to foster those tendencies which make for integrity and for a sense of responsibility to the public. We recommend that the Press itself should create a central organ for this purpose. We shall discuss the nature of this organ, which we propose to call the General Council of the Press, when we have considered in more detail the functions which it might perform.

2. Read the following passage carefully, and then, *briefly and to the point*, answer the questions beneath it:

On the same evening a message from the Orderly Room instructed me to proceed to the Fourth Army School for a month's refresher course. Barton saw me off at the cross-roads. "Lucky Kangaroo—to be hop-
5 ping away for a holiday!" he exclaimed, as I climbed into the elderly bus.

The Fourth Army School was at Flixécourt half-way between Amiens and Abbeville. Between Flixécourt and the War (which for my locally experienced mind meant
10 the Fricourt trenches) there were more than thirty English miles. Mentally, the distance became immeasurable during my first days at the School. Parades and lectures were all in the day's work, but they failed to convince me of their affinity with our long days and nights in the
15 Front Line. For instance, although I was closely acquainted with the mine-craters in the Fricourt sector, I would have welcomed a few practical hints on how to patrol those God-forsaken cavities. But the Army School instructors were all in favour of Open Warfare, which
20 was sure to come soon, they said. They had learnt all about it in peacetime; it was essential that we should be taught to "think in terms of mobility".

Sometimes a renowned big-game hunter gave us demonstrations of the art of sniping. He was genial and
25 enthusiastic; but I was no good at rifle-shooting, and as far as I was concerned he would have been more profitably employed in reducing the numerical strength of the enemy. He was an expert on loopholes and telescopic-sights; but telescopic-sights were a luxury
30 seldom enjoyed by an infantry battalion in the trenches.

The School was in reality only a holiday for officers

who needed a rest. It certainly seemed so when I awoke
on the first morning and became conscious of my clean
little room with its tiled floor and shuttered windows.
35 Wiping my face after a satisfactory shave, I stared out
of the window; on the other side of the street a blossom-
ing apple-tree leant over an old garden wall, and I
could see the friendly red roof of a dovecot. It was a
luxury to be alone, with plenty of space for my portable
40 property. There was a small table on which I could
arrange my few books. Hardy's *Far from the Madding
Crowd* was one of them. Books about England were all
that I wanted.

With half an hour to spare after breakfast, I strolled
45 up the hill and smoked my pipe under a quick-set
hedge. I looked at a chestnut tree in full leaf and listened
to the perfect performance of a nightingale. Such things
seemed miraculous after the devastation of the trenches.
It feels as if it's a place where I might get a chance to
call my soul my own, I thought, as I went down the hill
50 to my first parade. If only they don't chivvy us about
too much, I added. . . . It was not unlike the first day of
a public school term, and my form-master was a young-
ish major. He was an even-tempered man, pleasant to
55 obey. I cannot remember that any of us caused him
annoyance, though he more than once asked me to try
and be less absent-minded.

(Adapted from SASSOON, *Memoirs of an Infantry Officer*)

(*a*) What season of the year was it when these events
occurred? What is the evidence for your answer?

(*b*) Explain the meaning of "genial" (l. 24) and
"portable" (l. 39).

(*c*) In what ways did the writer think that the work
of the School had no real connection with the fighting in
the trenches?

(*d*) What does he mean when he tells us that the
distance between the School and the War became,
mentally, immeasurable (ll. 9–12)?

(*e*) Explain in your own words in what way he

thinks the big-game hunter could have been more profitably employed.

(*f*) Why does he want books exclusively about England (ll. 41–43)?

(*g*) Point out an instance of a play on words in the passage.

(*h*) Write three or four lines showing the most prominent features in the writer's character as revealed in this passage.

3. (*a*) Choose **five** of the following sentences and express the sense of the italicized words in each of those you choose by **one word** (you may, of course, change a relative clause into an adjective and you need not write out the whole sentence):

(i) She was left *without any means of support.*

(ii) The officer agreed to give his *word that he would not try to escape.*

(iii) He wrote an account of the incident *that was highly descriptive.*

(iv) The sun set behind a bank of clouds *that seemed to foretell bad weather.*

(v) The lecture was dull, and the lecturer's manner was *lacking in energy.*

(vi) He hoped to bequeath his good name to *those coming after him.*

(*b*) Each of the following passages contains a figure of speech; name it in each case:

(i) The sea saw that, and fled.

(ii) It seems to be one of those simple cases which are so extremely difficult.

(iii) Not louder shrieks to pitying heaven are cast
When husbands, or when lap-dogs breathe
their last.

(iv) His designs were strictly honourable: that is to say, to rob a lady of her fortune by way of marriage.

(v) The bare black cliff clang'd round him.

(*c*) Form adjectives (other than past participles) on the following nouns:

material, outrage, pessimism, quarter, style.

4. (*a*) Explain five of the following expressions:

crossing bridges before one comes to them; the writing on the wall; skating on thin ice; the biter bit; a Napoleon of finance; a Parthian shot.

(*b*) Write down a word identical in meaning with each of:

contemn, imply, procrastinate, stipend, superfluous.

5. (*a*) Correct any mistakes that you find in the following sentences:

(i) Mother is much better than me at finding accomodation for the holidays.

(ii) I am not only astonished at your excuse, but also at George and you refusing to help.

(iii) Being disinterested in cricket, I thought it alright to go home.

(iv) The burglar made every endeavour to effect an early entry, but perceiving the imminent arrival of the local man in blue he deemed it advisable to abandon the project in hand.

(*b*) Add punctuation, paragraphs and capital letters to:

as they left the churchyard patsy stopped look at those two old rats sitting up like wee old men theyre just saying which of us will be brought there first aunt charlotte gave a little scream you children have morbid minds you have made me quite nervous

SCOTTISH UNIVERSITIES ENTRANCE BOARD PRELIMINARY EXAMINATIONS

ENGLISH

First Paper

$2\frac{1}{2}$ Hours

Answer Questions 1 *and* 2 *and* TWO *others*

1. We have hitherto considered persons in their *natural capacities*, and have treated of their rights and duties. But, as all personal rights die with the person; and, as the necessary forms of investing a series of individuals, one after another, with the same identical rights, would be very inconvenient, if not impracticable; it has been found necessary, when it is for the advantage of the public to have any particular rights kept on foot and continued, to constitute *artificial persons*, who may maintain a perpetual succession, and enjoy a kind of legal immortality.

The artificial persons are called "bodies politic", "bodies corporate", or "Corporations": of which there is a great variety subsisting, for the advancement of religion, of learning and of commerce: in order to preserve entire and for ever those rights and immunities, which, if they were granted only to those individuals of which the body corporate is composed, would upon their death be utterly lost and extinct. To show the advantage of these incorporations, let us consider the case of a college in Oxford or Cambridge, founded for the encouragement and support of religion and learning. If this were a mere voluntary assembly, the individuals which compose it might indeed read, pray, study, and perform scholastic exercises together, so long as they could agree to do so; but they could neither frame, nor receive, any laws or rules of their conduct; none, at least, which would have any binding force, for want of a coercive power to create a sufficient obligation. Neither could they be capable of retaining any privileges or immunities; for, if such privileges be attacked, which of all this unconnected assembly has the right or ability to defend them?—and when they are dispersed by death or otherwise, how shall they transfer these advantages to another set of students, equally unconnected as themselves? So also with regard to holding estates or other property, if land be granted for the purposes of religion or learning to twenty individuals not incorporated, there is no legal way of continuing the property to any other persons for the same purposes, but by endless conveyances from one to the other, as often as the hands are changed. But, when they are consolidated and united into a *corporation*, they and their successors are then considered as ONE PERSON in law; as one person they have *one will*, which is collected from the sense of the majority of the individuals: this *one will* may establish rules and orders for the regulation of the whole, which are a sort of municipal laws of this little republic; or rules and statues may be prescribed to it at its creation, which are then in the place of natural laws: the privileges and immunities, the estates and possessions of the corporation, when once vested in them, will be for ever vested, without any new conveyance to new successors; for all the individual members that have existed from the foundation to the present time, or that shall ever hereafter exist, are but one person in law, a person that never dies; in like manner as the river Thames is still the same river, though the parts which compose it are changing every instant.— BLACKSTONE.

(*a*) Answer in your own words the following questions:

> (i) Why has the law created what are called *artificial persons*?
> (ii) What difficulties would confront a College were it not an incorporation?
> (iii) What justification is there for comparing a Corporation to the river Thames?

(*b*) Explain the meaning of the following phrases:

legal immortality, a sufficient obligation, the sense of the majority.

2. WITHIN KING'S COLLEGE CHAPEL, CAMBRIDGE

Tax not the royal Saint with vain expense,
With ill-match'd aims the Architect who plann'd
(Albeit labouring for a scanty band
Of white-robed Scholars only) this immense

And glorious work of fine intelligence!
—Give all thou canst; high Heaven rejects the lore
Of nicely-calculated less or more:—
So deem'd the man who fashion'd for the sense

These lofty pillars, spread that branching roof
Self-poised, and scoop'd into ten thousand cells
Where light and shade repose, where music dwells

Lingering—and wandering on as loth to die;
Like thoughts whose very sweetness yieldeth proof
That they were born for immortality.

(a) Give in your own words as much as you can of the sense of Wordsworth's sonnet.

(b) "In the commonest compound words in English the last element expresses a general meaning, which the prefixed element renders less general." Show how far this is illustrated by the compound words in the sonnet.

3. "The resemblance which an imitative word is felt to bear to the inarticulate noise which it names consists not so much in similarity of impression on the ear as in similarity of mental suggestion." Give a short list of these imitative or "echoic" words and consider briefly how far they illustrate Bradley's statement.

4. How does it come about that the *ox, sheep, calf, swine, deer,* when used for food are denoted by *beef, mutton, veal, pork, venison*?

5. "The distinction between such pairs of words as *paternal* and *fatherly*, *fraternity* and *brotherhood*, *celestial* and *heavenly*, *fortune* and *luck*, *felicity* and *happiness*, *royal* and *kingly* is very real to an Englishman who knows his own language." Select *five* of these pairs and compose short sentences that will show you understand the distinction between the paired words.

WELSH JOINT EDUCATION COMMITTEE
Y CYD-BWYLLGOR ADDYSG CYMREIG

ENGLISH ESSAY

1 HOUR

1. Select **one** of the following exercises, writing not more than **four** pages of your answer-book (about 500–600 words):

Either, Write an essay on **one** of the following subjects:

(*a*) The qualities you like and those you dislike in parents.

(*b*) Maps.

(*c*) Saturday.

(*d*) The ideal house.

(*e*) The greatest gift of science to mankind.

Or, (*f*) Write a letter to a friend, in correct English, urging the friend to spend a holiday with you, in the way you want, instead of having the very different holiday that the friend has suggested.

Or, (*g*) As though you were beginning a novel, write a description of a town or village you know, *as it appears to your principal character who is seeing it for the first time.*

Or, (*h*) Describe, as though you were writing to someone who has spent all his or her life on a small, remote, but English-speaking, island, **one** of the following:

(i) the crowd and scene at an important match;

(ii) a day in the life of a young man or woman who works in a Welsh town;

(iii) a big railway station.

ENGLISH LANGUAGE

2 HOURS

Answer Question 2 and THREE of the others.

2. Read the following passage carefully, noting the most important statements and rejecting what is unessential; then write its substance in a clear, simple, and logically connected version, *using your own words*. Your summary should not exceed 140 words or be less than 120 words. Write at the end of your answer the *exact number* of words you have used. If you exceed the word-limit, you will lose marks.

In the slow transition from village or provincial industry to city or cosmopolitan industry one sees a change, comparable to the geologic changes that are still altering the face of the earth; a change like them unnoticed, yet like them irresistible and cumulatively immense. Already, during the eighties and nineties of the nineteenth century, work was growing less interesting to the workman, although far more sure in its results. Whereas heretofore the village craftsman had been grappling adventurously and as a colonist pioneer with the materials of his own neighbourhood—the timber, the clay, the wool—, other materials to supersede the old ones were now arriving from multitudinous wage-earners in touch with no neighbourhood at all, but in the pay of capitalists. So the face of the country was being changed bit by bit. Incidentally, occasion was arising for the 'Unrest' of the present day,

Village life was dying out; intelligent interest in the country-side was being lost; the class-war was disturbing erstwhile quiet communities; yet nobody saw what was happening. What we saw was some apparently trivial thing, such as the incoming of tin pails instead of wooden buckets. Iron girders had hardly yet begun to oust oak beams from buildings; corrugated iron sheets were but just beginning to take the place of tiles or thatch. If an outhouse was boarded up with planed deal match-boarding from Norway instead of with "feather-edged" weather-boarding cut out locally by sawyers one knew, who was to imagine what an upheaval was implied in this sort of thing, accumulating for generations all over Europe? Seen in detail, the changes seemed so trumpery and, in most cases, such real improvements. That they were up-setting old forms of skill—producing a population of wage-slaves in place of a nation of self-supporting work-men—occurred to nobody.

Although in my old shop the flood of changes was not yet—the flood which at last has all but overwhelmed the ancient handicraft—, various smaller changes had begun to trickle in, as early as 1884. I bought no new paint-pots from the local pottery. The old ones, not renewed, were replaced by paint tins, improvised from the "empties" that had come originally from the manufacturer full of some special red or green paint. You couldn't burn the old paint out of these tins so well—they fell to pieces if the solder melted—; but why trouble? More and more came in their place—products of machine-work, made for nothing more dignified than the dust-hole.

3. (a) Analyse the following sentences into clauses; state the kind, and give the exact grammatical function of each clause:

If it is true that the essential quality of Suffolk is shyness—as a Suffolk writer has delightfully maintained—then East Bergholt, first made known by Constable's paintings, its charms once hidden as modestly as the rest, must blush for its modern and untypical prominence. It has become an attraction for the merely curious, who converge upon it, principally at week-ends, so that they may inspect the famous settings for themselves.

(*b*) Include the sentence or clause *The central part of Wales is thinly populated* in **four** separate sentences (according to the following directions) **without changing the words at all.**

(i) Include it in a sentence so that it becomes a Noun Clause; in doing this, avoid Direct Speech.

(ii) Add to it an Adverbial Clause of Cause.

(iii) Add to it an Adjectival Clause.

(iv) Insert inside it a phrase (not a clause) in parenthesis.

4. (*a*) The following are among the entries in a dictionary to explain the uses of the word *line* as a **noun.** Construct one sentence of at least seven words to illustrate each different use. Each answer must be a complete sentence, must include the word *line* or *lines*, and must use it as a noun. Keep to the same order as in the dictionary and use the same numbering, (i) to (iv).

(i) (With defining word, as *isothermal* ——) curve connecting all points having a specified common property.

(ii) *Read between the l——s*, detect hidden meaning in document, speech, &c.

(iii) Series or regular succession of steamers, omnibuses, &c., plying between certain places.

(iv) Department of activity, province, branch of business.

(*b*) Answer the following vocabulary questions by writing down in each case the word or phrase that gives the correct meaning. Put each answer on a separate line:

(v) *Tacit* means—

verbal; written; prejudiced; underlying; unspoken.

(vi) *Insatiable* means—

ridiculous; pretended; enthusiastic; curious; difficult to satisfy.

(vii) *Illusory* means—

dangerous; exaggerated; imaginary; impermanent; impossible to grasp.

(viii) *Depravity* means *extreme*—

decline; wickedness; intrigue; deterioration; aggressiveness.

(ix) *Postulating* means—

replacing; superseding; demanding; requesting; stressing.

(x) A *vendetta* is a—

cereal; kind of farm; religion; blood-feud; native custom.

(xi) *intrigue* means—

complicated plan; treachery; counter-revolution; underhand plotting; party politics.

(xii) The *Left* (in a political context) means the—

Conservative Party; Labour Party; Liberal Party.

5. Explain why the words in heavy type are unsuitable or incorrect in their present context in the following sentences.

(*a*) **Going** along the road, a gust of wind blew off his hat.

(*b*) After the Revival in Wales the minds of the people became **saturated** with the scriptures.

(*c*) The Roman Empire became **tainted** with Christianity.

(*d*) **Due** to the rain, the cricket match never began.

(*e*) All this is a form of training for adult life when a person has to go out into the world and fend for **themselves.**

(*f*) A judge ought not to be **disinterested** about what happens to criminals after they are sentenced.

(*g*) The singers thought it an honour to **partake** in this concert.

(*h*) His flood of oratory **electrified** his audience.

6. You are the Secretary of the Literary and Debating Society of King George V's School for Boys (or Girls),

Cambridge Road, Easthampton, Easthamptonshire. Write a letter to Mr. (or Miss) George (or Georgina) Brown, 103, Sale Road, St. Swithin's, Lancashire, a famous ex-pupil of the school, asking him (or her) to visit the school and talk to your society. Suggest possible dates and topics. Your letter must not exceed **ten sentences.**

In writing this letter give the complete lay-out of a formal letter.

7. The following passage gives the writer's very personal opinion of Baldwin, who was Prime Minister several times between 1918 and 1937, and Chamberlain, who was Prime Minister from 1937 to 1940. After reading the passage, answer the questions on it: *use your own words as much as possible*, and answer each question **in two or three sentences.**

Stanley Baldwin was the wiser, more comprehending personality but without detailed executive capacity. He was largely detached from foreign and military affairs. He knew little of Europe, and disliked what he knew. He had a deep knowledge of British party politics, and represented in a broad way some of the strengths and many of the infirmities of our Island race. He had a genius for waiting upon events and an imperturbability under adverse criticism. He seemed to me to revive the impressions history gives us of Sir Robert Walpole, without of course the eighteenth-century corruption, and he was master of British politics for nearly as long.

Neville Chamberlain, on the other hand, was alert, businesslike, opinionated and self-confident in a very high degree. Unlike Baldwin, he conceived himself able to comprehend the whole field of Europe, and indeed the world. Instead of a vague but none the less deep-seated intuition, we had now a narrow, sharp-edged efficiency within the limits of the policy in which he believed. He had formed decided judgments about all the political figures of the day, both at home and abroad, and felt himself capable of dealing with them. His all-pervading hope was to go down to history as the great Peace-maker,

and for this he was prepared to strive continually in the teeth of facts, and face great risks for himself and his country. Unhappily he ran into tides the force of which he could not measure, and met hurricanes from which he did not flinch, but with which he could not cope.

(a) Contrast the different ways in which, according to this writer, Baldwin and Chamberlain felt about Britain's relations with foreign countries.

(b) Quote and comment on **one** phrase or sentence in which the writer accuses Chamberlain of not realizing how difficult were the problems facing him.

(c) What were the better qualities of Chamberlain, according to this writer?

(d) Would it be fair to say that this writer writes with some bitterness or dislike? Offer evidence in support of your view.

8. Read the following poem carefully, and then answer the questions below:

> Fear no more the heat o' the sun,
>   Nor the furious winter's rages;
> Thou thy worldly task hast done,
>   Home art gone, and ta'en thy wages.
> 5 Golden lads and girls all must,
>   As chimney-sweepers, come to dust.
>
> Fear no more the frown o' the great,
>   Thou art past the tyrant's stroke;
> Care no more to clothe and eat,
> 10 To thee the reed is as the oak.
> The sceptre, learning, physic, must
> All follow this, and come to dust.
>
> Fear no more the lightning-flash,
>   Nor the all-dreaded thunder-stone;
> 15 Fear not slander, censure rash;
>   Thou has finished joy and moan,
> All lovers young, all lovers must
> Consign to thee, and come to dust.

(a) In line 5, what meaning has "golden" in addition to its literal sense?

(b) Put lines 9 and 10 into your own words.

(c) (i) In line 11, what exactly does Shakespeare mean by "sceptre, learning, physic"?

    (ii) Why do you think he chose these three?

(d) Put lines 15–16 into your own words.

ASSOCIATED EXAMINING BOARD

ENGLISH LANGUAGE

PAPER I

1½ HOURS

Answer both questions

1. Choose ONE of the following subjects for composition. About one hour should be spent on this question.

(a) Good and bad methods of advertising.

(b) "In this age of machinery there is no place for the craftsman." To what extent is this true?

(c) Write a letter to the editor of a paper complaining of the lack of facilities in your district for "keeping fit", and making suggestions to remedy this lack.

(d) Smugglers—ancient and modern.

(e) A character study of someone who has influenced you greatly.

(f) A great feat of engineering.

(g) Imagine yourself to be an inventor or explorer living in the past, present or future, who after long effort has achieved his aim. Give extracts from the diary in which you recorded your progress.

(h) An architect is to plan a house for you. Tell him what special features you would like him to include.

(j) Write for your school magazine a report of a school activity in which you have taken part.

2. Attempt ONE of the following:

(*a*) Describe accurately *in words* a spring balance *or* a vacuum flask *or* an electric iron *or* a telephone kiosk.

(*b*) Write in connected sentences clear instructions for inflating and lacing a football, *or* testing and adjusting brakes on a bicycle, *or* making your favourite dish *or* making a bed.

(*c*) Draft a notice which would be typed and displayed on your school notice board, announcing (with reasons) that, until further notice, the main entrance to the building will be closed during the dinner break. Students are to use the side entrances, one for either sex.

(*d*) You are secretary of your school Photographic Society, and have received the following letter. Write a suitable reply, with an appropriate heading and date, not exceeding 120 words.

"Dear Smith,

I see from the notice board that the Committee propose raising the Photographic Society subscription from 4/- to 5/- per annum. I wish to protest strongly. I have been a member for a few years and I consider that I get less value for my subscription now than I did when it was only 2/6.

I consider that economies could be made and money saved, thus making it unnecessary to ask members to pay a higher subscription.

Yours sincerely,

RALPH BROWN."

(*e*) Basing your account on the information given in the diagram below, write a short report on "Oil—Changes in Britain's position since 1938".

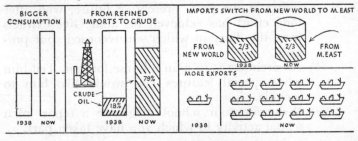

PAPER II

1½ Hours

Answer THREE *questions: Question* 1 *and any* TWO *of the remaining questions.*

1. Read the following passage carefully and then answer the questions which follow.

When we speak of workers we do not confine our words to those who work with their hands. Those who are engaged in supervision and other forms of management are quite as much workers as the weaver or miner.
5 And just as it is of importance to the nation that the handicraftsman should do good work, so it is important that the management of all forms of business and industry should be effective, honest and intelligent.

A man has a choice between doing honest work or
10 slovenly work, in book-keeping or in clerk's work, just as he has in carpentering or bricklaying. Indeed, the disasters which result from mismanagement and fraud in the conduct of a business are often more grievous than those which arise from bad hand-work. For example,
15 the man who, through folly and idleness, or fraud, ruins a great business, may bring misery on thousands, whereas the evils of a badly-joined door generally stop at injury to an individual.

What duty has the community as a whole to the
20 workers? Unquestionably, it is the duty of the community to sympathise with, and to help on, every fair and reasonable effort of the workers to improve their material condition and to develop their intelligence. And for this plain and common-sense reason among
25 others: if the workers of a nation are prosperous, intelligent and hopeful, they will do far more and far better work than if their condition is depressed.

It is then to the interest of the State—that is, of the community—that the workers should be well off in body

30   and mind. A healthy, skilful, intelligent body of workers,
upright and self-reliant in character, is a source of
strength to the nation. An unhealthy, depressed, ignorant body of working men, without independence or the
power of self-help, is a source of danger. That is why
35   the community should sympathise with the workers in
their efforts to secure better material conditions or, in
other words, to make the best of themselves.

One of the main objects of that association which we
call a State is the making of good citizens; for if the
40   greater part of the members of a State are not good
citizens, that State is as inevitably doomed to ruin as is
a rotten tree. How is the good citizen to be built up?
First, by a faithful discharge of the homelier duties of
life. Civic duty, the citizen's duty, begins in the life of
45   the family, and expands with his occupations in trade,
business, and profession. And especially can the duties
of the good citizen be learnt in the membership of self-
governing societies. In helping to manage the affairs
of a Trade Union, a Club, a Benefit Society, or a Co-
50   operative Store, a man is learning how to help to manage and control the affairs of the State. Every one of
these voluntary associations is a school of civic duty.

(approx. 490 words.)

(a) Summarise the above passage in about a quarter
of its length. State in brackets at the end the number of
words you have used.

(b) Explain what the writer means in lines 20 to 23.
"Unquestionably . . . intelligence."

(c) "Civic duty, the citizen's duty, begins in the life
of the family." In what ways do you think civic duty begins in the life of a family?

(d) Give briefly the meaning of FIVE of the following
words as they are used in the passage:

supervision (line 3); grievous (line 13); interest (line
28); association (line 38); inevitably (line 41); discharge
(line 43); voluntary (line 52).

2. (a) Use each of the following words in two separate

sentences to show the change in meaning of the word brought about by altering the stress from the first to the second syllable:

incense, discount, refuse, minute.

(*b*) Explain the force of the prefix in each of the following words: antiseptic, archbishop, bicycle, hexagon, submarine, television, transcontinental.

3. (*a*) Explain clearly what you understand by any FOUR of the following expressions:

to have an eye to business; to go against the grain; seasonal trade; to be a good Samaritan; an act of vandalism; to put in quarantine.

(*b*) Choose FIVE of the following words. Frame sentences in which each of them is used with the appropriate preposition.

absolve, implicate, submit, acquit, comply, dissent, concur, assent, different.

4. Transpose the following into Indirect (or Reported) speech:

"In the shop windows the figures on which the clothes are displayed make no attempt to represent us as we are, and are made from every kind of unlikely material —from lumps of wood, chunks of cork, from blocks of plaster. They are today as sub-human as their ancestors twenty years ago were super-human. Perhaps the present development is intended to hearten us. For however dissatisfied we may be with our own appearance we can at least feel tolerably certain that we are better looking than a lump of wood or a chunk of cork. Yes, but how much real satisfaction does that give us?"

APPENDIX A

WORDS COMMONLY MIS-SPELT

absence
accommodation
achievement
acquire
address
advertisement
affect
all right
allotted
analogy
analyse
Arctic
argument
armies
athlete
audience

believe
benefit
bicycle
Britain
business

carburettor
ceiling
chief
choose
chose
Christianity
colloquial
combatant
coming
committed

comparatively
concise
confusion
connection
conscientious
continually
council
counsel
criticism

deceit
definite
description
devil
different
disappear
disappoint
disapprove
disaster
disciple
disease
discusses
dispelled

effect
eligible
embarrassed
eminence
endeavour
erupt
exaggerate
examination
experience

facilities
fairly
family
February
finally
foreign
foretell
forty
fulfil
future

getting
grammar
guarantee

harass
height
humorous

illegible
immediately
immense
impossible
ineligible
instalment
irresponsible
its (of it)
it's (it is)

jealous

lawful
leisure

loosely
lose
lying

mathematics
medicine
metalled
miracle
mischievous

necessary
noticeable

occasion
occasionally
occurred
of
off
omission
opinion
opposite
originally

parliamentary
participate
passed
patrolling
piece
pinnacle
pleasant
possession
practice

practise
preferred
preparation
presence
principal
principle
privilege
profession
programme
prominent
promise
propeller
property

quarrel

receive
recognise
referring
relief
remember
repetition
representative
resound
responsibility
result

seize
separate
similar
speech
stationary

stationery
submitted
suburban
success
successful
supersede
surprising
symbol

teaching
temporary
territorial
their
there
to
too
totally
translation
typically

unnecessary
until

vegetation

weather
weird
whether
who's (who is)
whose
woollen

yield

APPENDIX B

WORDS TO BE DISTINGUISHED

Absence, abstinence
access, excess
adapt, adept, adopt
adherent, adhesive
admission, admittance
affect, effect
alliance, allegiance
allusion, illusion, delusion
alternate, alternative
amiable, amicable
anticipate, expect
apathy, antipathy
apprehend, reprehend
artist, artiste
astronomy, astrology
autocracy, autonomy
aviary, apiary

Barrister, solicitor
bellicose, belligerent
beneficent, benevolent
bereft, bereaved
bravado, bravery

Canon, cannon, canyon
capable, capacious
carefree, careless
cast, caste
censure, census, censor
champagne, champaign
character, reputation
check, cheque
childish, childlike

climate, weather
compile, compose
complement, compliment
composition, composure
composer, compositor
comprise, compose
consent, consensus
contagious, contiguous
contemptible,
    contemptuous
continual, continuous
council, counsel
cult, culture

Decidedly, decisively
defective, deficient
defer, differ
delusion, illusion
deprecate, depreciate
desert, dessert
destination, destiny
detract, distract
diseased, deceased
disinterested, uninterested
dissimulate, simulate
dominant, domineering
draft, draught

Eatable, edible
economic, economical
efficient, effective
eligible, illegible
elude, allude

emaciated, emancipated
eminence, imminence
emigrant, immigrant
enormity, enormousness
enumerate, remunerate
epigram, epitaph
exceedingly, excessively
exceptional, exceptionable
exert, exact
exhausting, exhaustive
expedient, expeditious

Facilities, faculties
faint, feint
fame, notoriety
fatal, fateful
forcible, forceful
formerly, formally

Historic, historical
honorary, honourable
human, humane
hypercritical, hypocritical

Imaginable, imaginary,
   imaginative
immunity, impunity
implicit, explicit
imply, infer
incredible, incredulous
industrial, industrious
inexpressive, inexpressible
infectious, contagious
inflammable,
   inflammatory
innocent, innocuous
insensible, insensitive
insight, incite
intelligent, intellectual

intense, intensive
interfere, intervene
intolerable, intolerant

Judicial, judicious
juvenile, puerile

Lightening, lightning
literate, literary, literally
lose, loose
luxuriant, luxurious

Masterful, masterly
militant, military
momentary, momentous

Nationalism, nationality
necessary, necessitous
negligent, negligible
noticeable, notable

Observation, observance
obsolete, obsolescent
oculist, optician
odious, odorous
official, officious
oral, aural
ordinance, ordnance

Palate, palette, pallet
peaceable, peaceful, pacific
persecute, prosecute
physic, physique
politician, statesman
populace, populous,
   popular
potent, potential
precede, proceed
precipitate, precipitous

prejudiced, prejudicial
prescribe, proscribe
principal, principle
profusion, diffusion
prophecy, prophesy
provision, prevision
punctilious, punctual

Recourse, resort, resource
recover, re-cover
refer, infer
replace, displace
respectable, respectful
responsible, responsive
reverend, reverent
rigid, rigorous
royal, regal
rudimentary, vestigial

Sacrifice, sacrilege
salubrious, salutary
sanguine, sanguinary
satiate, satisfy
satire, satyr
scarce, rare
sceptic, septic
seasonable, seasonal
seniority, senility
service, servitude
session, cession
single, singular
sociable, social

sophistry, sophistication
specie, species
spirited, spirituous
stationary, stationery
stimulant, stimulus
straight, strait
stratagem, strategy, tactics
subjective, objective
subsidence, subsidy
substance, sustenance
subtract, detract
success, succession
successfully, successively
suggested, suggestive
superfluous, superlative

Temperance, temperature
temporal, temporary
testament, testimony
transport, transportation
trilogy, triumvirate

Urban, urbane

Venal, venial
veracity, voracity
visible, visual

Waive, wave
wooded, wooden
wright, right, rite

Young, youthful

APPENDIX C

ONE or two examining bodies set questions that involve a knowledge of certain figures of speech and other means of expression. For convenience the possibilities are listed below.

Alliteration: the term used when a group of words begin with the same letter. It is common in early English poetry:

> In a somer season, when soft was the sun,
> I shope me in shroudes, as I a sheep were.

> > (LANGLAND)

It can be used for emphasis or speed:

> The lust of lucre and the dread of death.

> > (POPE)

To-day it is overworked by journalists.

Antithesis: the contrasting of two ideas by placing together two sharply opposed words:

> Penny wise, pound foolish

> A better farmer ne'er brush'd dew from lawn,
> A worse king never left a realm undone.

> > (BYRON, on George III)

Assonance: the similarity of vowel sounds in a group of words:

> Wiry and white-fiery and whirlwind-swivelled snow.
> > (G. M. HOPKINS)

> To swell the gourd and plump the hazel shells.

> > (KEATS)

Bathos: or anti-climax, i.e. coming down from a dignified level to something absurd or ridiculous. Pope speaks of the widely different activities of a queen:

Here thou, great Anna! whom three realms obey,
Dost sometimes counsel take—and sometimes tea.

Epigram: short witty saying, often in verse form:

Treason doth never prosper; what's the reason?
For if it prosper, none dare call it treason.

(J. HARRINGTON)

Epitaph: words intended, seriously or in jest, to be written on a tombstone:

Here lies our sovereign Lord the King,
   Whose word no man relies on,
Who never said a foolish thing
   Nor ever did a wise one.

(Said of Charles II)

Euphemism: a pleasant or veiled expression used in place of an unpleasant or forthright one, usually in order to tone down the unpleasantness. It is commonly said of a dead person that he or she has "passed away"; a lie was once called a "terminological inexactitude"—as I write this I notice that a deceitful politician is said to have "practised an official economy of truth"; and a person expelled from a country may be said to have "left in a hurry".

Exaggeration, or *Hyperbole:* an over-strong statement not meant to be taken literally:

He had tons of money.
The whole world lay at her feet.
It was an absolute miracle.

Irony: the use of language to convey a meaning exactly opposite to the literal sense of the words employed. When a father says to his son "You can't expect a decrepit old relic like me to go camping . . ." etc., etc., he does not himself believe that he is anything but fit and tough. And in his "Ode to a Pig while His Nose was being bored" Southey ironically concludes:

And when, at last, the deathwound yawning wide,
  Fainter and fainter grows the expiring cry,
Is there no grateful joy, no loyal pride,
  To think that for your master's good you die?

There is a good example in *Julius Cæsar*, Act III, sc. ii, in Antony's speech, "Friends, Romans, countrymen . . ."

Metaphor: a means of comparison; the attributes of one thing or process are used to describe another to which they are not literally applicable. In the sentence "Film star though he was, he got into hot water for not toeing the line" there are three metaphors. Metaphors are extremely common in everyday speech; millions of people use them without being able to explain what a metaphor is. Metaphors are often formed by compressing a simile: instead of saying "He learns his work like a parrot" we say "He parrots his work".

Metaphors enable a speaker or writer to say more in fewer words. Hence they are much used in poetry, which is one of the most condensed forms of expression.

Metonymy, or *Change of name:* a quality or attribute or part of a person is used instead of the whole:

  The Crown (i.e. the King or Queen) owns property in London.
  The Bench (i.e. the magistrates) gave their decision without retiring.
  Hands wanted in departments of this factory.

Onomatopœia: the imitation by words of the sounds they denote. *Boom, hiss, howl, babble* are all onomatopœic. Two examples from Tennyson:

  Blow, bugle, blow, set the wild echoes flying,
  And answer, echoes, answer, dying, dying, dying.

  The moan of doves in immemorial elms,
  And murmuring of innumerable bees.

Paradox: a statement which at first appears to contradict itself:

> I burned my hand on the frozen metal.
>
> Physics tells us that the solidest table leg consists of small particles in constant motion.

Personification: the giving of human qualities to abstractions or things:

> Fortune smiled on him.
> Father Time.
> Famine stalked the land.
> The tanker behaved well on her maiden voyage.

A special form of personification is the attribution of feelings to nature:

> A smiling landscape lay before us.
> Angry waves battered at the sea-wall.

This is known as the "pathetic fallacy".

Pleonasm: a superfluous expression:

> There is no *rational* reason why *carnivorous* meat-eaters should choose our food.

It is much the same as Tautology, which means saying the same thing twice:

> co-operate together
> final completion
> new innovation.

Pun: a play on words, sometimes labelled Paronomasia:

> I'll gild the faces of the grooms withal,
> For it must seem their guilt.

Simile: a comparison introduced by "like" or "as".

> His bones are like bars of iron.
> Love is strong as death; jealousy is cruel as the grave.
>
> (*The Authorised Version*)

Understatement (or *Meiosis*): Clearly she is no novice at making omelettes. (i.e. she is really experienced.)

    After three days camping in the rain, we were not exactly dry.

Zeugma: two incongruous ideas are linked by a verb or adjective:

    He swallowed his pride and a cough lozenge.

    His conceit and his front tyre were punctured in the first mile.

APPENDIX D

I

A MEMBER of Parliament must often feel himself in the position of a private in an army, or a player in a game, or an advocate in a law case. On many questions each party represents and defends the special interests of some particular classes in the country. When there are two plausible alternative courses to be pursued which divide public opinion, the Opposition is almost bound by its position to enforce the merits of the course opposed to that adopted by the Government. In theory nothing could seem more absurd than a system of government in which, as it has been said, the ablest men in Parliament are divided into two classes, one side being charged with the duty of carrying on the government and the other with that of obstructing and opposing them in their task, and in which, on a vast multitude of unconnected questions, these two great bodies of very competent men, with the same facts and arguments before them, habitually go into opposite lobbies. In practice, however, parliamentary government by great parties, in countries where it is fully understood and practised, is found to be admirably efficacious in representing every variety of political opinion; in securing a constant supervision and criticism of men and measures; and in forming a safety valve through which the dangerous humours of society can expand without evil to the community.

This, however, is only accomplished by constant compromises which are seldom successfully carried out without a long national experience. Party must exist. It must be maintained as an essential condition of good government, but it must be subordinated to the public interests, and in the public interests it must be in many cases suspended. There are subjects which cannot be introduced without the gravest danger into the arena of party controversy. Indian politics are a conspicuous example, and, although foreign policy cannot be kept wholly outside it, the dangers connected with its party treatment are extremely great. Many measures of a different kind are conducted with the concurrence of the two front benches. A cordial union on large classes of questions between the heads of the rival parties is one of the first conditions of successful parliamentary government. The Opposition leader must have a voice in the conduct of business, on the questions that should be brought forward, and on the questions that it is for the public interest to keep back. He is the official leader of systematic, organised opposition to the Government, yet he is on a large number of questions their most powerful ally. He must frequently have confidential relations with them, and one of his most useful functions is to prevent sections of his party from endeavouring to snatch party advantages by courses which might endanger public interests. If the country is to be well governed there must be a large amount of continuity in its policy; certain conditions and principles of administration must be inflexibly maintained, and in great national emergencies all parties must unite.

W. E. H. LECKY, The Map of Life

2

In these days of swift locomotion I may doubtless assume that most of my audience have been somewhere out of England—have been in Scotland, or France, or Switzerland. Whatever may have been their impression, on returning to their own country, of its superiority or inferiority in other respects, they cannot but have felt one thing about it—the comfortable look of towns and villages. Foreign towns are often very picturesque, very beautiful, but they never have quite that look of warm self-sufficiency and wholesome quiet with which our villages nestle themselves down among the green fields. If you will take the trouble to examine into the sources of this impression, you will find that by far the greater part of that warm and satisfactory appearance depends upon the rich scarlet colour of the bricks and tiles. It does not belong to the neat building—very neat building has an uncomfortable rather than a comfortable look—but it depends on the *warm* building; our villages are dressed in red tiles as our old women are in red cloaks; and it does not matter how worn the cloaks, or how bent and bowed the roof may be, so long as there are no holes in either one or the other, and the sober but unextinguishable colour still glows in the shadow of the hood, and burns among the green mosses of the gable. And what do you suppose dyes your tiles of cottage roof? You don't paint them. It is nature who puts all that lovely vermilion into the clay for you; and all that lovely vermilion is this oxide of iron. Think, therefore, what your streets or towns would become—ugly enough, indeed, already, some of them, but still comfortable-looking—if instead of that warm brick red, the houses became all pepper-and-salt colour. Fancy your country villages changing from that homely scarlet of theirs which, in its sweet suggestion of laborious peace, is as honourable as the soldier's scarlet of laborious battle —suppose all those cottage roofs, I say, turned at once into the colour of unbaked clay, the colour of street gutters in rainy weather. That's what they would be, without iron.

There is, however, yet another effect of colour in our English country towns which, perhaps, you may not all yourselves have noticed, but for which you must take the word of a sketcher. They are not so often merely warm scarlet as they are warm purple;—a more beautiful colour still: and they owe this colour to a mingling with the vermilion of the deep greyish or purple hue of our fine Welsh slates on the more respectable roofs, made more blue still by the colour of intervening atmosphere. If you examine one of these Welsh slates freshly broken, you will find its purple colour clear and vivid; and although never strikingly so after it has been long exposed to weather, it always retains enough of the tint to give rich harmonies of distant purple in opposition to the green of our woods and fields. Whatever brightness or power there is in the hue is entirely owing to the oxide of iron. Without it the slates would either be pale stone colour, or cold grey, or black.

JOHN RUSKIN, *The Two Paths*

3

Public penury, private ostentation—that, perhaps, is the heart of the complaint. A nation with the wealth of England can afford to spend, and spend royally. Only the end should be itself desirable, and the choice deliberate. The spectacle of a huge urban poverty confronts all this waste energy. That spectacle should not, indeed, forbid all luxuries and splendours: but it should condemn the less rewarding of them as things tawdry and mean. "Money! money!" cries the hero—a second-rate Government clerk —of a recent novel—"the good that can be done with it in the world! Only a little more: a little more!" It is the passionate cry of unnumbered thousands. Expenditure multiplies its return in human happiness as it is scattered amongst widening areas of population. And the only justification for the present unnatural heaping up of great possessions in the control of the very few would be some return in leisure, and the cultivation of the arts, and the more reputable magnificence of the luxurious life. We have called into existence a whole new industry in motor cars and quick travelling, and established populous cities to minister to our increasing demands for speed. We have converted half the Highlands into deer forests for our sport; and the amount annually spent on shooting, racing, golf—on apparatus, and train journeys and service— exceeds the total revenue of many a European princi- pality. We fling away in ugly white hotels, in uninspired dramatic entertainments, and in elaborate banquets of which every one is weary, the price of many poor men's yearly income. Yet we cannot build a new Cathedral. We cannot even preserve the Cathedrals bequeathed to us, and the finest of them are tumbling to pieces for lack of response to the demands for aid. We grumble freely at halfpenny increases in the rates for baths or libraries or pleasure-grounds. We assert—there are many of us who honestly believe it—that we cannot afford to set aside the necessary millions from our amazing revenues for the decent maintenance of our worn-out "veterans of in- dustry".

To the poor, any increase of income may mean a day's excursion, a summer holiday for the children; often the bare necessities of food and clothes and shelter. To the classes just above the industrial populations, who with an expanding standard of comfort are most obviously fretting against the limitation of their income, it may mean the gift of some of life's lesser goods which is now denied: music, the theatre, books, flowers. Its absence may mean also a deprivation of life's greater goods: scamped sick- nursing, absence of leisure, abandonment of the hope of wife or child. All these deprivations may be endured by a nation—have been endured by nations—for the sake of definite ends: in wars, at which existence is at stake, under the stress of national calamity, or as in the condition universal to Europe a few hundred years ago, when wealth and security were the heritage of the very few. But to-day that wealth is piling up into ever-increasing aggregation: is being scrutinized, as never before, by those who inquire with increasing insistence, where is the justice of these monstrous inequalities of fortune? Is the super-wealth of England expended in any adequate degree upon national service? Is the return to-day or to posterity a justification for this deflection of men and women's labour into ministering to the demands of a pleasure-loving society? Is it erecting works of permanent value, as the wealth of Florence in the fifteenth century? Is it, as in the England of Elizabeth, breeding men?

No honest inquirer could give a dogmatic reply. The present extravagance of England is associated with a strange mediocrity, a strange sterility of characters of supreme power in Church and State. It is accompanied, as all ages of security and luxury are accompanied, by a waning of the power of inspiration, a multiplying of the power of criticism. The more comfortable and opulent society becomes, the more cynicism proclaims the futility of it all, and the mind turns in despair from a vision of vanities.

C. F. G. MASTERMAN, The Condition of England

4

To a visitor from another country, London appears to be very well off for parks and open spaces, with the noble Thames winding through it, Royal Parks in the West End, Epping Forest close to its North-east district, and many fine squares. There is a total of 5,056 acres under the jurisdiction of the London County Council not including the Royal Parks, Richmond Park (2,358 acres) and Wool-wich Common (159 acres) which are owned by the government. But where the poorest live and most congestion exists London is unfortunate and few of these parks are really "far from the madding crowd".

When Oliver Cromwell wanted to have a private conversation with Ireton, who was very deaf, he chose Holland Park (only a mile west of Kensington Gardens) as a secluded spot where he could not be overheard. The middle of Holland Park might still serve for such a consultation to-day, for the park is roughly half a mile across from north to south and from east to west. But, whereas in Cromwell's day other suitable spots in or near London might have been found quite readily, to-day this is about the only large secluded private area anywhere in Greater London.

Fresh air and exercise are two essential requirements for healthy living. The purification of the atmosphere and the provision of facilities for recreation in the open air are two pressing problems for London's huge population. Smoke abatement is progressing and the means for its full accomplishment are well understood. But the means whereby the other problem can be tackled are not so clear, nor so easy to carry out. There are two solutions, viz., (1) the provision of reserved open spaces within the urban districts; and (2) journeyings to the open countryside, now rapidly becoming more distant from the centre. The bulk cost of travel to open country is generally found to be cheaper than the ever rising cost of providing open spaces in urban areas. But this cost too is mounting through inability to stop the spread of built-up areas and the breaking of the continuity of the urban districts by a Green Belt. Increased facilities for cheap travel and the acquisition by individual business firms of playing fields for their employees are only partially aiding matters.

Considering how Londoners are handicapped in many of these particulars London is a healthy town. The famous geographer, Ellsworth Huntington, extols the climate of England as "nearer to the ideal than almost any other place" and refers especially to the healthiness of London from a climatic point of view: "We are frequently told that the Riviera or Southern California has an ideal climate. . . . Two of the few regions which rarely assert their pre-eminence in this respect are Boston with its east winds, and London with its fogs. Yet in many ways they have a strong claim to high rank." Many of the drawbacks Londoners suffer from through lack of fresh air and ample space have been mitigated by the Englishman's love for a self-contained house with a back garden. Although this desire has increased the sprawl of London over a wide area, it has saved Londoners from some of the worst degrees of congestion. Many of the old boroughs are badly overcrowded, but it is more an overcrowding of persons in the house than of houses on the ground.

The more crowded districts have the fewest recreation grounds and are the furthest from the countryside. A friend of mine, not living in a slum, had to give up all games, at many of which he excelled, soon after he came to London because it took him too long to travel to and from the playing field. He had to take to skipping in a back yard. The average Londoner cannot often afford the time and money to get open-air exercise—say, for example, a walk in beautiful Epping Forest though it is only ten miles from the City. He is losing his desire for such health-giving pursuits and his joy in the beauties of nature. Many town dwellers who visit a forest are shy about penetrating into its depths, and their visits to the seaside are spent in the fun-fair. Holiday resorts are becoming just annexes to the towns in spite of bands of hikers and schoolboy climbers. The passing of a Physical Training and Recreation bill will not enable the town worker to forget his cares by arriving "at the gates of the forest (where) the surprised man of the world is forced to leave his city estimates of great and small, wise and foolish". Physical jerks and gymnastics are no substitutes for open-air exercise, though they render people more easily drilled.

S. V. PEARSON, *London's Overgrowth*

FINAL HINTS

If you have worked through a number of the examples and if you follow the advice given in this book, you should be in a strong position to succeed. But before you actually take the paper there are some reminders worth noting, especially about the presentation of your answers. Lack of care in setting down work can reduce the value of an otherwise good paper.

To take writing first. You may be a poor writer, but that is no reason for despair. You can still make your hand presentable by writing regularly, on the lines, not above or below, by making loops clear, by forming letters properly, and by finishing off "a"s and "o"s. Words must be sufficiently and evenly spaced.

Take care to note and follow any instructions about writing on one or both sides of the paper, and about margins. Do not start on the top line; indent all paragraphs about an inch; write up to the margin. Your work should have a frame of white space all round it. Good spacing and neatness make for ease of reading, even if the writing itself is not distinguished.

If you have any time left over, spend it on re-reading. You are certain to pick up a mis-punctuation, a spelling mistake, an inexact expression, or an error such as two nouns with a singular verb. Read your answers to yourself as if you were reading aloud, forming the words with your lips.

The general appearance of your work does count. It can predispose an examiner in the candidate's favour, or it can antagonise him. This is quite reasonable, when you consider that slovenly writing and presentation are a form of bad manners.

And lastly, a reminder that may seem so obvious that it is an insult to the candidate: be very careful to answer the question actually set. You can be confident that the marking of your papers will be fair and thorough and perhaps generous, but no marker can do much to help a candidate who puts in quantities of irrelevant matter or disregards the wording of a question.

INDEX

A